# ODSAL ODYSSEYS
## The History of Bradford Rugby League

### Phil Hodgson

VERTICAL EDITIONS

First published in the United Kingdom in 2006 by Vertical Editions, 7 Bell Busk,
Skipton, North Yorkshire BD23 4DT

ISBN
1-904091-14-8
978-1-904091-14-1

Jacket design and typeset by HBA, York

Printed and bound by the Cromwell Press, Trowbridge

# CONTENTS

In memory of Trevor Foster
A loving and loved adopted son of Bradford
1914–2005

# ACKNOWLEDGEMENTS

A wide-ranging history such as Odsal Odysseys could not be written without the extensive input, directly and indirectly, of a host of observers past and present.

Chroniclers of the deeds of the old Bradford club, of Manningham, of Bradford Northern and, for the past decade, of Bradford Bulls have all been referred to heavily in producing this book. None, perhaps, have been drawn on more than Nigel Williams, whose definitive *Bradford Northern, the History – 1863-1989* remains a classic of the genre.

I am also deeply grateful to David Pendleton and John Ashton, Bradford City men both, who have nevertheless ensured that Manningham, as the forerunner of that fine soccer side, are featured prominently at the club's impressive museum at Valley Parade and on the Bantams' website.

I would have loved to have been able to interview the early pioneers such as Oates Ingham and Alfred Firth at Bradford, Alfred Ayrton at Manningham and the latter club's George Lorimer, one of sport's first superstars who tragically died young.

Harry Hornby, one of the men who turned Bradford Northern into a real power, is another visionary whom I would have enjoyed meeting but Rugby League in the city has, happily, continued to produce men of great enthusiasm, ability and goodwill, all of whom have stepped forward readily with valuable insights.

The late Trevor Foster, who sadly passed away while this book was being written, was typically forthcoming and I am also grateful to figures from Northern's recent history such as Charlie Ebbage, Peter Fox, Len Haley, Keith Mumby and Tommy Smales for their input.

Present-day players, coaches and administrators who gave freely of their time and memories include Jamie Peacock, Robbie Paul, Stuart Fielden, Paul Deacon, Lesley Vainikolo, Steve McNamara, and Paul Medley.

Special thanks are due to Bulls Media Manager Stuart Duffy, who was a hugely enthusiastic supporter of the concept, and Community Development Manager, Chris Rostron.

Coach Brian Noble was affably forthcoming for interviews and I am delighted that he accepted my invitation to contribute the foreword.

Above all, in terms of the Bulls, I am indebted to Chris Caisley who, as Chairman, guided Bradford to the greatest era in the club's history.

Nothing can be achieved in sport without firm leadership from the very top and the fact that publication of Odsal Odysseys was delayed to include not only last season's glorious engage Super League championship success but the subsequent Carnegie World Club Challenge win over Wests Tigers can be traced directly to Caisley's coolness under pressure during June and July 2005, when he stood firmly by his tried and tested coaching team and deservedly reaped due reward.

I am grateful to Tim Butcher of *Rugby Leaguer and League Express*, who readily granted me permission to reproduce articles I wrote for the *Leaguer* prior to the merger of the two papers.

My long-suffering and infinitely patient publisher Karl Waddicor deserves a big kiss, but won't want one and won't get one. There is a peck, though, for my wife Julia (who has now got her life back) and children Sam (who came up with the title of this book), Jack and Sarah.

Others who made significant contributions, either directly or indirectly, and to whom I offer my heartfelt thanks, include: Brenda Bean, Steve Brady, James Brammer (Bradford Bulls), Phil Caplan, Dave Clark, Tony Collins, Dave Craven (*Telegraph & Argus*), Chris Deakin, John Downes (Bradford Bulls), Charlie Ebbage, Steve Fairhurst, Dennis Flatt, Raymond Fletcher, Simon Foster, Terry Frost, Len Garbett, Robert Gate, Sam Grundy, Roger Halstead, Martin Hawksworth, Ted Hodgson, Howard Hughes (Tyldesley RFC), Trevor Hunt, John Huxley, Harry Jepson, Rhodri Jones,

*League Weekly*, James Lowes, Jayne Marsden (*Yorkshire Post* Library), David Middleton (League Information Services), Geoffrey Moorhouse, Graham Morris, Maurice Oldroyd, Chris Park, Dave Parker, Sally Price (Rugby Football Union), Michael Rhodes (who sadly passed away as this book was going to press), Chris Roberts, *Rugby League Magazine*, *Rugby Leaguer*, *Rugby Leaguer & League Express*, Martyn Sadler, Irving Saxton, Charlie Seeling, Harry Sheard, Stuart Sheard, Kelvin Skerrett, Jed Smith (Rugby Football Union), Mike Sterriker, Vanessa Toulmin, Michael Turner, David Ward (*Pontefract & Castleford Express*), Gerald Webster, Denis Whittle, Donna Williams and Barry Wood.

Phil Hodgson
March 2006

# FOREWORD

It's a privilege, as a long-serving player, captain and now former coach, to be asked to write the foreword to a book covering the entire history of the game in Bradford.

As a Manningham lad I'm fully aware of the impact my 'local' club had in the early days of the Northern Union, winning the first championship; and the history of the Bradford club itself, while including a number of lows, involves several glorious eras.

I think, though, that this has been the most successful period in the club's history. The Bulls have appeared in two Challenge Cup finals, winning one, and five Super League Grand Finals of which three have been won. In my time we've had a couple of World Club championships in there and the League Leaders' Shield. And don't forget the Middlesex Sevens when we turned up on a wet and windy day and blew Rugby Union apart with a team that hadn't practised, hadn't slept and just went down to Twickenham and won!

We had great days before the new Millennium when Matthew Elliott was head coach. We won a Challenge Cup and a Super League and we got to another Grand Final when we lost against Saints through Rugby League's version of the Hand of God when Mick Withers allegedly touched the ball. The club's had a fantastic run of success in the last five or six years, one which is unprecedented in its history.

It's great, as a Manningham lad, to have been a part of this successful club. It's not just the coaching staff that achieve it; the Board of Directors should take full credit. The club shop, the lotteries, community development and marketing departments all play a part in the success of the Bulls. They are nice people at Bradford as well as good people and good rugby players. They stand for things at Bradford and rightly so.

They try to do the right thing all the time. Sometimes they get it wrong, but in the main this club tries to do the right thing by Rugby League and by everybody else. With that kind of principle and ethic they should be able to sustain success.

Brian Noble
April 2006

# INTRODUCTION

Can there be any other sporting story quite like the enduring tale that revolves around the sport of Rugby League in the city of Bradford?

Almost certainly not. Most sporting histories involve a litany of more or less unalleviated success, with perhaps the odd relative fall from grace from time to time. But any review of rugby in Bradford must, it has to be said, include accounts of the very depths of sporting despair followed only a few pages later by stories of stirring deeds.

Such a tale is, indeed, told in the closing chapter of this book, when the modern-day bearers of the torch rose from the misery of indifferent form highlighted by a 66-4 home defeat by St Helens to close the season as Super League champions.

The Bulls, in the roller coaster ride that was 2005, unwittingly encapsulated the story of not only their own club – as both Northern and the Bulls – but the intriguing tale of the former Bradford club, based at Park Avenue, that preceded the 'Northern Union' venture of 1907.

Brian Noble's side were also following in the footsteps of another leading light of the Victorian era, Manningham, whom I was keen to include in this book as an important part of not only the Bradford rugby story but also of the history of Rugby League.

It's ironic that both Manningham and Bradford Park Avenue were very successful Rugby Union (subsequently Northern Union) clubs but opted to switch to the burgeoning soccer code in the early part of the last century in pursuit of even greater glory.

The fact that neither Park Avenue or Bradford City (Manningham's successor) have managed to emulate their achievements with the oval ball is unfortunate.

Both have had their moments but arguably nothing to match City's feat, as Manningham, in winning the first Northern Union (Rugby League) championship in 1895–96, or Bradford's Division One title success eight years later.

The fact that neither club was happy to settle for what they had in the Northern Union could be seen as symptomatic of a trait, perhaps endemic in the city and its surrounds, towards stubbornness and independence of spirit.

It's a quality that renders the average Bradfordian the archetypal Yorkshireman. The character appears to have been attracted to the city's Rugby League clubs throughout the 143 years since Oates Ingham and Alfred Firth formed the first Bradford rugby club in 1863, right through to the present day, with the redoubtable Chris Caisley at the helm as Chairman and Brian Noble an unflappable and perspicacious coach.

The forthright Yorkshire approach has of course been leavened with a huge input from men from beyond, none more so than Welshman Trevor Foster who gave far, far more to the club (and to his beloved adopted city) than he ever received.

Foster was at great pains, when I interviewed him for this book in late 2004, to highlight the input of New Zealander Joe Phillips in re-forming the club in 1964.

The task of researching and relating the ups and downs of those men, their predecessors such as Harry Hornby, and Dai Rees, and subsequent Bradford Northern legends including Peter Fox, Harry Womersley, Keith Mumby, Karl Fairbank and, in later years, Brian Smith, Brian Noble, Peter Deakin, Matthew Elliott, Robbie and Henry Paul, James Lowes and many others has been illuminating, entertaining and, at times, harrowing.

Typical of the complex and convoluted tale that permeates the saga is the identity of the current club itself. A casual observer, for instance, could be forgiven for believing that Bradford Bulls is a new club, formed in 1996, which has little to do with the Bradford Northern that existed for 89 years from 1907 other than playing at the same ground and wearing, more or less, the same colours.

The reality, of course, is that the Bulls remain,

in legal terms, Bradford Northern (1964) Ltd, the club that was formed to take the place of the organisation that had been wound up in 1963. The fact that the new team bore exactly the same name, in usual usage, as the old club – and wore exactly the same colours and also played at Odsal – can only add to any confusion for the newcomer.

Happily, Bradford Bulls are now one of the most eminent names in the game (indeed, in any sport) matching – if not bettering – the feats of Manningham, Bradford, and the fine Northern teams of the 1940s and the late 1970s.

In those dark days in late 1963 it was often said that Rugby League needed a strong Bradford club.

That was certainly the case at the time (a fact that persuaded that fine man Trevor Foster and colleagues such as Joe Phillips to launch the new club in one of the most inspiring sporting stories ever told), it had been the case for many years before, and it remains the case now.

After a generally turbulent 150 years it's probably fair to say that Bradford Rugby League club, in whatever its guise now or previously, has never been in ruder health.

That fact can be attributed to a hard-working body of single-minded people in all sections of the Odsal complex, on and off the field; and, above all, to the man who has marshalled the unit with a deft – and, with regards to outsiders, occasionally forceful – hand for the best part of two decades.

Chris Caisley, the Bulls' Chairman from 1989, announced his retirement as this book was going to press and his departure will certainly herald the end of an era. His successor will have a hard act to follow. It's a truth too often overlooked that no club, in any sport, can enjoy any kind of sustained success without leadership of high quality. In Caisley, the Bulls have had just that and there can be no better illustration than the fact that the Chairman offered Brian Noble a new, two-year contract when results were indifferent midway through 2005 and calls were

being made for the coach's dismissal.

The reward for both men? As romantic and exhilarating a championship as has been achieved in the history of the game.

With a nice resonance from the perspective of this book, Bradford are the current champions of our game while the first Northern Union titleholders were none other than Manningham, the old adversaries of the Bulls' predecessors over a century ago.

It has been a huge pleasure for someone who, as a 13-year-old, was reduced to tears by Bradford Northern (the occasion: the 1965 Yorkshire Cup Final win over his team Hunslet) to recount an odyssey which, to this day, involves some of the most intriguing, committed, idealist, lovable and, yes, downright obstinate, trenchant and bolshie people – judging by some of the folk who liked to stand by the infamous Odsal steps as visiting players made their long way back to the changing rooms – it could ever be one's pleasure to meet.

# 1.
# 1863 – 1907

**Antecedents**

Bradford Rugby League Football Club, lauded in its guises as Northern and the Bulls as innovators for much of the twentieth century and the early years of the third millennium, has merely continued a trend instigated by its Victorian predecessor.

The first Bradford club – notionally a rugby club but playing a brand of football probably unrecognisable today – was formed in 1863 by a number of local philanthropists from Bramham College led by Oates Ingham and Alfred Firth.

So innovative, in fact, was the group that it had embarked on a pastime in which relatively few others were involved. Rugby clubs were a

> *Captain Fred Bonsor received a letter in 1885 from 'young ladies in Wakefield accusing his side of cowardice for their refusal to play Trinity that season'.*

> *Bradford were considered in 1887 to be the richest club in England, in any code of football. The assessment was implicitly endorsed six years later by the Inland Revenue which chose to investigate the Park Avenue organisation, together with only one Association Football club – Aston Villa – for non-payment of taxes.*

*The Yorkshire side that met England at Headingley in 1892 included three Bradford men and one Manningham player. Back row (left to right): JH Toothill (Bradford), E Dewhirst (Bradford), W Nichol (Brighouse R), D Jowett (Heckmondwike), F Wood (Brighouse R), W Goldthorpe (Hunslet). Middle row (left to right): H Bradshaw (Bramley), H Varley (Liversedge), WE Bromet (Tadcaster), T Broadley (Bingley), E Redman (Manningham), Barron Kilner (Wakefield T). Front row (left to right): A Briggs (Bradford), J Dyson (Huddersfield), RE Lockwood (Huddersfield), AE Goldthorpe (Hunslet).*

rarity in the mid-1860s, at least in the north of England. Liverpool, formed in 1857, were Bradford's closest neighbours while Edinburgh Academicals had been established in the same year. Blackheath, who remain among the most venerated of Rugby Union clubs, was launched in the capital 12 months later.

For several years, therefore, Bradford's members played largely among themselves, much in the manner of members of a golf or tennis club. Early games, perhaps between a Captain's side and a Secretary's team, were staged at Horton Cricket Club on All Saints Road, close to the present site of St Luke's Hospital, before the enthusiasts were asked to move on after a two-year tenure by hosts keen to protect the cricket square.

Laisterbridge Lane provided a temporary home, with further stopping-off points at North Park Road, Manningham, and Peel Park, Girlington, for games usually played 20-a-side

*John Thomas Toothill, Bradford's captain at the time of the Great Split. The England Rugby Union international played in the first three seasons of the Northern Union.*

# A match to remember
## Launch of the Northern Union

*Bradford 11 Wakefield 0*
*7 September 1895*
*Park Avenue, Bradford*
*Report from the Yorkshire Post*
*Cooper, Murgatroyd, Briggs, Wilding, Ward and Dobson did not turn out for the Bradford side. Croslan took the place of Smith among the Wakefield forwards. About 6,000 spectators were present when William Sugden started for Bradford, who lost the toss, and had to play with the sun to their faces. The home forwards soon dribbled into the Wakefield quarter, and Booth, picking up from a scrummage, passed finely to Crompton, who was only brought down on the line after a clever run. For some informality, the visitors were penalised in their own quarters, and Crompton had a shot at goal, the ball striking one of the uprights and rebounding into play. Bradford still kept up the attack and, after a good bout of passing by the backs, Crompton made an excellent attempt to drop a goal, the ball just falling short. At length Anderton kicked away from a scrummage, and reached midfield, and the same player directly afterwards made a couple of good kicks, with the result that for the first time Bradford had to defend. At this point Holden was injured and had to retire, and Bradford continued with only fourteen men. Bland, after a short run, passed to Grandage, who ran smartly up the touchline and scored in the corner, Firth failing to land the goal. Half time was called directly afterwards with the score – Bradford 1 try, Wakefield Trinity nil. In the second half Bradford soon attacked, owing to fine passing and running by Toothill and Wilson, and Booth getting the ball from a scrummage threw smartly to Crompton. The Bradford captain rounded his man brilliantly, and finished a pretty bit of play by scoring near the posts, but failed at goal. William Sugden scored for Bradford, Crompton converting.*

*Bradford: Burns; Crompton, Bland, Popplewell; Toothill, Booth; Grandage, William Sugden, Walter Sugden, Wilson, Holden, Bates, Robertson, Ramsden, Firth.*

*Wakefield: Kershaw; Wood, Howell, Gameson, Goldthorpe; Anderton, Milsom; Allchurch, Eyre, Day, Ducker, Binns, Crossland, Varley, Westerby.*

*Referee: Mr P F Farrar (Brighouse).*

*Rochdale Hornets confirmed their naked aggression in a game at Park Avenue in April 1896. A visiting player, after pulling off an interception, was tackled by a Bradford player who was left clutching the remnants of the Rochdale man's shorts as the Hornet sped away. A further, completed, tackle was followed by a hurried huddle to spare the Lancastrian's blushes until replacement shorts were brought onto the pitch.*

but occasionally incorporating up to 30 players in each team.

By 1866, however, Mr Ingham and his colleagues determined that the club would benefit from an organised fixture list. And firmer foundations led eight years later to another switch of venue, this time to Apperley Bridge where the team, now playing under the auspices of the Rugby Football Union which had been formed in 1871, boasted a 100 per cent record in 1874–75 and, incredibly, conceded not a single point.

Perhaps with envious eyes on this success, another club had been formed, and, from the

standpoint of Ingham and his colleagues, it was worryingly near to the centre of a city which, thanks to the burgeoning wool trade, was said to be among the most prosperous in Europe.

Formed in the late 1870s and playing at Park Avenue, the Bradford Cricket, Football & Athletic Club, which had access to a nearby railway line, was viewed as a real threat and, perhaps working to the maxim 'if you can't beat 'em, join 'em' the Bradford committee instigated initiatives which resulted in a merger, the new team playing at Park Avenue.

All this while yet another club had been formed in the city – Bradford Rangers. If the Park Avenue outfit assumed that they would automatically adopt the mantle of leading lights in the region, they were mistaken. Their first match, with Rangers the visitors, resulted in a defeat by six touchdowns to one.

Bradford, however, brushed that setback aside and went on to become a real power in the years before the Great Split of 1895. With a fixture list which included the likes of future Northern Union teams Broughton Rangers – who were to become the first club, in 1901–02, to achieve the Cup and League 'double' – Dewsbury, Halifax, Hull, Rochdale Hornets, Runcorn, and Salford, together with such as Blackheath, Cambridge University, Harlequins, London Scottish, Oxford University and

### 1895–96: Northern Rugby Football Union

| | P | W | D | L | F | A | Pts |
|---|---|---|---|---|---|---|---|
| Manningham | 42 | 33 | 0 | 9 | 367 | 158 | 66 |
| Halifax | 42 | 30 | 5 | 7 | 312 | 139 | 65 |
| Runcorn | 42 | 24 | 8 | 10 | 314 | 143 | 56 |
| Oldham | 42 | 27 | 2 | 13 | 374 | 194 | 56 |
| Brighouse Rangers | 42 | 22 | 9 | 11 | 247 | 129 | 53 |
| Tyldesley | 42 | 21 | 8 | 13 | 260 | 164 | 50 |
| Hunslet | 42 | 24 | 2 | 16 | 279 | 207 | 50 |
| Hull | 42 | 23 | 3 | 16 | 259 | 158 | 49 |
| Leigh | 42 | 21 | 4 | 17 | 214 | 269 | 46 |
| Wigan | 42 | 19 | 7 | 16 | 245 | 147 | 45 |
| Bradford | 42 | 18 | 9 | 15 | 254 | 175 | 45 |
| Leeds | 42 | 20 | 3 | 19 | 258 | 247 | 43 |
| Warrington | 42 | 17 | 5 | 20 | 198 | 240 | 39 |
| St Helens* | 42 | 15 | 8 | 19 | 195 | 230 | 36 |
| Liversedge | 42 | 15 | 4 | 23 | 261 | 355 | 34 |
| Widnes | 42 | 14 | 4 | 24 | 177 | 323 | 32 |
| Stockport | 42 | 12 | 8 | 22 | 171 | 315 | 32 |
| Batley | 42 | 12 | 7 | 23 | 137 | 298 | 31 |
| Wakefield Trinity | 42 | 13 | 4 | 25 | 156 | 318 | 30 |
| Huddersfield | 42 | 10 | 4 | 28 | 194 | 274 | 24 |
| Broughton Rangers | 42 | 8 | 8 | 26 | 165 | 244 | 24 |
| Rochdale Hornets | 42 | 4 | 8 | 30 | 78 | 388 | 16 |

* Deducted two points for playing ineligible player.

*Threequarter Tommy Dobson, who scored 34 tries in 116 appearances for Bradford in the first five seasons of the Northern Union.*

## A major attraction

The drawing power of the emerging Bradford side was vividly illustrated when Dewsbury opted to double admission prices for the game at Crown Flatt in 1886; an act which rebounded when the host club was rewarded with a disappointing gate.

Supporters, though, were equally ready to fleece their favourites. Bradford uncovered counterfeit season tickets in 1886 and, like other clubs, were undermined by the practice of fans passing their season tickets from within the ground to others outside.

Leeds Parish Church ended the fraud by introducing a match voucher – a solution which Bradford emulated.

There is no record of the type of 'supporter' who would attempt to fiddle his own club but reports from the era suggest that he or she could have emanated from practically any section of society.

The huge gate for the Yorkshire Cup tie with Manningham in 1884 included, it was said, 'clergy and ministers, pastors and deacons, very good people and some that were only so-so; lawyers, doctors, magistrates, tinkers and tailors, soldiers and sailors, rag, tag and bobtail'.

Three years earlier the *Yorkshire Post* revealed 'On the road near, an endless stream of people goes flowing on. There are enthusiasts munching the last mouthfuls of their dinners and speeding to be in time for the kick off. From all quarters and directions do they come. Old men and maidens, matrons and children, and young men of every degree. Already the lower walls of the field are surmounted by an unbroken line of spectators, who form a sort of human railing, and, regardless of the drizzle and biting wind, and the somewhat uncertain nature of their seats, amuse themselves with pipes, occasional bottles, and the interchange of not too delicate pleasantries with passers-by, while the belligerents in the grandstand strip for the fray.'

The Bradford crowd were entertained by

Sunderland, Bradford enjoyed local pre-eminence which extended county-wide when the Yorkshire Cup, better known as T'Owd Tin Pot, was won in 1884.

The first trophy to grace the Park Avenue cabinet was garnered with a 5-3 victory over Hull FC in the final at Cardigan Fields, Leeds. En route, Manningham had been beaten at Park Avenue before what contemporary reports described as a 'monster attendance'. The home side, determined to make their mark against the overwhelming favourites, had spent a week at Blackpool as part of their preparations and around 20,000 turned up to see if their initiative had been worthwhile.

The Yorkshire Cup success presaged a 10-year period in which Bradford became renowned as one of the best sides in the country, with Park Avenue a real citadel.

The club boasted internationals in captain John Thomas Toothill and Tommy Dobson, while Tom Broadley (1893) and Fred Cooper (1895) had England trials.

H Ward and H Duckett turned out for Yorkshire, together with Cooper and Dobson, and all were to become major figures in the assault on the Northern Union.

# A match to remember

## Challenge Cup

*Bradford 7 Oldham 3*
*Park Avenue*
*20 March 1897*
*Oldham, who had finished as runners-up in the inaugural Lancashire League in 1896–97, were strongly fancied to mount a serious bid for the Challenge Cup in its first season. Nobody told rank underdogs Bradford, who had finished the league campaign with four successive defeats but took the game to Oldham in the Roughyeds' own physical style and won 7-3. Full-back RL Smith was a pivotal figure with an astute kicking game on his own Park Avenue midden, and Foulds, Walker and Fearnley dominated the lineouts to allow half-backs Prole and Calvert to prosper. Bradford, who went close in the early stages when Calvert was denied – Oldham kicking dead after Robertson and Murgatroyd had launched an early raid – won the match with scores either side of half time.*
*Calvert dropped a goal after a heel against the head as the interval approached and Bradford stretched their*

*lead with their first attack of the second half, international winger Dobson racing away after Prole, Calvert, Pollard and Crompton had linked. Wilson and Foulds were obliged to retire as Oldham bristled and, five minutes from time, the Roughyeds came back into the game with a penalty goal by full-back Harry Eagland. But Bradford's valiant thirteen held out under immense pressure, to the delight of the majority of the 14,000 crowd, going on to beat amateur team Swinton Church 68-3 in the second round in a game switched from Manchester to Park Avenue in return for a persuasive £100.*

*Bradford: RL Smith; Dobson, Crompton, Murgatroyd, Pollard; Prole, Calvert; Broadley, Wilson, Robertson, Foulds, Walker, Sykes, Fearnley, Wright.*

*Oldham: Eagland; Walsh, S Lees, Taylor, Martin; Varley, A Lees; J Lees, Frater, Broome, Merrill, Etchells, Bonser, Edwards, Hughes.*

some quality players and Park Avenue, itself impressive, was selected by the RFU for representative games. Yorkshire beat England in February 1890 at the ground, following which the English Rugby Union Committee gathered at the Alexandria Hotel in Great Horton Road to select the England team for the following Saturday's game with Scotland. Two Bradford players, Toothill and Hickson, were called up, together with Manningham's Eddie Holmes, who had played for Yorkshire.

It was no surprise, therefore, when Bradford became the first winners of the Yorkshire Senior Competition in 1892–93.

### Launch of the Northern Union

Bradford, steered to a significant degree by the views of the players, was among the 22 clubs that made the historic decision at the George Hotel, Huddersfield, on 28 August 1895 to resign from the Rugby Football Union.

The revolutionary move, over the issue of 'broken time' payments to players who otherwise could ill afford to leave work early on Saturday afternoons, was one which affected several

*Tom Broadley, an England Rugby Union trialist before the advent of the Northern Union and a mainstay of the side from 1896 to 1904, captaining Bradford at the turn of the century.*

*Two Bradford players – John Toothill and Fred Bonsor, who was captain – together with Manningham's Eddie Holmes were selected for the Yorkshire side that met England at Halifax in February 1889. Back row (left to right): JW Sykes (Batley), M Newsome (Dewsbury, President), John Toothill (Bradford), FW Lowrie (Wakefield Trinity), G Jacketts (Hull), JA Miller (Hon. Sec.), H Wilkinson (Halifax). Middle row (left to right): W Stadden (Dewsbury), RE Lockwood (Heckmondwike), Fred Bonsor (Bradford), H Bedford (Batley), JH Jones (Wakefield Trinity), Eddie Holmes (Manningham). Front row (left to right): J Dodd (Halifax), JW Sutcliffe (Heckmondwike), AL Brooke (Heckmondwike), D Jowett (Heckmondwike).*

Bradford players. The RFU's stringent application of the rules on amateurism sat well with many of the affluent clubs in the south of England but could not be countenanced by most of the clubs in the north, whose players were largely drawn from the artisan classes.

Matters had come to a head in the late summer of 1895 – and within 10 days of the meeting at the George the first raft of fixtures was underway.

The kick-off for Bradford's first game, at home to Wakefield, was delayed. Trinity's journey had taken longer than expected after a wheel fell off their horse-drawn cart. The heat may also have been a factor, the author of the brochure celebrating Bradford Northern's successive Wembley appearances from 1947 to 1949 reflecting: 'There are still some who recall the occasion. Bright sunshine and a cloudless sky during the day delayed the kick-off until 4.50pm.'

It was agreed to play the game in two halves of only 35 minutes each, with the sides changing straight round at half time in a fiery game in which the referee found it necessary to speak to several players.

Many players throughout the north were hesitant about committing themselves to the Northern Union cause for fear of 'professionalising' themselves; not merely in relation to Rugby Union but in respect of other sports including cricket, athletics and cycling. Fred Cooper, Dobson, Pollard and Murgatroyd didn't take part in the Wakefield match and Bradford were forced to field a below-strength side in the early weeks of the 1895–96 season. Despite that, five successive wins led to the side sharing pole position with Halifax, both ironically losing their 100 per cent records on 5 October 1895. Problems quickly resurfaced as a number of leading players, some of whom also served on the committee, appeared to be 'picking' their matches. The issue came to a head in the fixture on 16 November 1895 at Halifax when Toothill insisted he was unfit to play despite having put in a full shift the previous day

*Bradford appealed in vain against the 8-4 defeat at the hands of Tyldesley in the 1896–97 Challenge Cup third round. The Park Avenue club's case was that a Tyldesley forward had been given refreshment from the touchline during play. The refreshment in question was alleged to have been a bottle of beer which witnesses claimed was shared by other players while the referee was distracted at the other end of the pitch. The appeal floundered for want of evidence and Bradford were left with £5 costs.*

*Over a century later, in early 1999, Bradford Bulls would secure sponsorship with General Nutrition, the 'world's largest nutrition company' when coach Matthew Elliott enthused: 'Players can take drugs to gain an edge over their team mates or their opponents but here at Bradford we can educate our players to a better option, and an option which is the natural way to fitness.*

*'Our players don't need to look elsewhere to get that vital edge. We have always had a strong anti-drug philosophy at Odsal. A good team needs good nutrition; access to a wide range of vitamins will certainly make a difference to the performances of my players.'*

as a dye house worker. JH Jenkinson turned up after the game had started, claiming that he understood he had been designated as a reserve. Both resigned from the committee as requested and were possibly relieved when Bradford's appeal against the result of the home game with Broughton Rangers in April 1896 – recorded as a draw by the referee and his touch judges – failed. Bradford's Secretary, in Russia on business, had forgotten to advise the Northern Rugby Union that his club would not be represented. The referee and his touch judges, however, did appear – and the NRU ruled that the official 3-3 result should stand.

Bradford would have argued that their only goal had been kicked from a 'mark' made after a 'fair catch' and had therefore been worth four points. The referee insisted that he had awarded Bradford a penalty; valued at only three points.

### Jam jars and the pursuit of trophies

Bradford's finances, robust several years earlier, were so poor at the end of the 1895–96 season that the committee warned that the club could

fold. The cost of life membership was increased to £20 but by October the club was £8,500 in debt to the bank and to a 'private investor' and had been given until 4 February the following year to pay off £2,600 of that sum. The committee and supporters organised jam jar collections in pubs and clubs and by the due date all but £20 had been raised. Bradford's creditors agreed to accept the £2,580 on the basis that the balance be settled by the end of February.

Supporters were also quickly on hand, later that month, to help quell what could have been a serious fire at Park Avenue. The match against Wakefield Trinity only beat freezing temperatures because of straw laid on the pitch during the week. The straw, piled up on the pitch surrounds on the morning of the game, caught alight through drifting sparks when a group of supporters decided to light a fire on the terraces to keep warm. Play stopped for 20 minutes while players and supporters jointly put out the blaze.

Putting their off-field troubles behind them, Bradford went 24 games unbeaten, with 23 wins and a draw, from mid-December to late April in a successful 1897–98 season only marred by defeat in two finals.

The Park Avenue side reached the Challenge Cup final, losing to Batley at Headingley, and were denied the Yorkshire League championship by Hunslet in a hastily arranged play-off – also at Headingley – after the Parksiders and Bradford had finished level at the top of the table.

Defeat in the Yorkshire decider, played seven days after the Challenge Cup Final, was particularly hard to swallow as Bradford had battled bravely in attempting to overhaul a Hunslet side that at one stage headed the table

*Bradford were fined 15 shillings when several players were late for the fixture at Heckmondwike on 27 December 1897.*

# A match to remember
## Challenge Cup Final

*Bradford 0 Batley 7*
*Headingley, Leeds*
*Saturday 23 April 1898*
*A crowd of 27,941 – over double the 13,492 that had gathered at the same venue 12 months earlier – turned up at Headingley to discover at first hand whether Bradford could wrest the Challenge Cup from the inaugural winners.*
*Batley had made history, in 1897, by winning the first Challenge Cup final (by 10-3, against St Helens) and the Gallant Youths were to secure immortality by prevailing, once again, by a seven-point margin.*
*The attendance was believed to be the highest recorded for any rugby match, anywhere in the world, up to that date and many of the spectators viewed Bradford, who had gone into the game on the back of a lengthy winning run, as favourites.*
*Batley had closed the season in indifferent form while Bradford had finished 11 points ahead of the third-placed Gallant Youths in the Yorkshire Senior Competition.*
*Bradford also held a slight advantage in the scrum and early possession gained partly through that superiority helped them dominate the opening stages. However, a disallowed try for Kelsey, who dropped on the ball following a scrummage, and two penalty misses by centre Fred Cooper proved to be costly.*
*Batley, also unable to open their account in a scoreless first half, exerted their authority after the interval to retain the Cup. The legendary Wattie Davies scored the game's first points with a drop goal and the men from Mount Pleasant were assured of victory when captain John Goodall crossed and added a drop goal.*

*Bradford: Patrick; Dobson, Cooper, W Murgatroyd, F Murgatroyd; Wood, Prole; Broadley, Fearnley, Robertson, Holden, Kelsey, Holt, McLoughlin, Toothill.*

*Batley: Garner; Davies, Fitzgerald, JB Goodall, Fozzard; Oakland, H Goodall; Shackleton, Gath, Maine, Spurr, Fisher, Stubley, Munns, Rodgers.*

*Referee: Mr J H Smith (Widnes).*

by seven clear points and still appeared to be in an unassailable position after drawing 10-10 with Bradford at Parkside. Steady progress in the later stages of the campaign, however, aided by a series of stumbles by Hunslet, left Bradford needing a win against Wakefield in the final game of the league season to share pole position.

That was duly achieved in a 12-6 success. Meanwhile, it took Bradford only two attempts to reach their first Challenge Cup Final. Beaten by Tyldesley in the third round in 1896–97, the side forced their way through to the 1898 decider with victories over Swinton, Birkenhead Wanderers, Hull, Broughton Rangers and Widnes.

Swinton, beaten 7-2 at home in the first round, represented perhaps the biggest hurdle

*Scottish winger Bill Sinton totalled 44 tries in 76 appearances for Bradford between 1901–02 and 1903–04 – a phenomenal strike-rate in the Northern Union era.*

and were to finish that season as runners-up in the Lancashire League. Amateurs Birkenhead, who turned down a £150 carrot to switch to Park Avenue, fought valiantly before conceding a try by Pollard in the last minute, converted by Patrick, as Bradford prevailed 5-0. Hull were beaten in the third round at the Boulevard, Murgatroyd and Calvert scoring a try each in a 6-2 win, and mighty Broughton were undone 7-0 on their own midden before Widnes were seen off in the semi-final at Halifax 13-0.

### Besieged at Hunslet

The players were attacked by a mob after the 16-12 win at Parkside on 17 September 1898. What was described as a 'large section of the Hunslet support' waited outside the pavilion, after the game, for the Bradford players to emerge. The visitors, on leaving their changing room, were met by a barrage of stones, bottles and bricks. Several of the team sustained cuts and bruises while Calvert, hit in the mouth by a full-size brick, was taken to hospital with a suspected broken jaw. The injury proved to be less serious than that, but Calvert was unable to play in the next game.

### Double success and the first 'Super League'

Bradford achieved what had been viewed as the near impossible by winning the Yorkshire championship – the Yorkshire Senior Competition – in consecutive seasons in 1899–1900 and 1900–01.

Their inaugural success was founded on a strong opening in which the first nine games of the season were won, to set the pace ahead of Halifax and Batley, before the side slipped to a first defeat of the season with a 13-3 setback at Castleford.

Bradford avoided the experience of the preceding campaign, when their inaugural defeat – again in the tenth game, but on this occasion at home to Hull – precipitated a decline in which only three of the next 10 fixtures were

---

## A match to remember
### Yorkshire Senior Competition Championship Play-off

*Bradford 2 Hunslet 5*
*Headingley, Leeds*
*Saturday 30 April 1898*
*The balmy conditions that had prevailed seven days earlier in the Challenge Cup Final gave way to 'wet, cold and very disagreeable weather' when Bradford met Hunslet in a hastily-arranged contest to determine the destiny of the Yorkshire title.*
*Bradford, after the Challenge Cup Final defeat seven days earlier at the hands of Batley, were left with little to show for their efforts when the Parksiders overcame a 2-0 interval deficit to secure victory and the role of top dog in the County of the Broad Acres with the only try of the match, scored shortly before the hour mark.*
*Bradford had looked on course for a notable win to atone for the disappointment of the Challenge Cup set-back when the players went in at half time with a narrow lead ('well deserved,' according to the Yorkshire Post) to reflect upon, courtesy of a goal by Fred Cooper.*
*The Yorkshire Post recorded that 'Hunslet were still in difficulties, Bradford playing much the superior game, but the latter's attacks continued to end in minor points only'.*
*But the 3,000 crowd was to witness a reversal of fortunes in the second half.*
*Hunslet took the lead for the first time when former Gala forward James Ramage forced his way over in the 58th minute, Albert Goldthorpe adding the goal. And, with no further score occurring, the title was to become the property of the south Leeds club.*

*Bradford: Patrick; Dobson, Cooper, W Murgatroyd, F Murgatroyd; Calvert, Prole; Broadley, Robertson, Fearnley, Holt, Holden, Kelsey, Robinson, Foulds.*

*Hunslet: Mitchell; Hannah, A Goldthorpe, W Goldthorpe, Wright; Robinson, Gillings; Barraclough, Bowley, Deacon, Kaye, Leach, Ramage, Walsh, Young.*

*Referee: Mr Farrar (Halifax).*

**1899/00: Yorkshire Senior Competition**

| | P | W | D | L | F | A | Pts |
|---|---|---|---|---|---|---|---|
| Bradford | 30 | 24 | 2 | 4 | 324 | 98 | 50 |
| Batley | 30 | 21 | 6 | 3 | 219 | 72 | 48 |
| Halifax | 30 | 20 | 3 | 7 | 193 | 120 | 43 |
| Wakefield Trinity | 30 | 18 | 5 | 7 | 203 | 120 | 41 |
| Huddersfield | 30 | 17 | 4 | 9 | 181 | 110 | 38 |
| Hull KR° | 30 | 15 | 4 | 11 | 181 | 129 | 32 |
| Hull | 30 | 15 | 0 | 15 | 249 | 154 | 30 |
| Hunslet | 30 | 14 | 2 | 14 | 182 | 168 | 30 |
| Manningham | 30 | 13 | 3 | 14 | 207 | 203 | 29 |
| Bramley | 30 | 13 | 0 | 17 | 121 | 190 | 26 |

°Two points deducted for a breach of professional rules.

won.

This time, although Batley were to inflict a second successive defeat, Bradford confirmed their mettle and maintained their form in what became a two-horse race with the Gallant Youths to set up what was in effect a title decider at Park Avenue on 3 March 1900.

Batley arrived in Bradford at the head of the standings, with a two-point lead and with one outstanding fixture, while the Park Avenue men had three remaining matches to complete in the following week. The result, a 0-0 draw in an absorbing clash, handed the initiative to Bradford and it was an opportunity that, despite the Gallant Youths' subsequent victory in their closing game, was not about to be wasted.

Huddersfield were seen off at Fartown and Hull at home to set up the fixture against Castleford, again at home, as the game that would secure the title. And Bradford duly delivered with a 13-2 victory.

The Park Avenue men began the 1900–01 season in fine fettle, winning each match – save for one draw – until a visit to Bramley in early December ended in defeat.

That reverse, coupled with the shared result at Hull, gave leaders Halifax something of an advantage and Bradford's difficulties were compounded when the Yorkshire Management deducted two points from their record for signing S Herberts from Normanton on amateur forms and subsequently persuading him to register as a professional.

The complaint, made by Leeds St Johns, was upheld on appeal with Bradford ordered to pay the £5 costs but the incident failed to disrupt the rhythm of the side which, other than a defeat at Hull KR at the beginning of February, brushed aside all comers.

With Hull not quite strong enough to mount a serious challenge, Bradford had the title won by the middle of March and eventually finished four points ahead of a Halifax side that had stumbled in the closing straight.

The Lancashire and Yorkshire Senior Competitions came to an end, other than as vehicles for A teams, at the close of the 1900–01 season. Leading clubs such as Bradford and their counterparts west of the Pennines, Oldham, were hungry for a higher level of competition and anticipated higher crowds as a result.

Bradford, naturally regarded as among the favourites to win the new championship – the forerunner by almost a century of the Super League as 14 clubs resigned from the two county leagues to form the Northern Rugby League –

**1903–04: Northern Rugby League (leading seven)**

| | P | W | D | L | F | A | Pts |
|---|---|---|---|---|---|---|---|
| Bradford | 34 | 25 | 2 | 7 | 303 | 96 | 52 |
| Salford | 34 | 25 | 2 | 7 | 366 | 108 | 52 |
| Broughton Rangers | 34 | 21 | 4 | 9 | 306 | 142 | 46 |
| Hunslet | 34 | 22 | 1 | 11 | 250 | 157 | 45 |
| Oldham | 34 | 20 | 3 | 11 | 215 | 110 | 43 |
| Leeds | 34 | 19 | 5 | 10 | 211 | 145 | 43 |
| Warrington | 34 | 17 | 3 | 14 | 214 | 153 | 37 |

# A match to remember
## Yorkshire Senior Competition

*Bradford 13 Castleford 2*
*Park Avenue, Bradford*
*13 March 1900*
*A scintillating solo try by star three-quarter Fred Cooper sent Bradford on the way to their first championship success.*

*The Park Avenue men went into the game needing only a draw to clinch the Yorkshire title in the fourth of five seasons in which the Northern Union was split into county competitions, and nerves were in evidence in the early stages in which, the Yorkshire Post reported, 'the home backs were mulling badly'.*

*With tension mounting before a crowd of just under 3,000, Castleford had added to the pressure on the aspirants, who had led 3-0 at the interval, when Smart dropped a goal early in the second half.*

*It is the nature of champions, however, to respond positively to intimations of pressure and Bradford, duly rankled, did just that, Cooper epitomising the title-winners' collective temperament with a score that was perhaps the finest of his glittering career.*

*The visitors were under no real pressure when a scrum was formed on the half way line. But Cooper spotted an opening unseen by anyone else. In the words of the Post, 'dashing off, he dodged at top speed through his opponents, registering one of the finest tries of his career'.*

*The hero of the hour was unable to add the conversion but Castleford were finished. Cooper set up another attack which only resulted in a minor point, but 'pretty passing' by Wood and Prole led to Tom Broadley racing over, Cooper improving. And it was, of course, Cooper who sealed victory and the championship with a late penalty.*

*In a tense first half, Cooper and Len Dobson had been wide with drop goal attempts, while the latter had been bundled into touch close to the Castleford line and Hutt had had a try ruled out for a forward pass. Broadley, however, had put the side ahead at the break with an unconverted try.*

*Bradford: Ward; Pollard, F Murgatroyd, Cooper, TH Dobson; Prole, Wood; Broadley, Laidlaw, Hutt, Barraclough, Wright, Holden, Grayson, Feather.*

*Castleford: Townend; Salmani, Smith, Dalton, Niel; Brady, Smart; H Speed, Holland, Church, Webster, Ball, Dixon, Walton, Foster.*

*Referee: Mr W Eddison (Leeds).*

eventually finished sixth in the table, way behind Manchester side Broughton Rangers who not only took the title but also won the Challenge Cup to become the first team to record the 'double'.

Broughton had been 15 points clear of Bradford, who were then lying second, by late January; and a bleak February in which a draw and two defeats were sustained effectively ended the Park Avenue bid.

In a frustrating close to the campaign, Bradford closed their programme in the runners-up slot but could do nothing to prevent a drift down the table as Salford and Runcorn, both still in action, each won their last games. And matters took another turn for the worse when Northern Union officials ruled that the unemployed Harry Feather had been selected in contravention of the Northern Union's 'broken time' rules. The deduction of two points left them below Halifax in the standings.

## Champions

The Northern Rugby League championship, however, came to Park Avenue for the first and only time when Bradford took the Division One title in 1903–04 after a play-off at Halifax with joint leaders Salford.

In the second of three seasons in which Northern Union leaders toyed with two divisions (a concept which led to the departure of Holbeck, who missed out on promotion from Division Two after losing a play-off with St Helens and, piqued, switched to soccer as Leeds City, the forerunner of Leeds United) Bradford overcame a relatively indifferent opening to surge to the higher reaches of the table.

A potent mix of experience in the shape of

*James Dechan. The former Hawick Rugby Union winger who retains the club's record for tries in a match with seven in the 68-7 Yorkshire Cup victory over Bramley in October 1906.*

Tom Broadley, Bill Eagers, Harry Feather, Alex Laidlaw, George Marsden and Smales from the Yorkshire Senior Competition championship campaign, and younger players such as former Hawick Rugby Union winger James Dechan, Dunbavin, Gomer Gunn and Scottish winger Bill Sinton helped Park Avenue reach new heights.

Mosby set a new goalkicking record with 45, of which 41 were scored in league football, narrow defeats at Hull KR, Halifax and Wigan in the first eight games being put to one side as the team stepped into gear.

An unbeaten run of nine wins in 10 games from mid-January to late March left Bradford

| **The First Championship** | | | |
|---|---|---|---|
| **How the title was won – 1903–04** | | | |
| Sept | 5 | Widnes | (a) W 23 - 5 |
| | 12 | Swinton | (h) W 6 - 0 |
| | 19 | Hull KR | (a) L 3 - 9 |
| | 26 | Oldham | (h) W 5 - 3 |
| Oct | 3 | Halifax | (a) L 5 - 8 |
| | 10 | Huddersfield | (h) W 11 - 3 |
| | 17 | Hull | (h) W 19 - 0 |
| | 24 | Wigan | (a) L 2 - 3 |
| | 31 | Leeds | (h) W 13 - 5 |
| Nov | 7 | Runcorn | (a) W 14 - 2 |
| | 21 | Leigh | (a) W 9 - 8 |
| | 28 | Warrington | (h) W 14 - 0 |
| Dec | 5 | Batley | (a) L 0 - 2 |
| | 12 | Keighley | (h) W 8 - 2 |
| | 19 | Broughton R | (a) D 3- 3 |
| | 25 | Salford | (h) W 9 - 0 |
| | 26 | Hunslet | (h) L 0 - 3 |
| Jan | 2 | Widnes | (h) W 20 - 3 |
| | 9 | Swinton | (a) L 3 -10 |
| | 16 | Hull KR | (h) W 3 - 0 |
| | 23 | Oldham | (a) W 5 - 2 |
| | 30 | Halifax | (h) W 5 - 2 |
| Feb | 6 | Huddersfield | (a) W 20 - 3 |
| | 13 | Hull | (a) D 0 - 0 |
| | 20 | Wigan | (h) W 25 - 0 |
| | 27 | Leeds | (a) W 11 - 0 |
| Mar | 5 | Runcorn | (h) W 13 - 2 |
| | 22 | Leigh | (h) W 17 - 5 |
| | 26 | Warrington | (a) W 2 - 0 |
| | 28 | Salford | (a) L 2 - 4 |
| April | 9 | Keighley | (a) W 10 - 7 |
| | 12 | Batley | (h) W 5 - 0 |
| | 23 | Hunslet | (a) W 13 - 2 |
| | 25 | Broughton R | (h) W 5 - 0 |

# A match to remember
## Northern Rugby League Championship Playoff

*Bradford 5 Salford 0*
*Thrum Hall, Halifax*
*28 April 1904*
*A tremendous backs-to-the-wall performance in which sustained pressure by Salford was repelled, and the one real try-scoring opportunity taken, helped Bradford to a richly-deserved first full championship success before a 12,000 crowd.*

*Salford could legitimately contend that their superior points difference should have earned them the reward of the title after having finished as runners-up in each of the previous two seasons. Bradford, for their part, could point to the fact that they had enjoyed a slight edge in that season's league games between the sides, having beaten the Lancastrians 9-0 at home and lost only 4-2 away.*

*Several key men, injured in the victory only three days earlier over Broughton, were absent but the loss of the likes of Brear, Gomer Gunn and Scotsman Bill Sinton was met with stern resolve.*

*Full-back Ward epitomised the approach, pulling off a series of try-saving tackles that inspired those around him to even greater efforts.*

*Ward also relieved the pressure on a number of occasions with intelligent clearing kicks and that factor, together with a tendency by Salford to throw wayward final passes, helped Bradford keep their goal line intact.*

*As the first half progressed, winger Dunbavin began increasingly to worry Salford's defenders with a series of incisive breaks but there was no score to break the deadlock until left centre Mosby kicked a penalty early in the second half after Sharratt had been tackled late. The goal led a Salford team desperate to avoid a repeat of the previous two seasons' failures to yet more determined attacks but Ward, aided by the likes of Bill Eagers and George Marsden, were up to the task. And it was Dunbavin who, eight minutes from time, clinched the championship with an interception on his own 25 yard line that not only thwarted a possible Salford try but secured a touchdown for Hutt who was on hand to collect and race over the line when Dunbavin was hauled down 15 yards short.*

*Mosby's conversion attempt inexplicably failed but the season had been a success – with the championship trophy on board as confirmation.*

*Bradford: Ward; Dechan, Eagers, Mosby, Dunbavin; Marsden, Surman; Broadley, Laidlaw, Hutt, Rees, Upton, Sharratt, Greenwood, Barker.*

*Salford: D Smith; Bedford, Lomas, Thomas, Lewis; Ezekiel, Harter; Preston, Bebbington, Brown, Buckler, Heath, Rhapps, Shaw, Tunney, Williams.*

*Referee: Mr W McCutcheon (Oldham).*

---

facing a crucial and tough run-in of fixtures at Salford – silver medallists in each of the previous two seasons – Keighley and Hunslet, with home games against Batley and Broughton also to come.

The task took on a darker hue when Salford won 4-2 to go two points clear at the head of the table. But, in a heady April, Bradford won 10-7 at Keighley and beat Batley 5-0 at home to keep their bid alive.

Salford's surprise 7-0 defeat at Hull, whom they had beaten 23-5 at the Boulevard on 19 March in the Challenge Cup, provided a timely boost to morale as the men from Park Avenue contemplated fixtures against three of the major powers. Batley, the first hurdle, was cleared with a 5-0 win over the Gallant Youths, leaving testing closing fixtures at Hunslet, on Saturday 23 April, followed by the visit of Broughton Rangers two days later. Hunslet were summarily disposed of, 13-2, and the effort did Bradford little harm as Rangers were kept at bay the following Monday in a 5-0 win.

The result ensured that Bradford and Salford – who had won 11-3 and 19-3 at Runcorn and Warrington respectively, and 28-6 at home to Leigh – shared top billing on 52 points. And the fact that the Lancastrians enjoyed a superior points difference meant nothing as Northern Union chiefs ruled that what was effectively the first Championship Final should be played to settle the issue.

The date – Thursday 28 April, only three days after their game against Broughton – added to the pressure on the Park Avenue men but the team was at full steam and Salford were to be condemned, by Bradford's 5-0 win, to the runners-up role for a third consecutive season.

The following year, however, it was Bradford's turn to experience the feeling of 'so near and yet so far'. The retirement of Sinton hardly helped the cause but a number of other veterans were clearly hungry to enjoy their swansong with silverware as a two-point lead was established in the championship by Christmas.

Defeats in their final two games, against Batley and Swinton teams both languishing in the lower regions of the section, proved to be very costly. Oldham won the championship for the first time with 51 points to Bradford's 48.

Broadley, meanwhile, had, like Sinton, retired following the championship win over Salford. The Bradford captain, a Park Avenue man in the days before the launch of the Northern Union, had wavered over the 'Great Split' in 1895 and initially remained a Rugby Union player despite repeated blandishments by Bradford.

He was appointed Yorkshire captain in 1896 and was tipped for the same role with England.

---

*Bradford's involvement in the inaugural Yorkshire Cup of 1905–06 was tinged with controversy after the side had drawn 0-0 at Dewsbury in the first round on 14 October. A new date of 24 October had been agreed but the decision was over-ruled by the Yorkshire Committee which reminded both clubs that any replay should be played the following Wednesday, 18 October.*
*Bradford appealed successfully but Dewsbury, ignoring advice from Park Avenue, duly travelled over on that date in a bid to claim the game by default.*
*The Yorkshire Management turned down the claim – and Bradford progressed 5-0 when the match finally went ahead.*

---

Belatedly, however, Broadley opted to join the breakaway organisation, turning out for the first time in the 'derby' game with Manningham on 30 October 1896. His appearance had been disguised by the naming of 'A N Other' on the team sheet but rumours abounding in the area were confirmed when he ran out with the rest of the side.

Bradford's status as a continuing power was vividly illustrated when, on 12 November 1904, the club had six players selected to play for Yorkshire yet still won their game at Runcorn. Gunn, Dechan, Laidlaw, Marsden, Mosby and Tom Surman were the missing sextet but their absence was barely noticed as the Park Avenue side eased to an 11-0 win against a team admittedly destined to finish the season bottom of Division One.

Later that season, on 2 January, seven Bradford players were called up for the England v Other Nationalities game played on their own ground. Three – Feather, Marsden and Mosby – appeared for England, who won 26-11. Dechan, Gunn, Laidlaw and Rees were in the Other Nationalities' ranks.

**Challenge Cup glory**

Indifferent league form, after the heady days of the early 1900s, was more than made up for by the club's first success in the Challenge Cup.

Bradford, runners-up in 1898, went one better in 1905–06; a season in which they ironically finished in their lowest position (twelfth) since the launch of the Northern Union.

Wakefield Trinity were beaten 5-0 in the first round, courtesy of a try in the first half by Dunbavin and a goal for Marsden which proved to be enough despite heavy Trinity pressure in the second period.

Bradford entertained eventual champions Leigh at the next stage and pulled off a shock 15-0 success. The Lancastrians, who won the title controversially on a percentage basis – leading to the subsequent formalisation of fixtures by the

# A match to remember
## Challenge Cup Final

Bradford 5 Salford 0
Headingley, Leeds
28 April 1906
Bradford, in the last Challenge Cup Final to be played on a 15-a-side basis, served a huge helping of déjà vu on Salford, who had been beaten by the same scoreline in the Championship play-off two years earlier to the day. That win had secured Bradford's first title and the second dose ensured inaugural Challenge Cup glory for the Park Avenue side.

A 15,834 crowd – a little over 100 more than had watched the semi-final as heavy rain and sleet deterred potential spectators from eclipsing the 1903 record of 32,507 – turned up at Headingley with the Bradford contingent hoping for a repeat of the 33-0 league win a month earlier.

The conditions dictated otherwise and Bradford, facing the strong wind in the first half, had an escape when Salford captain Jim Lomas missed a penalty from in front of the posts. The Park Avenue men could, however, have been in front by half time, centre Connell twice failing to supply his winger James Dechan when a try was in the offing, and Bill Sinton being bundled into touch after a powerful run.

With the wind at their backs as the second half began, Bradford began to enjoy sustained territorial dominance and were unfortunate not to go in front when George Marsden crashed over, only to be turned on his back. As the tension began to mount Bradford's Harry Feather and Silas Warwick, of Salford, were sent off after a fracas but the Yorkshire side reacted better to the departures – despite Marsden missing a goal from in front of the posts – with Brear ploughing through two tackles for the opening score with only eight minutes left.

Marsden was unable to improve but an Alex Laidlaw penalty with two minutes remaining added to Bradford's authority. And the tactic of passing the ball around on their own line to deny Salford possession in the closing seconds ensured that the Lancastrians would suffer a fourth defeat in seven Challenge Cup Final appearances.

Bradford: Gunn; Sinton, Heseltine, Connell, Dechan; Brear, Marsden; Sharratt, Francis, Turner, Smales, Grayson, Feather, Greenwood, Laidlaw.

Salford: Cochrane; Hampson, Lomas, Thomas, McWhirter; Preston, John; Rhapps, EJ Thomas, Spencer, Lewis, Warwick, Brown, Foster.

Referee: Mr W McCutcheon (Oldham).

authorities – went into the game as favourites but trailed by 12 points at half time as an expansive approach by Bradford was rewarded with two tries each for Dechan and Dunbavin. And in a tight second period Dunbavin's hat-trick score three minutes from time sealed a notable win.

A record crowd of around 28,000 gathered at Park Avenue for the attractive quarter-final pairing with Halifax. All went home without a single point to debate but a healthy 20,000 turned out for the replay, which Bradford won 8-2 with the help of a try in each half for Dechan, Laidlaw adding a conversion.

That victory secured a semi-final pairing with Batley, Bradford's nemesis in the 1898 Cup Final, at Fartown, Huddersfield. Bradford, who had a league fixture at York the previous day, elected to send a side comprising 11 second team men to the Minster City, together with two trialists and a couple of players who had featured with the first team the previous season.

The club, called to account by the Northern Union, pointed to the fact that they had won 10-6 but were nevertheless fined £20. As far as Bradford's supporters were concerned, though, the decision was vindicated by an 11-3 victory over Batley in which Marsden netted two tries, Brear nipped over and Gunn kicked a goal.

The early and enduring romance of the Challenge Cup was captured by the storybook return to action of Bill Sinton for the 1906 Cup Final.

Sinton, who had missed the Championship play-off win against Salford in 1904 after being injured in the league win against Broughton

*Welsh full back Gomer Gunn. A brave defender who gave Bradford fine service from 1903 to 1908.*

continuation of the 13-a-side code in the city – was mainly notable for the action off the pitch.

On the field of play, however, the team, while slipping down the league rankings, made history by winning the Yorkshire Cup for the first time.

Although struggling Bramley were expected to present few problems in the first round tie at Park Avenue, no one expected the phenomenal 68-2 victory which represented a new winning margin for the club, edging by a point the 68-3 Challenge Cup success over amateurs Swinton Church in 1897.

Scottish winger James Dechan rattled up seven tries to set another record and J Marsland, in his sole appearance for Bradford, equalled Fred Cooper's total of seven goals in a game, in addition to creating three tries.

Bradford went on to account for strong favourites Leeds 21-5 in the second round and, in a tight derby semi-final, made full use of home advantage with a 6-4 win over Halifax.

Bradford's decision, meanwhile, to turn to the burgeoning Association Football code, so emulating the transformation of Manningham into Bradford City in 1903, appeared to have had its roots in a general downturn in fortunes on the field of play after the Challenge Cup victory of 1905–06, abetted by concerns voiced by a significant number of members over the reduction in players from the 1906–07 season from 15-a-side to 13-a-side.

The club had supported the formation of the Northern Union in 1895 but many members had backed the initiative on the understanding that the game itself would not differ from Rugby Union. The concept of playing with only 13 men was unacceptable to diehards, led by former player Laurie Hickson and the Reverend JE Leighton, who also longed for the return of the line-out. A motion for a reversion of rules received only three votes. Bradford, meanwhile, had been given confirmation by the Rugby Football Union that the club – but not the players, who had been professionalised – would be welcomed back to the fold.

Rangers three days earlier, had subsequently retired to concentrate on his work but had remained in the city.

The club's thoughts turned to him for the semi-final when Dunbavin sustained a bad ankle injury the previous week against Oldham. With their only other winger, Mosby, also on the sidelines Sinton's qualities and big match experience could not be overlooked and the piece of lateral thinking earned due reward, both in the semi-final and the final itself.

**Park Avenue swansong – the switch to soccer**

The 1906–07 campaign – Bradford's last before the switch to soccer compelled rugby enthusiasts to form Bradford Northern to ensure the

# A match to remember

## Yorkshire Cup Final

*Bradford 8 Hull KR 5*
*Belle Vue, Wakefield*
*1 December 1906*
*The inaugural success in the Yorkshire Cup turned out to be the last piece of silverware to be secured by the original Bradford club.*
*Rovers went into the game boosted by a 17-8 league victory over the Park Avenue men seven days earlier but the absence of such pivotal figures as James Dechan, Connell, Heseltine, Tom Surman, Greenwood and Francis suggested that it could be a different story in the more important meeting.*
*So it proved, even if Hull KR confirmed their status as favourites with a powerful opening in which Bradford were denied entry to the Robins' half until midway through the opening period through solid defence by the likes of full-back Gomer Gunn, Mosby, and Heseltine, with Alfred Mann and Harry Feather earning the wrath of the referee for vigorous tackles.*
*Alex Laidlaw put his side in front with a penalty in the twenty-third minute when Rovers were caught offside in a rare Bradford raid, but a smart switch of play led to Hull KR going in front when winger George (Titch) West – who had set a record, which still stands, of 53 points in a match with 11 tries and 10 goals in the Challenge Cup against amateurs Brookland Rovers 21 months earlier – crossed in the corner.*
*The Robins' lead wasn't to last for long. Bradford, who had seen a Gunn drop goal attempt drift wide of a post,*

*took a lead they were not going to lose when Walton popped up on the end of an attack launched by Tom Surman and Greenwood to beat Rovers full-back Alfred Carmichael in a thrilling arcing run to the corner.*
*That score, which Laidlaw was unable to convert, was supplemented before the interval with a quality touchdown for Dechan, who was first to an intelligent kick by Connell.*
*Mosby, this time, failed with the touchline conversion and Rovers forced their way back into an epic contest with a Billy Phipps drop goal five minutes after the resumption.*
*That, however, proved to be the last score of the game as Hull KR missed a couple of kickable penalties and Laidlaw, who otherwise had a magnificent match, was also wide.*
*Dechan was unable to take a pass with the tryline at his mercy but, inspired by Gunn, Bradford's defence held out for a magnificent victory before an 11,000 crowd.*

*Bradford: Gunn; Dechan, Mosby, Heseltine, Connell; Brear, Surman; Laidlaw, Greenwood, Francis, Mann, Feather, Walton.*

*Hull KR: Alfred Carmichael; West, Phipps, Rees, Madley; Barry, Lofthouse, Gath, Hambrecht, Sherwood, Spackman, H Smith, Windle.*

*Referee: Mr W McCutcheon (Oldham).*

---

The side, while winning the Yorkshire Cup, slipped to a new low of eighteenth in the table and envious eyes perhaps turned towards Valley Parade, where Manningham in their new guise of Bradford City were attracting national interest and, with a round ball, bigger crowds.

Attention, it seems, was focusing behind the scenes on a switch to the Football League, which became the favoured option of the committee.

In March 1907 a special meeting was called to resolve the issue. The committee's response to the members' vote for a return to Rugby Union was to declare the meeting illegal, on the basis that it had contravened the club's articles of association.

Ballot papers were issued which secured a majority in favour of soccer and that mandate was followed, on 7 May 1907, by an 18-2 vote on the same lines by the club's Finance and Property Committee which insisted, 'association is the best paying game from a financial point of view'.

The initial excitement was immediately quashed when Bradford's application for membership of the Football League was turned down. The club, perhaps outmanoeuvred in a complex game of brinkmanship, joined the Southern League, with Oldham Athletic. Ironically – given that a motivating factor in the change of codes was the desire to maintain parity

*An artist's review of the first Bradford Charity Cup Final.*

with their old rivals at Valley Parade – Bradford (Park Avenue) never quite regained their former ascendancy.

Given that during the furore Bradford possessed the Challenge Cup and, from early December, the Yorkshire Cup, it could be argued that continued membership of the Northern Rugby League had perhaps been the best option.

The future of the professional rugby code in the city would, however, be safeguarded by the immediate formation by a number of stalwarts of a new club which could not have been more aptly or better-named; although they were to face 30 years of struggle before any real light was to dawn.

Further down the track, in fact exactly one hundred years after the opening of Park Avenue, plans to turn Odsal back into a rubbish dump fell through when the old Park Avenue ground – envisaged as Bradford Northern's new home by Bradford Council – was found to be in a dangerous state of disrepair.

The announcement that the main stand and the changing rooms complex would have to be bulldozed was made, sadly, only a few days prior to the centenary of Bradford's first game at the stadium on 25 September 1980. And Park Avenue was levelled in just one week, between 13 and 20 October 1980.

# 2.
# Manningham

Manningham, thought to have been formed in 1872 and – as Bradford City soccer club – still a vibrant concern in the early years of the 21st century, occupies a special niche in Rugby League history.

The club, as the first champions of the Northern Union, is guaranteed a central place on the Rugby League pantheon; a position, perhaps in an echo of the great poet or musician who dies young, that cannot be tarnished by subsequent failure or by a painfully slow demise.

Although many commentators believe that Manningham was formed in 1876 certain Victorian sources suggest that the club, based in what was regarded one of the more salubrious suburbs of Bradford, may have been launched four years earlier.

The Bradford Observer provided evidence in its reportage of the club's annual dinner in 1885 in which Chairman William Lister offered an important clue in his speech.

In looking back, he stated '... as the Manningham Albion club for eight years and the Manningham club for the past few years'.

> *Manningham's game at Horton Alexandria in late 1880 was abandoned in rare circumstances. The visitors scored an early try, which the Horton captain contested.*
>
> *His Manningham counterpart, C H Nelson, acceded to the objection but refused to back down when a second away try was disputed. Horton simply walked off the field, bringing the game to a premature close.*

> *The 1883–84 Yorkshire Cup campaign opened with home successes against Barnsley and Batley Mountaineers, the latter victory setting up a dream tie with Bradford. Manningham spent a week in Blackpool as part of their pre-match preparations and the tie attracted a 20,000 crowd. Bradford, however, won the game and went on to win the competition.*

Given that the suffix 'Albion' was dropped in 1880, Mr Lister's statement suggests that the original launch must have been in 1872.

'Albion' was discarded in 1880 when Manningham moved to Carlisle Road, on a site since occupied by Drummond Road Schools, playing in black jerseys and socks and white shorts and winning sixteen and drawing two of their 21 games in their first season at their new home.

*F Lister, an early administrator of the successful Manningham club.*

Manningham's headquarters and changing facilities, by 1884, was at the Junction Hotel on Heaton Road but the club subsequently encountered a period of uncertainty, with irregular fixtures because of a shortage of players.

The club, though, continued to grow in stature and by mid-1892 were of sufficient standing to be at the forefront of the Yorkshire Alliance, a competitive league that perhaps presaged in part the subsequent formation of the Northern Union.

Manningham had entered the Rugby Union's Yorkshire Cup (T'Owd Tin Pot) for the first time in 1881–82 and the side's growing popularity was illustrated by the decision to stage the first round tie against Gildersome & Morley at Bradford's spacious Park Avenue ground. Harrogate were dispensed with in the second round, after a replay which went to extra time before 'a very large assemblage of spectators, in whom the contest seemed to arouse the greatest of enthusiasm' before the adventure ended with a controversial defeat at Kirkstall.

Twelve months later, Manningham slipped out of the competition at the first hurdle. But a 3,000 crowd at Carlisle Road for the visit of Ossett once again suggested a bright future and,

*The legendary Eddie Holmes, a hero of the pre-Northern Union era.*

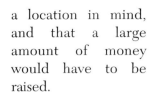

*Fred Clegg, a key member of the Manningham pack in the glorious 90s.*

perhaps, not one envisaged as being entirely focused on sport, a view confirmed in 1885 when Manningham became the first club in Yorkshire to open its own news and reading room, a facility based at the Thorncliffe Hotel.

The prime *raison d'être* of the club was, however, indisputably rugby football. As Manningham's prominence grew and crowds increased accordingly – 8,000 turned up for the visit of Dewsbury early in the 1885–86 season and 7,000 paid to see Halifax beaten in November, when the new grandstand was opened – the team ratified its newfound notoriety by accounting for Pudsey, Liversedge and Hull before taking on Bradford at Park Avenue in front of an 18,000 gate.

Manningham's own Carlisle Road ground was, however, under threat from the School Board, which had targeted the site as ideal for a new school.

Most of the 4,000 crowd for the visit of Brighouse in late April 1886 knew well enough that the game would be the last played at Carlisle Road. On 7 May Chairman William Lister informed attendees at the annual dinner that a new ground had to be found, that the committee had

a location in mind, and that a large amount of money would have to be raised.

Fourteen days later, at the annual meeting, the site was identified as Valley Parade. The ground, a former quarry with a capacity of 18,000, was hacked out of the hillside in less than three months and housed one wooden stand, transferred from Carlisle Road.

*Alfred Ayrton, the Manningham chairman. Ayrton's sure hand and vision steered the club to early Northern Union glory. Those qualities helped precipitate the switch to Bradford City.*

*Manningham supporters unable to get to the Yorkshire Cup Final against Batley in 1884 gathered in the centre of Bradford to await news of the result by telegram.*
*So many assembled that the Salvation Army struggled to complete its planned march through the town and tempers flared on both sides.*
*The Bradford Daily Telegraph reflected, 15 years later: 'Natural result – a collision in which the Army suffered a reverse with the loss of their flag, which was torn up. A football crowd is not to be trifled with.'*
*The fact that an estimated quarter of the 5,000 crowd at Cardigan Fields, Leeds, were women may have had something to do with the rowdy atmosphere back home. One can only speculate.*

*A 5,000 crowd assembled at a revamped Carlisle Road for the visit of Hull for the opening game of 1884–85, vindicating the time and money spent on improvements to the ground during the summer. The side wore, for the first time, claret and amber – based on the colours of the Prince of Wales Own (West Yorkshire) Regiment – and continues to do so as Bradford City.*

*Manningham, 1893–94. Perhaps the last known photograph of the Valley Paraders as a rugby union side.*

The opening game was on 25 September 1886 when visitors Wakefield Trinity enjoyed a narrow win before a near full house. The next fixture, when Manningham entertained Huddersfield, also ended in defeat but was rather harder to swallow, the crucial drop goal coming 'from the foot of despised ex-Manninghamite H. Archer'. Twenty-eight games were played in the first season at Valley Parade. Sixteen were won and four drawn, a profit of £137 was made on turnover of £1,907, and an increased membership of 1,146 was recorded.

# The tussle for a Welshman

*Manningham and Bradford found themselves in contention for the services of a Welshman from Newport in 1885. Over 50 years before another son of the Valleys – Trevor Foster – headed north from the same town, the Newport and Wales back James Bridie took the route to Bradford where he managed to turn out for both clubs.*

*Bridie, who had already secured work in the city, signed for Manningham and then played for Bradford. Manningham supporters, not best pleased, rewrote a popular music hall song of the time to the refrain:*

*'Bridie was a Welshman,*
*Bradford was a thief,*
*Bradford came to our house,*
*And now we are in grief.'*

*The Welshman, perhaps thoroughly embarrassed by the furore, returned to Manningham.*

The ground, despite problems with the pitch which would continue for decades, had been completed in amazingly quick time, with the construction contract signed on 11 June 1886 and the first game played in late September, at a cost of around £1,600 – £400 more than the original estimate because of the need to erect changing rooms and build a stone wall around the ground.

The drive to build a new stadium, and a new future, at Valley Parade was helped by an initiative in which free membership for seven years was offered to the person attracting most new recruits. The winner, a Mr Jackson, beat all comers to the prize with a total of 95; the runner up attracted 35.

Membership was doubled to 1,200 by the exercise, and by the club's continued success on the field of play.

**Expenses**

The Valley Paraders, viewed as one of the sides guilty of paying players in contravention of Rugby Union rules, escaped censure when Pudsey launched a formal complaint following defeat in the first round of the Yorkshire Cup in

*Manningham, the first Northern Union Champions in 1895–96, pose proudly. The Northern Union had not commissioned a trophy by the close of the competition's first campaign. The bounty on show is the Yorkshire Shield, which Manningham also won that season. Back row (left to right): H Jowett, T Bamford, H Tolson, T Wilkinson, J Thomas, F Clegg, A Proctor, H Whiteoak, W Robson, club doctor. Middle row: A Leach, W Atkinson, J Brown, A Barraclough, GE Lorimer, A Padgett, J Newton. Front row: W Needham, J Williamson, R Sunderland, H Pickles.*

# No common ground

*Manningham beat Bradford in the third round of the 1886–87 Yorkshire Cup – with the teams miles apart.*

*The dream-tie-turned-nightmare was settled in bizarre fashion after the first game failed to go ahead because of snow on the ground. Other matches in Yorkshire had survived as workers cleared pitches; however, no attempt had been made to do so at Park Avenue.*

*There was a suspicion that Bradford had simply not wanted to play and the Yorkshire Rugby Union County Football Committee ruled that they should lose home advantage and that the game be played at Leeds St John's.*

*Bradford objected, claiming unsuccessfully that no rule compelled them to clear their pitch and that the cost would have been £30, and offered to entertain Manningham on a date of their opponents' choosing. They also stated that in the absence of a reply they would be on the Park Avenue pitch at 3.30pm on*

*Saturday 16 March.*

*Manningham responded that they would abide by the County Committee's instructions and that if the ruling body stipulated that the game should take place in Leeds, that was where they would be.*

*Bradford's members, who blamed their opponents for 'the whole fiasco', gathered at the railway station on the day of the game to 'hoot' at the departing Manningham side.*

*Manningham's train was stopped specially at Armley, the team disembarking for Leeds St John's Cardigan Fields ground. Bradford, meanwhile, lined up at Park Avenue and, at the same time, the respective captains each kicked the 'winning' goal.*

*The County Committee ruled in favour of Manningham but the issue was far from over, Bradford going to court over the matter. The judge rejected their case.*

*Manningham went on to lose at Ossett in the next round.*

---

1886. Pudsey insisted that J Birmingham and W Pulleyn, both of whom had previously played for Selby, had been paid 'more than expenses'. One witness testified that the pair had 'received broken time payments, rail fare and a sovereign' in return for turning out for Manningham. Another witness claimed that Pulleyn had said that he would play for the club that paid him best and that 'football paid better than working'. The Yorkshire Committee found the case 'not proven'. In the same year the Rugby Football Union, concerned at the growing dominance of the largely working-class northern clubs, introduced strict amateur rules.

Players could still adhere to the old amateur ethos of simply turning out for whoever they liked. The 'inventive genius of an irresponsible news vendor' led to confusion when Fred Bonsor, one of Bradford's leading players and the Yorkshire captain to boot, featured for Manningham against Manchester Rangers in October 1889. Rumours had been rife that Bonsor had transferred from Bradford and there was a huge roar when the county player ran out in a Manningham shirt, and equally resounding cheers when he helped steer the side to victory. The signing was, however, an illusion; Bonsor, who had not been selected for Bradford's game

that day, had merely opted to spend the afternoon helping out a Manningham team struggling with injuries.

## Trouble and truculence

Two perhaps complementary social revolutions got underway in the 1890s, with Bradford and Manningham centrally involved in each.

Rising crowds, coupled with the issue of 'broken time' which occasionally made it difficult for working men to play on Saturday afternoons, were pointing clubs in the north inexorably towards a collision course with the Rugby Football Union. Manningham President James Freeman, at his club's annual meeting in

*The men who represented Manningham in the 1899–1900 season.*

May 1891, insisted to thunderous applause: 'It is only right that a working man who plays football for the entertainment of others should be paid'.

Mr Freeman may have also had in mind, or at least been inspired by, the famous Manningham Mills strike which laid the foundations for the formation of the Labour Party. And he will no doubt have noted the cancellation of the Boxing Day fixture at Valley Parade with Hawick, who were unable to travel because 4,000 Scottish railwaymen were on strike.

The 1890–91 season, played against that backdrop of social unrest, was hit by trouble on the field as general ill temper spilled over into football.

It took the prompt actions of players and police to rescue the referee from angry home supporters after Manningham won narrowly at Leeds Parish Church – and the side's continuing progress in the Yorkshire Cup was fraught with problems of one kind or another.

A spectator collapsed and died shortly before the kick off of the first round game at Hull Britannia, played before a 10,000 crowd, while Heckmondwike – beaten at the next stage –

*John Beckram, in Manningham kit, was pictured on the cover of Bradford City's first handbook, in which the rules of Association Football were explained to the new initiates. City wore Manningham's shirts for their first home game, against Gainsborough Trinity, and possibly for several subsequent matches.*

mounted a three-pronged appeal against the result.

Their first point, that Manningham's winning try had been scored by a player who was outside the pitch perimeter because a corner flag had been knocked down and not replaced, was dismissed. The second allegation – that Manningham secretary Mr S Naylor had thrown a pair of drawers onto the field so that the goalkicker Firth could clean his boots before converting the try – was also contested.

# A death on Christmas Day

*Valley Parade, quickly deemed a fine venue by the authorities, housed 12,000 for the 1887 Yorkshire Cup semi-final between Halifax and Huddersfield and was allocated the game between Yorkshire and the touring Maoris in mid-December, a match watched by 7,000 supporters.*

*Another big attendance led to tragedy at the match against Heckmondwike on Christmas Day 1888. An estimated 16,000 crowd packed the ground and children were passed over the heads of adults to sit in front of the pitch perimeter fencing for a better view. After seven minutes a sudden surge in the crowd at the Midland Road end led to the barrier collapsing, trapping several boys. The match was halted and players joined spectators in rescuing four youngsters. Three had suffered relatively minor injuries, the worst being a broken limb. But 12-year-old Thomas Coyl, who had sustained a broken neck, was pronounced dead.*

*The game, which had restarted, was brought to a halt when word of the fatality spread through the crowd, and the gate receipts of £115 were donated to the dead boy's family. A verdict of accidental death was subsequently returned, Manningham officials testifying at the inquest that spectators had been informed of the existence of a separate boys' pen.*

*Bradford City 1903–04. The Valley Paraders' first soccer team.*

## The Pink 'Un

*The Bradford Daily Telegraph introduced the 'Pink 'Un' in 1889 in response to popular demand by rugby fans. The newspaper had, for several years, printed a late 'football edition' on Saturday evenings which included the day's results. Supporters, however, all too often bought an earlier edition in error. From Saturday 14 September the Telegraph's football edition was printed on pink paper to avoid confusion.*

Mr Naylor produced a blue silk handkerchief to the committee as the item in question; the issue was considered trivial by the committee and also thrown out.

But the third objection, that Manningham had selected a player – Rhodes – who was ineligible, having played for Heckmondwike at Valley Parade on Christmas Day (well after the 1 December transfer deadline) was treated as having some substance. Rhodes was banned for the season and the cup-tie was ordered to be replayed at Halifax. Manningham won, only to lose to Pontefract at the next stage.

### Yorkshire Senior Competition glory

Bradford and Manningham renewed acquaintance, six years after the celebrated Yorkshire Cup affair, with two closely-fought games in 1892-93. Bradford justified their role of favourites with a 2-0 win at Park Avenue on 2 December, securing their victory by denying Manningham captain Ike Newton a late try, holding him up on their own goal line. And Bradford also won the return – this time 4-2 – as 18,000 packed Valley Parade for the Christmas Eve clash and thousands more remained locked out.

Manningham, though, put those defeats behind them by reaching the semi-final of the Yorkshire Cup, facing Halifax at Huddersfield before a 20,000 crowd and establishing a half time lead before losing 12-4.

The side, however, confirmed its qualities by withstanding a strong finish by Brighouse, the team of the season, before a crowd reckoned to be higher than the 18,000 who gathered for the Bradford game. The home supporters were forced to endure a tense last few minutes after George Lorimer had a goal disallowed by the referee, with Manningham 7-2 ahead, because

*Glory in the round-ball code came quickly to Bradford City. The Division Two championship was won in 1907–08 and, three years later, City reached their peak as a soccer club by winning the FA Cup. The immortal Jimmy Speirs, a Scottish international and holder of the Military Medal, scored the only goal in the victory over Newcastle United. He is pictured with the rest of the side, balanced precariously on the steps to the Old Trafford podium, awaiting his reward.*

## Fattorinis

*The clebrated sportsman and Olympic timekeeper Mr Antonio Fattorini was a key figure in Manningham's rise to prominence.*

*In addition to proving himself one of the soundest administrators in the Northern Union, he was a member of the renowned jewellery and sports trophy manufacturing firm of Fattorini and Sons, which produced the Rugby League Challenge Cup and the FA Cup.*

*Quite apart from also founding Grattans and Empire Stores, Antonio Fattorini was also centrally involved in the discussions which led to the club joining the Second Division of the Football League, as Bradford City, in May 1903.*

# A match to remember

*Leeds v Manningham*
*Headingley*
*Saturday 20 September 1890*
*Leeds opened their new Headingley ground at the beginning of the 1890-91 season. To Manningham fell the honour of being the first visitors to one of the most famous stadiums in the world.*
*As befits such an occasion, victory went to the home side by one try, one goal and two minors to the two minor points registered by their guests.*
*Manningham, however, contributed fully to an entertaining game in which Leeds largely owed their win to excellent defence.*
*The Yorkshire Post reflected, in criticising Leeds for confusion over the allocation of seating for members and poor facilities for the press: 'The players, at all events, realised to the full the expectations of their followers, scoring a decisive victory. It must not be supposed, however, that the score really indicates the run of play, as the visitors had quite as much of the game as the home team. In one respect the new Leeds fifteen appear to have one advantage over the late St Johns – they make better use of their opportunities'.*
*Leeds scored the only try of the game, through GM Naylor, who was sent in at the corner flag after fine approach work by centre Fletcher, while the home side*

*had resisted attacks inspired by Manningham centres Ike Newton and Robertshaw. Visiting stand off Pocock – who displayed tactics of a 'smart nature' throughout – also threatened with a 50-yard raid and was later tackled on the home line in the closing seconds.*
*Perhaps the key moment, shortly after Manningham forward Heaton had been held short, came when Robertshaw 'got past every opposition, when all hopes of saving a goal seemed over, Southall started off with long strides and overtook the flying three-quarter, who had the field to himself, and brought him down on the verge of the line'.*
*Southall had earlier denied an attack by Manningham forwards who were 'full of dash' while winger Summersgill clinched Leeds' win with a drop goal.*

*Leeds: Wilkinson; Southall, Fletcher, Summersgill; Burrell, Field; Broadbent, Fowler, Hoyle, Hudson, Naylor, Sumner, Todd, Wood, Load.*

*Manningham: Brown; Newton, Robertshaw, Firth; Pocock, Beardsall; Holmes, Toothill, Hardaker, Heaton, Boulton, Brayshaw, Clegg, Carey, Graham.*

*Referee: Mr B Kilner (Wakefield).*

the Brighouse forwards had charged at him. The match official ordered the kick to be retaken and Lorimer's second attempt bounced out off a post.

Manningham duly established themselves as the premier football team east of the Pennines by winning the Rugby Union's Yorkshire Senior competition in 1893–94; an achievement that set the agenda for the higher accolade of the inaugural Northern Union championship two years later.

A 34-0 hammering of Broughton Rangers (who, in 1901–02, would become the first side to win the Cup and League 'double') should have sent alarm bells ringing through the rest of the county and there were certainly alarm bells ringing in London, where the annual general meeting of the Rugby Football Union voted against a proposal for broken time payments by 282 votes to 136; a stance which would be continued and which would cost the RFU dear

less than two years later.

Manningham finished the season joint level at the head of the table, with 33 points from 14 wins and five draws, with Brighouse, who had drawn three and lost four of their 22 games.

Those 14 victories included two memorable successes over Bradford, the first by 6-4 in late September at Valley Parade. Manningham fell behind to a JH Jenkinson drop goal from half way which sent the Bradford contingent in the 17,000 crowd into raptures but the home side hit back to win with a converted try and set up the chance of a 'double' when the trip to Park Avenue came around on Boxing Day.

That was achieved with a 3-0 win before an 18,408 crowd, which paid record receipts of £416 9s 0d. And there was a sign of what was to come at the end of the season when Brighouse travelled to Valley Parade on 30 December and forced a 0-0 draw.

*Chairman Alfred Ayrton was highly regarded by stalwarts of the club in each of its guises as Manningham and Bradford City. That fact is vividly illustrated by the loving care taken over the magnificent citation commissioned in his honour.*

There was nothing to separate the two teams in the standings at the close of the campaign and that was how it remained after a play-off game, ordered by the Yorkshire Rugby Union to settle the title, when another scoreless draw was recorded.

Manningham went on to win the replay, staged at Belle Vue, Wakefield, on 20 March, 9-3 with the help of a try by Australian George Stephenson which Lorimer improved.

The team returned home to wondrous scenes. An estimated 10,000 crowd met the players at the Exchange station and thousands more lined the route back to Belle Vue where the Manningham Brass Band played 'See the conquering heroes come'.

The general excitement was to lead, unerringly, to the formation of the Northern Union in 1895 as 22 leading clubs broke away from the Rugby Football Union, with Manningham to the fore. Tony Fattorini was as enthusiastic as anyone. He told his members: 'If the new Union is properly conducted, the Rugby Union will have to recognise professionalism in some form or another or they will find ere long the only support they will receive will be from the universities and the public schools'.

Fattorini's enthusiasm was well founded. His club was firmly among the leading lights in the new code and would confirm that status by becoming the inaugural champions of the Northern Union.

Manningham laid the foundations for their historic success with 27 victories from 35 games up to the end of March 1896. The championship was still in the balance when the team, with matches at Widnes and Hunslet still to play, hosted Hull in their last home game of the

*Bradford City 1910–11: the men who brought the FA Cup to Bradford for the one and only time.*

# A match to remember
## Launch of the Northern Union

*Tyldesley 6 Manningham 0*
*Well Street, Tyldesley*
*Saturday September 7 1895*
*Report from the Yorkshire Post*
*The above organisations met at Tyldesley before about 3,000 spectators. Barraclough started, but no return was made. The home contingent, however, quickly succeeded in removing the ball out of danger. The visitors again assailed the home line, Needham showing up prominently. J Berry then got possession, and took the game into his opponents' quarters, where Worthington scored. Shaw took the place but failed to convert. On the resumption the visitors were to the fore and for a considerable time pressed their opponents. Then a free kick was allowed them, but Lorimer's attempt was a failure. For some time interesting play was witnessed, and then Miller showed up prominently, but Lorimer impeded his progress, the game still remaining in the visitors' territory.*

*Manningham now had a turn and invaded the home citadel, where Harris returned. Again, and again, the visitors tried, but all efforts proved futile. Half time was called with the score – Tyldesley 1 try; Manningham, nil. On the resumption play settled down at the centre. Presently matters were improved for the home contingent by Shaw, who showed some conspicuous play. For a long time Tyldesley were kept busily acting on the defensive. L Berry improved matters, transferring play to the centre. Worthington dribbled over and scored, no goal resulting. Tyldesley therefore won by 2 tries (6 points) to Manningham nil.*

*Tyldesley (squad): Backs: Shaw, J Berry, W Roberts, W Berry, Shepherd, Harris, Evans, Fox, R Berry. Forwards: Bell, J Roberts, Worthington, Miller, Smith, G Woodward, W Woodward, Cooper, Lawton.*

*Manningham: Lorimer; Needham, Maxfield, Atkinson, Pickles; Williamson, Sunderland; Clegg, Barraclough, Lambert, Wilson, Bamford, Whiteoak, Fisher, Robinson.*

*Thousands pay their respects at the memorial service following Valley Parade's darkest hour – the fire on May 11 1985 in which 56 people perished and many hundreds more were injured.*

season on 18 April 1896.

Rivals Halifax, without a fixture, were present on the touchline and the Thrum Hallers commissioned a special train for their supporters.

The Manningham Brass Band entertained the 8,000 crowd while the Paraders also delighted the Valley faithful, maintaining their title bid with an 8-6 win.

Association Football was first played at Valley Parade on 14 March 1886 when 3,000 witnessed a replayed Leeds Hospital Cup semi-final between Bradford FC, who were based at Park Avenue, and Leeds FC, Bradford winning 4-0. Over 12 months later, on 3 April 1897, the ground hosted the Bradford Schools Competition semi-finals; Lilycroft and Chapel Street drew 1-1, and Whetley Lane overcame Lorne Street 1-0.

Tony Fattorini, who was on the committee of the West Yorkshire Football Association, represented a club operating under the name of Manningham which, although affiliated, did not have any results published.

Manningham Chairman James Freeman then called, in 1900, for a return to 'that free and independent style of amateur play'. His plea may merely have been a natural reflection, common to many at the turn of any century, on what has been lost. Subsequent events, however, cast a more intriguing light on his dissatisfaction.

The rise of Association Football, previously very much the second cousin to both forms of rugby and to cricket in the north of England, had not gone unnoticed in Bradford.

A facet of the round-ball code which was

# A match to remember
## Northern Union

*Hunslet 0 Manningham 4*
*Parkside*
*25 April 1896*
*Centre Jack Brown, with a drop goal deep into injury time, ensured that Manningham won the inaugural Northern Union championship without recourse to a play-off against neighbours Halifax.*
*Manningham and Halifax had gone into their final games of the season with the Bradford club a point clear at the top of the table.*
*The game at Parkside appeared to be heading for a scoreless draw when, with news of Halifax's 8-0 win at Warrington emerging, Brown attempted his late match-winner.*
*Manningham's right to the title appeared to be pre-ordained as the centre's shot hit an upright before bouncing over the crossbar for a dramatic goal which ensured the Bradford club's retention of pole position. The incident delighted the new champions' many supporters in the 15,000 crowd, not to mention the club's committee, which had watched the team depart from the Midland Station at 2.10pm before heading for south Leeds in two stagecoaches.*
*Inspired by banners, flags and Chinese umbrellas sporting Manningham's claret and amber, Manningham gave as good as they got against a tough Hunslet side and the match was halted at one stage as the referee cautioned both sets of players. No penalty goals were kicked, however, leaving the way open for Brown to register the all-important score.*
*The champions returned by road to Bradford and were cheered by crowds all along Leeds Road, Well Street, Forster Square, Market Street, Tyrrel Street, Bank Street, Manningham Lane, Bowland Street, Lumb Lane, Carlisle Road, Silver Street, Heaton Road, Victor Road and North Park Road until they reached Belle Vue, where around 5,000 exulted in speeches by the likes of George Lorimer – who had scored a third of the side's points for the season – James Freeman, Alf Barraclough, Ike Newton, Fred Clegg and Brown.*

*Hunslet: W Goldthorpe; Hannah, Robinson, AE Goldthorpe, Mitchell; Wright, Fletcher; Barraclough, Deacon, Greenwood, Kaye, Leach, Mawson, Rubrey, Walsh.*

*Manningham: Lorimer; Newton, Brown, Atkinson, Needham; Sunderland, Williamson; Bradley, Padgett, Clegg, Barraclough, Bamford, Proctor, Wilkinson, Leach.*

### How the title was won - 1895-96

| | | | |
|---|---|---|---|
| Sept | 7 Tyldesley | (a) | L 0 - 6 |
| | 14 Batley | (h) | W 5 - 3 |
| | 21 Leigh | (a) | L 0 -11 |
| | 28 Runcorn | (h) | W 13 - 9 |
| Oct | 5 Wakefield T | (a) | W 16 - 3 |
| | 8 Huddersfield | (h) | W 6 - 0 |
| | 12 Brighouse R | (h) | L 0 - 3 |
| | 19 Wigan | (h) | W 5 - 0 |
| | 26 Bradford | (h) | W 8 - 4 |
| Nov | 2 Oldham | (a) | L 0 - 10 |
| | 9 Halifax | (h) | W 16 - 4 |
| | 16 Leeds | (a) | W 3 - 0 |
| | 23 Tyldesley | (h) | W 6 - 0 |
| | 30 Hull | (a) | W 6 - 3 |
| Dec | 7 Warrington | (h) | W 3 - 0 |
| | 14 Liversedge | (a) | W 17 - 5 |
| | 21 Stockport | (h) | W 16 - 0 |
| | 25 Hunslet | (h) | W 3 - 0 |
| | 26 Broughton R | (a) | L 3 - 10 |
| | 28 Widnes | (h) | W 33 - 3 |
| Jan | 1 St Helens | (a) | W 8 - 3 |
| | 4 Rochdale H | (h) | W 7 - 5 |
| | 11 Batley | (a) | W 4 - 0 |
| | 18 Brighouse R | (a) | W 9 - 8 |
| | 25 Halifax | (a) | L 0 - 5 |
| Feb | 1 Wakefield T | (h) | W 15 - 0 |
| | 8 Wigan | (a) | W 7 - 4 |
| | 15 St Helens | (h) | W 9 - 5 |
| | 18 Huddersfield | (a) | W 3 - 0 |
| | 22 Bradford | (a) | L 3 - 10 |
| | 29 Runcorn | (a) | L 0 - 8 |
| Mar | 7 Oldham | (h) | W 7 - 4 |
| | 14 Warrington | (a) | W 8 - 6 |
| | 21 Leeds | (h) | W 21 - 5 |
| | 28 Rochdale H | (a) | W 24 - 0 |
| | (played at Manningham) | | |
| April | 3 Liversedge | (h) | W 14 - 5 |
| | 4 Stockport | (a) | L 0 - 4 |
| | 7 Broughton R | (h) | W 3 - 0 |
| | 11 Leigh | (h) | W 40 - 3 |
| | 18 Hull | (h) | W 8 - 6 |
| | 21 Widnes | (a) | W 14 - 3 |
| | 25 Hunslet | (a) | W 4 - 0 |

# A hero dies young

*The champions' celebration season was blighted at the turn of the year by the death, just 18 days short of what would have been his twenty-fifth birthday, of George Lorimer.*

*The loss was felt way beyond Bradford as Lorimer had made his mark on the Northern Union's first season, 12 months earlier, by heading the fledgling code's goal-scoring lists with 35 successes. The full-back had also finished joint top scorer, with 106 points, with Fred Cooper of Bradford.*

*Lorimer had already earned representative honours with Yorkshire and appeared set for a glittering career when fate took a hand after what turned out to be his last match, against Brighouse Rangers, on 16 January 1897. The player fell ill shortly afterwards and concerns grew the following month when his condition worsened and typhoid was diagnosed.*

*Confined to his bed at the Bavaria public house, where club secretary Ike Newton was the landlord, George*

*Lorimer passed away at 5.00am on 8 February – two days after his team mates had lost 8-0 to Bradford at Valley Parade before a 15,000 gate – with Manningham President James Freeman, committee member Antonio Fattorini and Newton at his bedside.*

*Lorimer's teammate Eddie Holmes, an undertaker, conducted the funeral, which was held two days later. Huge crowds gathered, and hundreds of mourners walked in front of the horse drawn hearse. Businesses along the route, from Springcliffe Street to Heaton Baptist Chapel via Heaton Road, Parkside Road, Wilmer Road and Emm Lane, closed out of respect, and blinds were drawn. An estimated 8,000 lined the roads and Manningham players, eight of whom acted as pallbearers, wore claret and amber badges of crape and ribbons which were dropped one by one into the family grave.*

*A 'Lorimer cot' was donated, in his memory, to a Bradford hospital.*

---

beyond the Northern Union and the Rugby Union was a potent combination of national competition and working class involvement. Soccer, perhaps, was a 'mix' of the two varieties of rugby in an age when the three football codes were very similar.

Bradford, together with Leeds and Halifax, rooted themselves to the Northern Union cause in 1901 by disbanding their soccer sections but Manningham took a different tack, informing the West Yorkshire Football Association that 'we are doing all we possibly can to help the Association game,' and pledging to 'look again later' at the question.

They certainly did that, against a background in which the Football League was seeking a foothold in the cities of Leeds and Bradford.

South Leeds club Holbeck – denied promotion from Division Two in 1904 after losing a play-off with St Helens – metamorphosed into Leeds City, the forerunner of Leeds United.

Manningham had made the switch 12 months earlier, reducing fortunes and falling gates since the championship season of 1895–96 – allied to the threat of Bradford, who had won the Yorkshire Senior Competition in 1900 and 1901 – serving to concentrate minds.

The Paraders, who had shelved their second team in 1901, had been dealt a further blow when (their championship feat of the Northern Union's inaugural season just five years earlier seemingly counting for little) they were denied entry, during the summer of 1902, into the top flight of the new two-division competition.

Many chroniclers, including Rugby Football League historian Tony Collins, believe that the club subsequently made approaches to the Football League, forging links late in 1902 with key soccer figures in the city including local headmaster Charles Brunt and a Scottish sub-editor on the Bradford Observer by the name of James Whyte.

Matters moved apace and in recommending a

*Bradford City 2005–06. The men currently representing the club formed in 1872.*

# Rugby League games at Valley Parade

*(excluding Manningham and Bradford Bulls fixtures)*

| | |
|---|---|
| *21 February 1921 (Challenge Cup):* | *Bradford Northern v Oldham* |
| *13 February 1926 (Challenge Cup):* | *Bradford Northern v Keighley* |
| *17 February 1926 (Challenge Cup replay):* | *Bradford Northern v Keighley* |
| *13 November 1929:* | *Bradford Northern v Australia* |
| *11 October 1933:* | *Bradford Northern v Australia* |
| *30 October 1933:* | *Bradford Northern v Australia* |
| *3 March 1937 (Challenge Cup):* | *Bradford Northern v Huddersfield* |
| *6 March 1937 (League):* | *Bradford Northern v Oldham* |
| *10 April 1988 (League):* | *Bradford Northern v Wigan* |
| *2 September 1990 (Yorkshire Cup):* | *Bradford Northern v Castleford* |
| *17 February 1991 (Challenge Cup):* | *Bradford Northern v Leigh* |
| *7 December 1991 (Regal Trophy semi-final):* | *Leeds v Salford* |

switch of codes Secretary Harry Jowett said: 'It had been realised that Manningham had no chance if they were not in the same rugby league as Bradford. They were ready to leave the rugby game to the Bradford club and put their energies into the Association game if they received enough support.'

At the club's AGM at St John's Church School, Manningham, on 29 May 1903 he told members: 'It is a sad thing to have to do but I propose that Manningham Football Club should abandon the rugby code for the present.'

The motion was carried 75-34 and Manningham were able to announce to a stunned rugby world that they had been accepted into Division Two of the Football League, despite not having played a single match with a round ball.

The Football League had accepted the Bradford club by a comparatively narrow margin – 35 votes to 30 – but Collins, in *Rugby's Great Split*, maintains that the move was underpinned by guarantees by soccer's governing body. He also makes the point that Manningham, in profit for four of

*Manningham legend George Lorimer, an early sporting superstar, who died of typhoid at the age of 24.*

its eight years as a Northern Union operation, lost £1,638 in its first three seasons as a soccer club – an almost identical figure to the total deficit in the Northern Union.

The national stage, however, had been the main temptation and there were few remaining doubters when City won the Football League's Division Two championship in 1907–08. The *Leeds Mercury*, reporting on the club's celebration dinner, reflected: 'Bradford has indeed gone over wholeheartedly to soccer and one saw such old Rugby men as Messrs Alf Ayrton, Harry Jowett, Arthur Lancaster, Tom Robinson and Fred Buckley cheering and flag waving with the rest, while even so old a Rugger enthusiast as Mr Percy Illingworth, the Member for Shipley, who was unable to be present, sent his congratulations and expressed his pride in the distinction that had been brought to Bradford by the City club.

'Mr Harry Jowett, once as keen a Rugby enthusiast as could be found in Yorkshire, set the ball rolling in proposing "The Bradford City Association Football Club" recalling how the old Manningham organisation had, in about 20 years, risen from being a roadside club to one of the best in the country, and he was proud of the fact that Bradford City had made such rapid progress.'

# 3.
# To Him Who Waits

In a precursor to the actions of like-minded visionaries almost 60 years later, 13-a-side activists moved quickly to ensure that Rugby League would be kept alive in the city following the decision of Bradford to switch to soccer.

A meeting was held at the Mechanics Institute on 24 May 1907 at which it was announced that the Northern Rugby Football League had granted approval in principle for the launch of a new club.

Vitally, other clubs would not be allowed to sign players who had been registered with the old Bradford side.

Fund-raising schemes were launched and on 26 June 1907 it was confirmed that a team, playing at the Greenfield Stadium, Dudley Hill, would represent the city the following season.

Despite the solid support of the authorities, however, the fledgling club was hit by the departure of two star men. Prolific Scottish winger James Dechan, keen to move to a bigger club but thwarted by the RFL's embargo, opted to retire. J Dunbavin elected to stay at Park Avenue, subsequently evolving into a talented soccer player. Former captain George Marsden, meanwhile, declined to come out of retirement after having hung up his boots the previous January because of work commitments.

*A Bradford Northern team badge. A statement, in 1907, of the club's commitment to the Northern Union following the switch to soccer by both Bradford (Park Avenue) and Manningham.*

The new club's first match, on 2 September 1907, brought Huddersfield to the Greenfield Stadium where a disappointing crowd of 4,000 – 10,000 down on the norm for the fixture in Bradford's heyday – raised immediate concerns for the future.

It was felt that following the switch of the Park Avenue club to soccer, and Manningham's earlier decision to take the same route, a strong statement had to be made that professional rugby was still alive and well in the city.

On that basis the suffix was agreed upon, intended as a temporary measure only until such time as the club had consolidated, of 'Northern' to align Bradford firmly to the Northern Union (by 1907, Northern Rugby League) cause and end any confusion of

*An artist reviews Northern's tussle, in the club's first season, with mighty Hunslet.*

identity with the Association Football clubs at Valley Parade and Park Avenue.

The name 'Bradford Northern' was formally adopted on 10 September 1907 and was embraced by the reborn club in 1964. Bradford Northern (1964) Ltd remains the incorporated name of the Bradford Bulls.

### A Secretary vanishes

Bradford Northern quickly came to regret their initial choice of full-time Secretary.

Mr W Bayliss, appointed in February 1908, arranged the transfer the following November of club captain Tom Surman and international forward Alfred Mann to Hull KR, informing both players that they had to move because of Northern's 'serious financial plight'.

The transfers, for a total of £120 paid in cash, came as a shock a couple of days later to the Northern board which, while selecting the team for the following Saturday's fixture at St Helens, queried why the duo were not at training.

Bradford's board was further surprised to learn that Bayliss – who had previously attempted to sell the two players to Leeds for £150 in gold coins – had given Surman and Mann £25 and £20 respectively as a 'bonus for long and faithful service'.

Hull KR, informed that the transfers had not been properly authorised and were null and void, responded that the men had been bought in good faith and that appropriate documentation had been signed by Northern's Secretary.

Bayliss was never traced – nor was the £75 outstanding from the deal.

The Northern Union later ruled that Mann and Surman should hand back to Hull KR the money given to them; its committee also stipulated that although the pair were now Rovers players, they should return to Bradford.

Northern, meanwhile, were instructed to pay Hull KR £82 10s 0d, comprising a £45 transfer fee and £37 10s 0d (half of the 'missing' £75).

Bradford were, in essence, being told to buy back their own players, while Rovers profited by

---

# A match to remember
## New Zealand Tour

*Bradford Northern 7 New Zealand 2*
*Greenfield Stadium, Bradford*
*10 December 1907*
*Northern had the honour of becoming the first Yorkshire team to beat a touring side with the victory over Albert Baskerville's New Zealand 'All Golds'.*
*The pioneering party, making history as the first Rugby League tourists and including the legendary Australian centre Dally Messenger, had lost at Wigan, Barrow, Leigh, Oldham and Runcorn but had enjoyed more success east of the Pennines where Bramley – in the first game of the tour – Huddersfield, Wakefield Trinity, Leeds and Hull had been among the victims.*
*The great Hunslet team that was to become the first to win 'All Four Cups' were among those unable to defeat the All Golds, who drew 11-11 at Parkside, but Bradford were able to achieve what had been beyond Albert Goldthorpe and his colleagues in a match played in heavy rain which transformed the Greenfield pitch into something resembling a duck pond.*
*A small crowd of 2,000 turned up for the game, with the absentees deterred by the inclement weather, to witness a contest punctuated by a series of niggly incidents in which Northern took an early lead with a Gomer Gunn penalty.*
*New Zealand failed with two attempts in response, one effort remaining rooted in the cloying mud, before equalising with a successful penalty assisted by the crossbar. But Bradford went in front by the break with an enterprising try for forward Alfred Mann who was rewarded for supporting a Gunn kick and feeding winger Neil by being on hand to collect the return crosskick after a supporting colleague had hacked on. Tom Surman was unable to convert but the damage had, effectively, been done.*
*Continued pressure in the second period was repelled by a courageous rearguard action in which Gunn, at full-back, was typically prominent. And victory was sealed when Surman landed a drop goal with two minutes remaining.*

*Northern: Gunn; Neil, Francis, Davison, Connell; Brear, Surman; Feather, Rees, Mann, Walton, Wilkinson, Haley.*

*New Zealand: Turtill; Gleeson, Rowe, Lavery; R Wynyard, Wrigley; Kelly; Gilchrist, Lile, Pearce, Johnston, Byrne, Cross.*

*Referee: Mr E Tonge (Swinton)*

*Northern generally found the going hard for the first 25 years of the new club's existence. The above side struggled in the seasons prior to the Great War.*

£7 10s 0d. Northern, however, reluctantly agreed to the compromise. The Rugby League, for its part, amended its byelaws; future transfers had to be authorised by the Chairman, or a leading committeeman or director, rather than by the Secretary.

## To Birch Lane and Odsal

Northern ended their term of tenure at Greenfield Stadium after only one year. Difficulties in reaching the ground – which was not on a bus route – and a fundamental lack of amenities outweighed the fact that the rent was only £8 a year, with income of £50 promised by a local brewery in return for the sale of beer.

The decision, made easier by the poor drainage conditions at Greenfield, was to move to Birch Lane, albeit at an annual rent of £30. It was felt that the new stadium offered superior facilities and more possibilities for the improvements that would be necessary as and when the great days returned.

Those were to prove some way off, despite the Trojan efforts of the stalwarts who kept the flag flying for Bradford through setback after setback over most of the next 30 years.

Northern had, apart from a few isolated moments, little success at Birch Lane, hitting a new low immediately by finishing twenty-third in 1908–09 (five places below Bradford's previous worst, two years previously, when the winning of the Yorkshire Cup had been a saving grace).

The side at least achieved consistency, remaining in twenty-third position for the next two years before a brief improvement to seventeenth in 1912–13 heralded a false dawn.

Perhaps suffering from a policy of signing great players who were past their best – epitomised by the later acquisition, in the twilight of his career, of record try scorer Albert Rosenfeld from Huddersfield – and a habit of persuading such as Alex Laidlaw and George Marsden to come out of retirement, Northern generally struggled.

Bradford finished twenty-fourth and nineteenth in the last two seasons before the Great War and occasional moments of joy, including a league victory over mighty Huddersfield in 1913–14, did little to alleviate the overall gloom. That season closed with a vote of no confidence in the directors and the appointment of a new board.

The welcome return to peacetime in 1918

# A match to remember
## Tour Match

*Bradford Northern 11 Australia 12*
*Birch Lane, Bradford*
*7 October 1908*
*Only a last-minute goal miss by Downs denied Northern a notable success against the first Australian tourists.*
*The loose forward, who had already landed a conversion from the touchline, was given the chance to win the game when Ramsden charged down a clearance kick and collected to romp over for a stunning try.*
*But Downs mishit his conversion attempt from the side of the posts, leaving the Kangaroos unbeaten after two games following their opening 20-6 success at Mid-Rhonda.*
*The match had opened with a performance of the Aboriginal war dance the 'Wallee Mullara' by the tourists whose superior techniques and imposing physical presence ensured a five-point lead at the interval through a try for hooker Alex Burdon and a conversion by Herbert 'Dally' Messenger, who had failed with a couple of relatively simple penalty attempts.*
*Northern, however, hit back in the second period with a short-range solo touchdown for scrum-half Brear, who bustled over in the corner after winger Cluderay had gone close.*
*That score inspired Bradford to new heights and by the hour mark the home side had nosed ahead, courtesy of a touchdown by right winger Neil, who squeezed in at the corner off Alfred Mann's astute long pass, and Downs' superb goal.*
*The Australians, however, bounced back with a Dan Frawley try and Messenger goal, and a drop goal to right centre Andy Morton seemed to have settled the issue. Ramsden had other ideas but the Kangaroos were to wriggle off the hook, and embark on a six-match unbeaten run, when Downs couldn't add the goal.*

*Northern: Davison; Neil, Ramsden, Schofield, Cluderay; Surman, Brear; Mann, Feather, Haley, Stancliffe, Sharratt, Downs.*

*Australia: Bolewski; Messenger, Morton, Frawley, Heidke; Halloway, Deane; Graves, Burdon, Hennessy, Davis, O'Malley, Lutge.*

brought no improvement. Instead, Bradford plunged into an ever-downwards spiral both on the field and off it, where the club regularly fell foul of the authorities over late payments of transfer fees and fines.

The first campaign after the closure of hostilities was played on a county league basis and Northern duly propped up the rest in eleventh spot.

The reversion to a single league in 1919–20 failed to inspire an upturn in fortunes. Bradford, in consecutive campaigns, came twenty-fourth, twenty-fifth and, in 1921–22, twenty-sixth (the wooden spoon role that season).

Only Bramley, for three years in succession,

*Long-serving stand off Teddy Melling reaches out for a try against Batley at Mount Pleasant in the mid-1920s.*

separated Northern from the 'ignominy' of retaining the wooden spoon before – after coming twenty-third and twenty-eighth – Bradford suggested with a heady rise to sixteenth in 1927–28 that the bad days could be over.

They weren't. Other than the subsequent nadir with the complete collapse in 1963, Northern reached what remains probably the lowest point in the history of any of the clubs in the city by coming bottom in each of the four seasons from 1928–29 to 1931–32.

During that period Northern won 21 league games, losing 123. Only Liverpool, adrift of the rest for six consecutive seasons (as Stanley from

# A match to remember
## Yorkshire Cup Final

Bradford Northern 3 Huddersfield 19
Thrum Hall, Halifax
29 November 1913

Northern made a mockery of the ratings by reaching their first major final during a season in which they finished second-from-bottom, in twenty-fourth position, with only seven victories from 34 games.

Opponents Huddersfield would, the following year, emulate Hunslet by lifting All Four Cups and were in the middle of a five-season period in which they topped the Northern Rugby League table each time.

Bradford had enjoyed, en route to the final, a touch of the good fortune needed by all teams hoping for cup success. All three of their opponents were in residence in the bottom half of the table, with Keighley being beaten 11-4 at home and wooden spoonists York going down 9-4 at Clarence Street before mighty Wakefield Trinity, in something of a lull but still boasting players of high quality, were disposed of 13-2 at the penultimate stage.

Huddersfield represented a formidable challenge. Harold Wagstaff's side had, after all, beaten Bradford 61-7 (scoring 15 tries) only 10 days before the final and had denied any of their opponents a solitary point in the preceding rounds.

It was, however, to be a different story at Thrum Hall where Northern hooker Haley and his pack secured the lions' share of possession for a revamped back line which included four new selections after the Fartown battering.

Despite a strong opening in which Carter, Wilby and Haley were all held short and McEwan was wide with a penalty attempt, Bradford found themselves behind against the run of play when the pacey Huddersfield side broke from their own half for a converted try by centre Bob Habron and then pulled off a long-range interception for winger George Todd to extend their lead to eight points.

Northern hit back early in the second half when Wilby crashed over direct from a scrum to atone for having knocked on earlier with the tryline beckoning and, with Carter, having missed a penalty shot.

More pressure, however, came to nothing as resilient Fartown scored tries by Habron, Todd and winger Albert Rosenfeld in the last 12 minutes, full back Major Holland kicking his second goal. The Team of All the Talents, though, had been made fully aware before an 18,000 crowd that they had been involved, despite the scoreline, in a hard-fought final that could so easily have gone the other way.

Bradford: Schofield; Irving, Hall, Wilby, Wilson; McEwan, Carter; Winterburn, Haley, Mitchell, Feather, Ruck, Simmons.

Huddersfield: Holland; Rosenfeld, Gleeson, Habron, Todd; Davies, Rogers; Gronow, Longstaff, Chilcott, Clark, Swinden, Higson.

---

1948–49 to 1950–51, and City from 1951–52 to 1953–54) and Doncaster, who had a five-year horror sequence from 1956–57 to 1960–61, can reflect on a worse record.

The nightmare, however, was soon to end. Northern languished in the lower reaches of the league for the next three years, coming twenty-second, twenty-seventh and twenty-fifth, but two wonderful displays against the 1933 Australian tourists in the middle season of those three campaigns can be seen as the catalyst for a remarkable change in fortunes.

### The Marshall Plan

The Rugby Football League, increasingly concerned throughout the late 1920s by Bradford's ongoing financial problems and perennial requests for handouts, formed a three-man action committee in December 1930 charged with saving, within a month, Northern from extinction. In a heartening episode which would be repeated over 60 years later, a number of clubs loaned players or organised collections and there was immediate reward when a new-look side ended a 29-match losing run with a 14-2 home victory over Keighley on Christmas Day.

That success, and significant additions at boardroom level, helped persuade the RFL to grant a stay of execution. Their officials remained at Birch Lane for a further month; Northern were on something like an even keel; and Rugby League was still alive in the city, albeit not in the best of health.

The initiative, however, strengthened the governing body's belief, echoed by the club, that a change of ground was necessary if Northern's struggles were to be brought to an end.

Cash that could have been earmarked towards a new stadium had been used to bolster an ailing side for the best part of a decade. And after a proposed switch to any one of potential sites at Bankfoot, Girlington and Undercliffe had been put on the back burner funds had been ploughed, in 1924, into the erection of an embankment for 6,000 spectators which increased Birch Lane's capacity to 15,000.

Talks involving Northern, the Rugby Football League and Bradford Council in 1929 for a move back to Greenfield Stadium floundered when the club was unable to raise its £700 contribution to the total £2,100 cost.

That setback, ironically, paved the way for an opportunity that would lead to the transformation of Bradford Northern.

Mr Marshall, a member of Northern's board who had a background in the building trade, offered the inspired idea in the spring of 1933 of asking Bradford Council if the huge rubbish tip at Odsal could be converted into a stadium for the club's use, rather than be filled in as originally envisaged. By midsummer, terms had been agreed. Northern were granted tenancy on a 10-year lease from 1 January 1934.

*H Young, Bradford Northern's first tourist. Young scored six tries in nine appearances on Great Britain's 1928 tour of Australia and New Zealand.*

> *An ugly episode at Birch Lane on 14 March 1914 eclipsed any subsequent incidents at Odsal, which with its long walk to the dressing rooms was generally recognised as a bear pit for referees.*
>
> *The general opinion among home supporters that day was that the match official had been at fault for their favourites' 17-3 defeat at the hands of Salford. Bradford, in their view, had been dealt with harshly in the scrums, and the vetoing of two or three 'tries' hardly helped the mood.*
>
> *Their frustration came to a head at the final whistle when a section of the crowd raced onto the field and struck the referee, throwing objects at him and pushing the hapless whistler to the floor.*
>
> *The police and Northern officials came to his rescue, hustling him to the dressing rooms. An hour later, he managed to avoid the waiting and still hostile crowd by climbing through a back window whence he was spirited away in a hansom cab to the railway station.*
>
> *Bradford, fined £20 by the Northern Union, were ordered to post warning notices and were advised that Birch Lane would be closed for an indefinite period should there be any repetition.*
>
> *There were, however, recurrences of crowd trouble in December 1923 and January 1924. And when the 23-3 defeat by Dewsbury on 17 April 1926 was followed by assaults on the referee and a number of visiting players Northern were instructed to play the first two home games of the following season outside a five-mile radius of Bradford.*
>
> *Northern switched their 'home' game with Halifax to their opponents' Thrum Hall ground and played York at Keighley.*

## Two games that changed the course of history – Kangaroos courted

If any one single episode led to a revival in Bradford's fortunes, it was the game against the 1933 Australian tourists which turned into two matches.

The Kangaroos went into the allocated fixture on 11 October 1933, which had been switched to Valley Parade, having lost the First Test 4-0 at Belle Vue, Manchester, the previous Saturday.

That had been the first defeat of a tour which had opened with victories against nine club teams in addition to the Yorkshire and Lancashire county sides.

Northern, by contrast, were destined to finish

second from bottom of the twenty-eight team pile, eight points ahead of Featherstone but seven points shy of Bramley. The team had, including the pre-season Lazenby Cup win over Keighley, prevailed in only three games, with seven lost including five in the build-up to the visit of the Australians.

The fact that the game was an obvious no-contest was perhaps reflected in the 3,328 gate, the second lowest of the tour, but the diehards who bothered to turn up were treated to one of the great club performances of all time.

The *Yorkshire Post* reported: 'The fighting roar of 'feet, forwards, feet' heard here so often when the Manningham club, a power in the land in those days, had the Valley Parade ground as its home, raised itself this afternoon, and with this echo from the past came a sweep from Bradford Northern which took the ball up the field in the movement which proved decisive'.

Northern, belying their ragbag appearance in sewn-up shirts, shorts and socks, played in the manner of champions in the heavy rain and testing conditions and served a real shock for the ecstatic crowd with a 7-5 victory earned with a drop goal two minutes from time by loose forward Sherwood, from the position established by that mighty 'sweep'.

That score, earned with a heel against the head on the Kangaroos' line by hooker Turner and secured with the help of a five-man-scrum ploy with Sherwood standing back (and knocking on the first pass) broke the stalemate. The players were carried aloft from the pitch by their joyous supporters and then on to the Queens Hotel for a celebratory dinner at the expense of the club.

The *Yorkshire Post* reporter added: 'No match-winning score was ever schemed for more deliberately than this', but the defeat was difficult to accept for the tourists, who had lost the first half scrums 3-1 but had led by three points after having responded to an early goal by prop Charlie Litt with a Wally Prigg try, converted by Les Mead.

That score should have set the scene for a

*Only nine people watched the fixture at Brighouse Rangers on 9 February 1918.*

*A reported eight inches of snow covered Rangers' pitch when Bradford arrived but Northern, undeterred, insisted that the game should go ahead. A couple of groundsmen marked out the pitch while the players stripped but the one missing ingredient when the teams emerged from the dressing rooms was the supporters. Sensibly, perhaps, not a single soul had turned up for a match which had never seemed likely to take place after two days of continuous snowfall.*

*The 26 players, referee and two touch judges heavily outnumbered the watching 'throng' of three journalists, two officials from each club and the two Brighouse ground staff.*

*In the event, the fans were proved correct. Conditions quickly deteriorated and, in grim blizzard conditions, play was abandoned after 35 minutes following appeals to the referee by the players.*

*Bradford, however, had played a good hand. The side had battled back from an early 11-3 deficit to lead 13-11, and the sport's authorities subsequently ruled that the result should stand.*

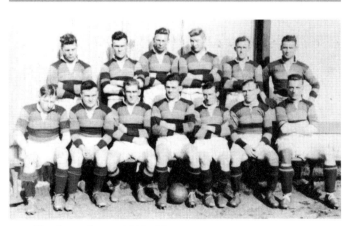

*Bradford Northern, 1929–30.*

comfortable Australian win. It didn't materialise. Roared on by fans who recognised and fully appreciated their favourites' mighty efforts, Northern hit back in the closing seconds of the half through scrum-half Bradbury, who bustled over in the corner for a score that Litt couldn't improve.

The scene was set for a climactic second period and so it proved, Sherwood's magical moment in the closing stages earning Bradford Northern the victory they richly deserved.

# Harry Sheard, supporter from the 1930s

*'Birch Lane was just below Dudley Hill. I was only quite young when my father used to take me and many a time he used to say, "Oh no, it isn't fit for you to go." If you got a decent crowd it was a bit dodgy. It wasn't set up for crowds, it was more or less an amateur type rugby field. There were no sleepers or anything like that, I don't remember any anyway. 'They were called the Steam Pigs. That came from the pack, they spent a lot more time in the scrums in those days and when they were down and sweating you could see the steam rising.'*

It was, however, a result that did not sit well with the Australians, who contended that they had been hampered by the heavy rain and mudbound conditions.

Manager Harry Sunderland, a charismatic figure who would later return to England and make such an impact that the Man of the Match trophy in the championship final would be named in his honour, asked for a return game. The Rugby Football League acquiesced; and the fixture was arranged for 30 October 1933, again at Valley Parade.

Bradford coach Ben Gronow, a man who knew a great deal about how to win games after his experiences as a player with Huddersfield's 'Team of all the Talents' that won All Four Cups in 1914–15 had no qualms about agreeing to take on the Australians again and the pride within the camp at their fine performance was reflected in a groundswell of public and local pride in Northern's feat.

Gracie Fields, appearing in the city at the time, joined the Bishop of Bradford, the Lord Mayor, and hundreds of others in helping buy the team a kit fit for the occasion.

*Singer Gracie Fields, a huge star of the era, backed Bradford Northern's bid to beat Australia twice in 1933.*

The Kangaroos, who won three and lost two of the games between the two matches in Bradford, were determined not to be humbled a second time and fielded nine of their Test team in the following line-up: McMillan; Ridley, Brown, Why, Neumann; Hey, Thicknesse; Curran, Folwell, Stehr, O'Connor, Doyle, Prigg.

Northern, meanwhile, called up Thornburrow in place of injured winger Bush. Almost three times the original crowd – 9,937 – assembled for the Monday afternoon fixture, and Bradford would, again, not disappoint despite a controversial 10-7 defeat.

Pre-match entertainment included war cries by both the Australian side and (with more of a challenging yell) Bradford, which followed music from the Black Dyke Mills band. And the importance of the occasion was not lost on others, with a special message of encouragement to both sides from the king.

The match, as in the opening game, appeared to be heading for a draw when the teams went into the closing stages level at 7-7. That was the way many observers felt the contest would end when Australia 'won' a scrum close to the home line with the help of what appeared to be a feed into the second row, with a hand palming the ball back to Joe Doyle who scampered over Northern's line and touched down.

Bradford's players, who should perhaps have played to the whistle, had merely stood by in anticipation of a penalty in their favour. The score, however, was allowed to stand

| *1928–29: Northern Rugby League (bottom three)* | | | | | | | | |
|---|---|---|---|---|---|---|---|---|
| | P | W | D | L | F | A | Pts | % |
| *Rochdale Hornets* | 34 | 10 | 0 | 24 | 235 | 434 | 20 | 29.41 |
| *Keighley* | 34 | 8 | 2 | 24 | 209 | 422 | 18 | 26.47 |
| *Bradford Northern* | 38 | 5 | 3 | 30 | 242 | 871 | 13 | 17.10 |
| *(final positions determined on a percentage basis)* | | | | | | | | |

*An aerial shot of Odsal, days before the opening of the ground in 1934. The move from Birch Lane was to herald a remarkable transformation in Bradford Northern's fortunes.*

and the Kangaroos had won 10-7. Moreover, they resisted overtures from Northern for a third game, claiming there was no date available in the remainder of the tour.

The result may arguably have been affected by outside influences which added to the pressure on Manchester referee, Mr A E Harding.

The tour was taking place at the same time as the infamous 'Bodyline' cricket tour of Australia, which was threatening to seriously undermine already fragile diplomatic relations between the two countries. The *Yorkshire Post* reported on 11 October: 'English player's remarks calculated to do much harm' and quoted England fast bowler Harold Larwood as saying: 'If I am picked for the Test match with the Australians next year I shall bowl leg-theory when the wicket is right unless I am expressly ordered no to do so. And I do not think the MCC will ever order me or anyone else not to bowl to a packed leg trap.'

The Rugby Football League had also come under fire from the Australian tour

In the circumstances it was perhaps understandable that Mr Webb opted to allow Doyle's try.

The defeat was hard to take but Bradford Northern, who had sensibly played to their limitations and adopted an astute kicking game, could nevertheless claim a moral victory. More importantly, the two games had served to reignite interest in a club that had struggled for far too long. Inspired by renditions from the touchlines of *'Ilkley Moor B'Aht 'At'* Bradford had led 7-2 at the interval through a try for Bradbury, who dummied his way over from short range, and two Litt goals. The lead wasn't to last as the Kangaroos hit back with a Prigg touchdown and Dave Brown goal before that controversial late score; but the fervour engendered by the two great performances would help propel the club forward for two decades of previously unparalleled glory.

Motivated by the achievement, Northern set about strengthening the side and established a new club record with the capture of Tom Winnard from St Helens in December 1933. The acquisition of the three-quarter for £385

*1929–30: Northern Rugby League (bottom three)*

| | P | W | D | L | F | A | Pts | % |
|---|---|---|---|---|---|---|---|---|
| Castleford | 36 | 10 | 2 | 24 | 230 | 535 | 22 | 30.55 |
| Batley | 36 | 7 | 2 | 27 | 221 | 543 | 16 | 22.22 |
| Bradford Northern | 38 | 7 | 2 | 29 | 299 | 718 | 16 | 21.05 |

*(final positions determined on a percentage basis)*

management, Sunderland writing: 'Of the 15 games so far "line referees" have gone onto the field over 20 times against Australia and only once in favour. These figures suggest that our team commits many more breaches of a reprehensible nature than your teams do, and that your players by comparison with ours are perfect.

'Yet, when your players are competing among themselves, we find that there are many more breaches, and that your Council has had to take action against them.'

*Struggling Northern hit a new low with the league fixture at Leigh in February 1931. The Lancashire club, hit by a players' strike, fielded a side consisting of second team men and youth players. Bradford still contrived to lose 8-0.*

| 1930–31: Northern Rugby League (bottom three) | | | | | | | |
| --- | --- | --- | --- | --- | --- | --- | --- |
| | P | W | D | L | F | A | Pts |
| Featherstone Rovers | 38 | 7 | 1 | 30 | 265 | 536 | 15 |
| Bramley | 38 | 5 | 3 | 30 | 251 | 636 | 13 |
| Bradford Northern | 38 | 4 | 1 | 33 | 227 | 809 | 9 |

| 1931–32: Northern Rugby League (bottom three) | | | | | | | |
| --- | --- | --- | --- | --- | --- | --- | --- |
| | P | W | D | L | F | A | Pts |
| Keighley | 38 | 10 | 0 | 28 | 228 | 630 | 20 |
| Wigan Highfield | 38 | 6 | 2 | 30 | 350 | 707 | 14 |
| Bradford Northern | 38 | 5 | 1 | 32 | 313 | 854 | 11 |

sent out a clear message that the board meant business as a new era approached.

The Odsal Stadium Fund, launched in early November 1933, ensured that the ground would be properly equipped and that the club would begin life in their new home free of debt.

Bradford also pleased their long-suffering supporters with the re-signing of former star player Harold Young from Castleford, who had reluctantly left Odsal for Huddersfield five years earlier.

### Two Greats

Two other men joined Northern in the early 1930s – and both were to have a huge influence on the club.

Harry Hornby was the driving force behind the regeneration of Northern and the club's subsequent rise to the heights. A visionary, he joined the board in the early 1930s, becoming Chairman and Managing Director.

While ensuring that Rugby League remained the prime focus, he made certain that Odsal was utilised to the full.

Hornby opened the ground, to Northern's financial benefit, to events such as speedway, baseball, cricket, trotting, boxing and tennis. And he made another highly important decision by enlisting former Halifax and Wales forward Dai Rees as coach in 1936. With Rees, Hornby set about moulding a side to match and perhaps better that which had graced Park Avenue at the turn of the century.

Rees, a tactical maestro who introduced the concept of a scrum-half operating at dummy half to facilitate speed at the play-the-ball, worked closely with his Chairman to recruit some of the best players around.

Within a fortnight of his arrival Rees, on 30 July 1936, signed promising local centre Ernest Ward on his sixteenth birthday. Ward, one of the most important of Rees' captures, went on to lead both Northern and Great Britain to wonderful deeds.

George Harrison and George Bennett were enticed from Wigan, while Bradford broke new ground by becoming the first club to sign overseas nationals who were still resident in their own country with the capture of New Zealand duo George Gilbert and Robert Hohia.

The signings were added to those, before Rees' arrival, of the likes of full-back George Carmichael from Hull KR, with Vince Dilorenzo, Sandy Orford and Ted Spillane joining Bradford during the first Odsal campaign.

The biggest coup, however, arguably came when Rees returned home to the Valleys as war clouds gathered and came back with two forwards and a back

*Action from 1935–36. Winger CL Grainge is given space to show his speed.*

*Elusive winger Jackson evades a tackle in the 1936-37 season.*

who would become all-time greats.

The first forward was Trevor Foster, a dynamic back-rower from Newport, who put pen to paper on 16 September 1938 and recalled the episode shortly before his death in 2005.

He said: 'I signed in my home in Newport, South Wales, alongside my mum and my dad, my brothers and my sisters. We lived in a lovely old public house called "The Church House" where, incidentally, a poet was born many, many years before us named William Henry Davies, the Tramp Poet.

'After one full season for Newport I was the highest try-scorer as a wing forward and according to the critics I was well in line for a Welsh international cap the following season. I came home from training in early September 1938 and there was this big Buick car outside our public house. Mr Hornby, the Bradford Northern Managing Director, had travelled down with one or two other directors, and he was talking to my dad. My dad was an ex-rugby player and a great soldier – he'd spent 26 years in the army and had been awarded the DCM for his service in the South African War.

'I went straight into the bar where my mam was with customers and said, "I'm not going Mam, I've changed my mind." All I could think about was a Welsh cap. My mam said, "Do the right thing, go into the sitting room and tell Mr

## A match to remember
### Northern Rugby League

*Bradford Northern 16 Huddersfield 31*
*Odsal Stadium, Bradford*
*1 September 1934*
*With the help of a £2,000 loan from the Rugby Football League and nearly £900 by public subscription towards the laying of the pitch, Bradford Northern were ready for their first game at Odsal against, ironically, the side that had provided the opposition for the opening match at Birch Lane.*
*In a nice touch Sir Joseph Turner KBE, the Huddersfield President, opened a stadium which impressed an estimated 20,000 crowd with its sheer size and which immediately became known as the 'Wembley of the North'.*
*Northern winger Robert Walker scored the first-ever try at the ground but Huddersfield, who had won the Challenge Cup 12 months earlier, proved to be too strong for their hosts, particularly on the wide, flat pitch, and eased to a comfortable victory in which Fartown winger Ray Markham netted four tries. Bradford, in fact, took some time to settle into their new surroundings, losing their first 10 games and not winning at Odsal until 17 November 1934, with the 14-2 success over Featherstone Rovers.*

*Bradford: Taylor; Pilling, Bradbury, Winnard, Walker; Marsh, Hayes; Green, Cotton, Collins, Morgan, Parr, Sherwood.*

*Huddersfield: Bowkett; Rhoades, Towill, Fiddes, Markham; Royston, Spencer; Roberts, Halliday, Sherwood, Tiffany, Talbot, Brindle.*

Hornby what you're going to do." I walked into the kitchen, and there was my dad sat on the chair with a glass of beer and Mr Hornby and one of the other directors. And I said to Mr Hornby, "I'm not going, Mr Hornby." He went red, white and blue, tore a strip off me and said, "You've brought us all the way from Bradford and now you're not going! What's made you change your mind?" I said, "One thing, I want a Welsh cap." He said "Here, £100, £300, £400, go and buy six caps!" At that moment my sister with her young family who lived a few doors away from our public house came into the room and she said, "Mum says you're not going to sign for Bradford Northern?" I said, "Yes, that's right."

*Welshman Trevor Foster, destined to become one of Bradford's 'greats'*

She said "What if you break your leg next Saturday playing against Penarth?" And I picked up the pen and signed. Just like that, changed my mind. That was the beginning of my wonderful trip to the great city of Bradford.'

The second signing, two days before Christmas in the same year, was heavyweight Cardiff prop Frank Whitcombe.

Eight months later Rees was back in Wales, this time at Swansea, where he persuaded Walsh stand-off Willie Davies to take the professional ticket.

Despite the intervention of World War Two, all three – and particularly Foster – were to give Bradford Northern glorious service. And the trio were joining a club, under Hornby, that was clearly on the rise. A new record crowd for Odsal of 28,843 paid to watch the Yorkshire Cup second round tie with Leeds in September 1937, when an estimated 5,000 broke through the

## A legend remembers
### Trevor Foster

'I found, very early on, the warmth of the people of Yorkshire, particularly in Bradford, and particularly of Rugby League followers. There is something special about the affinity between spectators and players.

'I went into lodgings with two lovely old ladies, Miss Hainsworth and Miss Norcliffe, who were related to Northern's Managing Director, Mr Hornby. They made me and other players such as Frank Whitcombe, Emlyn Walters and Billy Davis, very welcome.

'I had 10 or 12 very happy years there, it was like being at home in Wales where we are all very close together, especially in the rugby.

'That was an important factor, leaving home for the first time. They were very similar to the people back home, they went out of their way to ensure that we had a good life off the field.'

perimeter fences, and that figure was eclipsed the following March with 31,317 for the Challenge Cup round two replay with Halifax.

Average gates had risen to over 10,000 and the board opted to instal sleepers at the Rooley Lane end to add to spectator comfort. That initiative was rewarded when Odsal was allocated its first final, in October 1938, Huddersfield and Hull meeting in the Yorkshire Cup decider before a 28,714 attendance.

*Huddersfield and Hull line up before the 1938 Yorkshire Cup Final. The occasion was the first on which Odsal staged a major final.*

# 4.
# Into the Sunlight

The plans of Harry Hornby, his board and his coach Dai Rees for the immediate future of Bradford Northern were thrown into disarray, together with those of their counterparts around the Rugby Football League, by the rather more compelling matter of the outbreak of World War Two.

Many clubs closed down for the duration while others such as Dewsbury prospered through the RFL's ruling that guest players could be selected. Bradford took some advantage of this dispensation by fielding former player Stan Brogden, who played for Hull but still lived in Bradford. Essentially, however, Rees sought to field a team comprising bona fide Northern players and his policy reaped rich rewards as Northern secured seven major trophies between 1939 and 1945 in an unprecedented run of success which would form the prelude to the glory days of the immediate post-war period.

Northern won the Championship in 1939–40, topping the Yorkshire Section of the War Emergency League by three clear points ahead of Huddersfield and beating Lancashire counterparts Swinton in a two-legged final by 21-13 at Station Road and 16-9 at Odsal for an aggregate score of 37-22.

The following year, Bradford won the Yorkshire Cup for the first time since the last season of the Park Avenue club in 1906–07. Surprise packets Dewsbury, who were to develop into a fine side during the war as manager Eddie Waring attracted players of the highest calibre, had forced their way through to the final at Fartown, Huddersfield where 13,316 witnessed a 15-5 win for Northern secured with tries by Trevor Foster, who raced over off an astute Don Ward pass, and Walter Best.

Bradford, with the immortal Gus Risman in their ranks, also had the better of the second period, Foster netting his second try and reliable full-back George Carmichael kicked three goals to seal a notable success.

The championship was retained the following season, Bradford once again heading the Yorkshire table and disposing, this time, of Wigan 17-6 at Central Park (Risman again guesting) and 28-9 at home for a 45-15 aggregate verdict. And Northern also kept their grip on the Yorkshire Cup – which included three Lancashire sides, Oldham going down to Bradford over two legs in the second round –

*The Bradford team that beat Swinton in the second leg of the 1939–40 Championship Final.*

**1939–40: War Emergency League – Yorkshire Section (leading four)**

| | P | W | D | L | F | A | Pts |
|---|---|---|---|---|---|---|---|
| Bradford Northern | 28 | 21 | 0 | 7 | 574 | 302 | 42 |
| Huddersfield | 28 | 19 | 1 | 8 | 545 | 340 | 39 |
| Hull | 26 | 18 | 0 | 8 | 376 | 265 | 36 |
| Halifax | 28 | 17 | 0 | 11 | 462 | 339 | 34 |

beating Halifax 24-0 in the final at Fartown.

Bradford were limited to a Willie Davies try and a Carmichael conversion in the first half but it was more conclusive in the second period as Davies, at his constructive best, sparked the assault with a long range solo score and then orchestrated touchdowns by Best, the second row pairing of Foster and Herbert Smith, and hooker Cliff Carter.

The county league sections were dropped for the 1942–43 season but that did little to curtail Northern's success. Bradford finished the campaign in second spot and beat third-placed Halifax 15-8 in the semi-final before losing out to Eddie Waring's Dewsbury 13-0 at Headingley in the Championship Final.

Rees and his men appeared to be on course to retrieve the title the following year when, after having rested up in third spot, Northern travelled to Dewsbury in the semi-final and carved out an 8-3 verdict at Crown Flatt. That, however, was where Bradford's tilt ended. Dewsbury lodged a complaint, which the Rugby Football League upheld, that Sandy Orford – a former Northern player who had been transferred to Wakefield Trinity – had only played three league matches for Bradford (one short of the required four) and was therefore ineligible.

Dewsbury, awarded the game, went on to beat Halifax in the two-legged final. However they in turn fell foul of the authorities when it was established that an ineligible player had been fielded against Bradford. The Rugby Football League ruled the 1942–43 Championship null and void.

Northern made no such slip-ups two years later when, having missed out on the 1943–44 title through finishing sixth, the side regained pole position and edged Wigan 18-15 in the semi-final to book a two-legged decider with Halifax.

The team that faced Fax at Thrum Hall was one of classical strength with Ernest Ward at full-back, Eric Batten in the centre and Alan Edwards on the wing; but Northern were placed on the back foot for the return when their old rivals prevailed 9-2.

## A match to remember
### Challenge Cup Final (second leg)

*Bradford Northern 8 Wigan 0*
*Odsal*
*22 April 1944*
*A huge crowd, against the backdrop of the war, of 30,000 descended on Odsal for the final match of the 1944 competition, with Northern viewed by most as slight favourites to prevail after having held Wigan to a 3-0 scoreline in the first leg at Central Park. Bradford, whose last success in the competition had been exactly 40 years earlier, welcomed back second row Trevor Foster. Eric Batten, who had injured a shoulder the previous week, remained in the side while Wigan lacked legendary full-back Jim Sullivan. Batten was quick to confirm his fitness, swooping on a loose ball at a scrum and diving over the visitors' line before any defenders had woken up to the threat. There was no further score, thanks to a try-saving tackle by centre Jack Kitching and a successful move to smother a Wigan drop goal attempt, until full-back George Carmichael landed a penalty – putting his side ahead on aggregate for the first time – after hooker Vic Darlison had been the victim of a high tackle. With Wigan rarely threatening, Northern remained in firm control and completed their victory when prop Frank Whitcombe ploughed over in the closing seconds for an unconverted try.*

*Bradford: Carmichael; Batten, Kitching, E Ward, Walters; Bennett, D Ward; Whitcombe, Darlison, Higson, Foster, Roberts, Hutchinson.*

*Wigan: Jones; Lawrenson, Belshaw, Maloney, Ashcroft; Ryan, H Gee; K Gee, Egan, Blan, Featherstone, Watkins, Bowen.*

*Referee: Mr A Cowell (Warrington).*

# A match to remember
## Yorkshire Cup Final

*Bradford Northern 5 Wakefield Trinity 2*
*Thrum Hall, Halifax*
*3 November 1945*

*Northern retrieved the Yorkshire Cup, which they had won in the war-time campaigns of 1940, 1941 and 1943, with a compelling, defence-dominated display which confirmed to coach Dai Rees that his players were capable of pragmatism as well as panache.*

*The result also owed much to Rees' lateral strategic approach and a masterstroke of imaginative tactical thinking at the beginning of the second half.*

*A 24,292 crowd was treated to a match which was in many ways redolent of the Northern Union era when tries were often at a premium.*

*The first half was contested almost entirely in midfield as both Northern and Trinity refused to concede ground. And the only points went to Wakefield who went into the famous tiled Thrum Hall changing rooms at the interval two points ahead through a Billy Stott penalty.*

*Rees, however, instigated the only try of the game with a ploy that totally outwitted Wakefield.*

*Instead of remaining in the dressing rooms for the customary 10 minutes or so, the Northern players returned to the pitch – and to their positions – inside a couple of minutes. There they remained, to the bemusement of the crowd – but there was method to the apparent madness.*

*Wakefield, ambling back onto the pitch, weren't quite ready when the referee blew for play and a large space was left unprotected in front of Trinity's posts. Bradford scrum-half Don Ward booted the ball into the area where Wakefield centre Johnny Jones, dithering with his full-back Billy Teall, fumbled under unexpected pressure from Ernest Ward.*

*Prop Frank Whitcombe, belying his 18 stone frame, hacked on and beat a posse of straggling Wakefield players to a spectacular touchdown. George Carmichael improved – and that was enough to secure victory as the contest reverted to type.*

*Bradford: Carmichael; Batten, Kitching, E Ward, Best; Bennett, D Ward; Whitcombe, Darlison, Higson, Roberts, Marklew, Hutchinson.*

*Wakefield: Teall; Copley, Stott, Jones, Baddeley; Rylance, Goodfellow; Wilkinson, Marson, Higgins, Murphy, Moore, Bratley.*

*Referee: Mr G S Phillips (Widnes).*

*Northern coach Dai Rees instructs the relaxed but attentive 1946 Great Britain 'Indomitables' touring party. Ernest Ward and Trevor Foster are seated together, third and second from the right.*

It was a different story, however, at Odsal where Bradford, with Davies at stand off instead of George Bennett, overcame a strong opening by Halifax to take the lead with a long-range touchdown for winger Best, Ernest Ward adding the extras.

Batten, with a trademark leap over an opponent, set up another raid by Best who sent second row Alf Marklew over with an inside ball, and Bradford rammed home their advantage with a Jack Kitching try.

Edwards was next to cross, courtesy of a move involving loose forward Bill Hutchinson, Kitching and Batten. And although Halifax hit back to within three points on aggregate with a Tommy McHugh try and four Hubert Lockwood goals Bradford, who had kept in front through a Don Ward touchdown, remained in the ascendancy with Don Ward's second try and Ernest Ward's fourth goal.

Bradford, meanwhile, had snapped up the Yorkshire Cup the previous year, toppling Keighley over two legs after having disposed of Dewsbury, Leeds and guest Lancastrians Barrow on the way to the final.

It was close at Odsal in the opening game, when Keighley kept Northern to a 5-2 advantage in which Foster grabbed the only try after intelligently supporting an attack by winger

# A match to remember

## Yorkshire Cup Final

*Bradford Northern 18 Castleford 9*
*Headingley, Leeds*
*30 October 1948*

*A young Castleford side, featuring in the club's first Yorkshire Cup Final, threatened to stage an upset before the old heads in the Northern camp ensured that the cup was retrieved after a three-year gap. The upstarts, abjuring the undoubted pedigrees of their opponents, raced into a 9-2 lead at the interval with a try and a goal by Des Foreman, a Charlie Staines penalty and a George Langfield drop goal, while Northern had been limited to a sole Alan Edwards drop goal in response.*

*The pattern continued when hostilities were resumed after the interval, Castleford again pressing strongly. Northern, though, effectively won the game in this testing period. Valiant defence in which Ron Greaves, Frank Whitcombe and Trevor Foster were prominent denied Cas what would probably have been the clinching score. And, remarkably, it was to be the older side that was to hold sway in the closing stages of the game.*

*Castleford, showing signs that they had over-extended themselves, slowed to Bradford's pace and with captain and centre Ernest Ward dictating matters Northern swung the issue with eight points in a blistering 11-minute spell.*

*Edwards was the beneficiary, racing over for two tries and adding a conversion to put his side ahead on the hour, Foster crashed over with 10 minutes left and, as Castleford wilted, left centre Bill Leake raced through, Edwards adding the goal to complete an 18-9 win.*

*There was, though, a less than happy ending for Edwards who was unable to respond to the fans' post-match exhortations for a celebratory appearance. Edwards, instead, was confined to the dressing rooms awaiting an ambulance after having dislocated his shoulder while being tackled in the closing stages.*

*Bradford: Carmichael; Batten, Leake, E Ward, Edwards; Davies, D Ward; Whitcombe, Darlison, Greaves, Foster, Tyler, Traill.*

*Castleford: Lewis; Bastow, Guest, Skidmore, Lloyd; Alf Fisher, Langfield; Harris, Jones, Crossley, Staines, Foreman, Mugglestone.*

*One of Rugby League's more celebrated action shots. Winger Eric Batten leaps over his brother Bob, the Leeds winger, in a league match at Headingley in 1947, played before the Loiners' record crowd of 40,175.*

Emlyn Walters, centre James adding a drop goal in the second half.

The return, at Lawkholme Lane, was equally keenly contested, Keighley taking an early lead with a try by veteran centre Idris Towill before Ernest Ward crossed to restore Bradford's overall advantage.

Hooker Vic Darlison nosed Northern further in front with a rare drop goal and although the home side replied with a Mel De Lloyd penalty,

# Harry Sheard, supporter from the 1930s

*'Frank Whitcombe was a long distance lorry driver; he eventually got a pub when he'd got a bob or two. We were playing at Dewsbury and Frank rolled up with his big wagon, parked in the car park and went straight onto the field. Harry Royal was their scrum-half. They never liked one another. Harry was a midget at the side of Frank but he wouldn't let go and if Frank did out to him Harry would have a crack back.*

*'In one of the first scrums Frank brought his leg out as Harry was putting the ball in and he caught Harry on the top of the head. Well, Harry ran straight into the pack, let him have a peg and then they had a little bit of a set-to.'*

# A match to remember
## Challenge Cup Final

*Bradford Northern 8 Leeds 4*
*Wembley*
*3 May 1947*
*A try in the final minute by Welsh second row forward Trevor Foster sealed a memorable victory against the fancied Loiners.*
*Northern, who had last won the Challenge Cup in 1944 (in peace-time, in 1906) were facing a side that, incredibly, had not conceded a single point en route to Wembley.*
*The Rugby League public, perhaps sensing an upset and keen to put post-war deprivations to one side, headed south in droves in anticipation of something special.*
*A world record crowd of 77,605 turned up expecting a mighty tussle between the redoubtable Leeds pack, which included such as loose forward Ike Owens and Australian second row Arthur Clues, and a Northern six headed by prop Frank Whitcombe and Foster, with quality backs on hand in the form of centre and skipper Ernest Ward, stand off Willie Davies and winger Eric Batten.*
*Bradford were not to disappoint, despite a sluggish start in which the Loiners dominated territorially.*
*Superb defence, with Whitcombe controlling matters in the centre of the pitch and Foster energetic out wide, thwarted every gambit Leeds attempted before*

*Northern slowly but surely gained the upper hand. The Loiners, limited to a penalty by New Zealand full-back Bert Cook – the only score of the first half – found themselves behind for the first time nine minutes into the second half. Ernest Ward, playing a true captain's game, raced through but was denied a yard short of Leeds' tryline. From the play-the-ball, however, the ball was fed to Ward's co-centre Jack Kitching who sent Welsh winger Emlyn Walters over in the corner. Cook put Leeds ahead once more with his second penalty but the lead was short-lived, Ernest Ward edging Bradford in front with a drop goal.*
*And, with time running out, a kick by Northern full-back George Carmichael was fumbled by Cook – and Foster was on hand to collect and cross for the clinching try.*

*Bradford: Carmichael; Batten, Kitching, E Ward, Walters; Davies, D Ward; Whitcombe, Darlison, Smith, Tyler, Foster, Evans.*

*Leeds: Cook; Cornelius, Price, Les Williams, Whitehead; Dickie Williams, Jenkins; Brereton, Murphy, Prosser, Watson, Clues, Owens.*

*Referee: Mr P Cowell (Warrington).*

Bradford were not to be denied, holding out for a 10-7 win which secured a 15-9 aggregate success and a cup victory in which the side, in the two-legged era, had won each of its eight ties.

### A quick return

Having waited nearly four decades for a repeat of the 1906 Challenge Cup Final outing, Bradford were back in the limelight in double-quick time with an appearance in the 1944–45 decider; the last in war-time and the third in succession to be played over two legs.

Northern, who were to also head the War Emergency League and retrieve the championship, were viewed as strong favourites to outwit a Huddersfield side that closed exactly halfway down the table – but the absence of full-back Carmichael through injury necessitated a shuffle in which Ernest Ward moved to the rear, Edwards switching from the wing and Best covering out wide.

The pack, lacking its usual ferocity, generally played second fiddle to the Huddersfield six and against that background the first leg at Fartown finished 7-4 in the Claret & Golds' favour, future Northern full-back Bill Leake scoring a try and winger Jeff Bawden adding a couple of goals, while Bradford were limited to two Ernest Ward penalties.

That scoreline need not have unduly worried Northern, who had already overturned an identical deficit to deny Wigan the Challenge Cup and could boast a 34-match unbeaten record at Odsal, when the second leg arrived.

A moribund first half

*The 1947 Challenge Cup Final programme.*

# A legend remembers
## Trevor Foster

*'The wonderful thing about our victory in the 1947 Challenge Cup final was that when our great captain Ernest Ward came into the dressing room and put the Cup on the table our manager Dai Rees followed him in and said: "Do you know what? You chaps have never asked about money". And that was a fact. At no time at all in our stay in London was money ever discussed. You had one thing on your mind: win the Cup for Bradford, for yourselves, for your red, amber and black jersey and for your family. Money was secondary. That was the way we played; they gave us a reasonable sum of money for what we achieved. 'When we came back on the Monday night to the City Hall at Bradford, right through the city on an open decked coach, you could not move in Town Hall square, you could not put a pin down, it was jam packed with men, women and children. A great occasion. 1947. Bradford Northern had won the Cup.'*

which not only lacked any score but also any worthwhile attack by either side was largely forgotten when stand off Davies beat two men in a blistering run before drawing the remnants of the defence to send Batten over, Ernest Ward's conversion giving Bradford a 9-7 aggregate lead. But Huddersfield hit back immediately, collecting the ball at the restart and finding touch near Northern's line with an intelligent kick.

Bradford's woes increased when Fartown won the scrum, and the misery intensified when the ball was moved wide for Bawden to beat Ernest Ward in a race to the corner to put Huddersfield a point ahead.

Any hopes Northern may have harboured of rescuing the situation evaporated when a move broke down, Bawden intercepting and hacking on for a touchdown that confirmed a 6-5 defeat for Northern – the first reverse at home since April 1944 – and a 13-9 aggregate victory for Huddersfield.

Batten's score, however, helped the former Hunslet flyer to match the 35 registered by Walters in 1940–41. Batten's fellow-winger had eclipsed the previous record of 29 set by James Dechan and, with 105 points, had become the first Bradford player to pass the century mark in a season.

There was, however, a less pleasant experience for another winger as long-standing supporter Harry Sheard recalls: 'Alan Edwards, the Salford winger, was guesting with Bradford.

*A first Challenge Cup success for Bradford Northern. Coach Dai Rees takes the matter seriously as skipper Ernest Ward hoists the silverware in 1947.*

*George Carmichael gets in the shade as he celebrates the first of Northern's three successive Wembley appearances with the Challenge Cup. The full back is escorted by stand off Willie Davies, winger Eric Batten and coach Dai Rees; prop Frank Whitcombe is thoughtful at the rear.*

We were playing Hunslet at Parkside where they had benches in front of the stands with an iron rail at each end. One of the ruddy Hunslet lads picked Edwards up and dropped him on this bench and he'd a bad shoulder for the rest of his career.'

Sheard has fonder memories of another great Northern character, the hooker Vince Dilorenzo. 'I would have felt that Trevor Foster would have been the officer during the war and Billy would have been one of the privates. But he wasn't, apparently Dilorenzo was the officer and Trevor Foster was the private.

'Dilorenzo was like a young tank, ambling about the field. If there was a scrum on the right hand side and then they had another on the left, Dilorenzo wouldn't have got out of the first scrum by the time it happened. The props would pick him up, put his arms round their shoulders and they'd amble towards the scrum across the field!

'The biggest cheer I ever heard at Odsal, and I've heard a few, was when Dilorenzo scored a

## A match to remember
### Championship Semi-Final

Wigan 3 Bradford Northern 15
Central Park, Wigan
24 April 1948

*Wigan, bidding to become the first team to win the championship in three successive seasons, were denied by Northern just seven days before the sides met in the Challenge Cup Final.*

*Bradford, seeking their first title since the pre-Northern era, were well served in an epic game, perhaps one of the club's finest performances, by full-back Bill Leake who, with a superlative display, forced his way into the Wembley line-up in place of the injured George Carmichael.*

*Wigan, who lacked Gordon Ratcliffe, Ernie Ashcroft and Jack Hilton, were – despite playing well – unable to cope with what the Yorkshire Post described as Northern's 'firm mastery' and the Pie Eaters' 'many-pointed and intricate' attack was regularly thwarted. Northern were at their expansive best, clearing their lines with 'breathtaking moves' with passing that rippled with 'almost insolent ease' and which gave wingers Eric Batten and Alan Edwards regular opportunities. Edwards blotted his copybook by spilling possession on more than one occasion with the tryline begging but the flyer made amends, to the delight of Bradford's fans in the 32,671 crowd, with a sensational try after a 20-yard run in which he was 'never more than a couple of inches from touch'. Batten also swept in, courtesy of a five-man passing move and a strong finish, and a wonderful victory was sealed by a late try by second row Trevor Foster. Ernest Ward kicked three goals, while Johnny Lawrenson crossed for the home side.*

*Wigan's Billy Blan was sent off in the last minute after a fracas involving several players.*

*The effort, and the long season, may have taken too much out of Northern, who lost to Wigan the following week at Wembley. Charlie Ebbage provides a telling insight. 'When Northern played Warrington in the championship final at Maine Road, Manchester in 1947–48 they were beaten before they started. Don Ward told me afterwards that he knew in the dressing room, prior to kick off, that Northern had no chance. The players were worn out. "Their eyes were just dead," he said.'*

*Wigan: Ryan; Nordgren, Ward, Cunliffe, Lawrenson; Mountford, Bradshaw; Gee, Egan, Barton, White, Blan, Hudson.*

*Bradford: Leake; Batten, Case, E Ward, Edwards; Davies, D Ward; Whitcombe, Darlison, Smith, Foster, Tyler, Traill.*

# A match to remember
## Challenge Cup Final

Bradford Northern 3 Wigan 8
Wembley
1 May 1948
The tables were turned on Northern, just seven days after their epic Championship semi-final win at Wigan, by a Pie Eaters outfit that boasted many great players in its ranks but which perhaps also benefited from one of those omens that suggest that sporting results can perhaps occasionally be pre-ordained.

Bradford's mascot, nine-year-old Tony Halliday, had not seen Bradford lose that season while performing his duties and was distraught when he learned that Wembley rules would prevent him from taking on his usual role at the Empire stadium.

His parents wrote to the guest of honour, King George VI, for help in their plight but His Majesty, while assured of his own right to be on the pitch before kick off as the first reigning monarch to attend a Challenge Cup final, was unable to assist young Tony.

Sir Arthur Elvin, Wembley's Managing Director, eased the boy's anguish with two 10s 6d tickets, but he could do nothing about the result as Tony's fears proved justified.

Ill-fortune befell Bradford midway through the first half when winger Eric Batten, seeking to recover from a slip with a kick-through, saw his attempt charged down by Wigan left-winger Jack Hilton who dribbled on for a try at the corner that centre Ted Ward, who had missed a couple of earlier penalties, improved.

Northern hit back immediately when loose forward Ken Traill kicked to the flag, winger Alan Edwards collecting to touch down, but a chance to take the lead went begging when Batten was unable, in the wet conditions, to take a pass when clear.

Second row Trevor Foster went close, only to be denied by a tackle by Wigan full-back Martin Ryan. And despite the efforts of prop Frank Whitcombe, who won the Lance Todd Trophy, Bradford were denied by a second, scrappy, Pie Eaters try when Les White and Billy Blan dribbled a drop out back to the Northern line, prop Frank Barton pouncing for the clinching score. Ward's simple conversion attempt bounced out off a post but the fates, despite that setback, had been, quite simply, against Bradford – as Tony Halliday could have foretold.

Bradford: Leake; Batten, Case, E Ward, Edwards; Davies, D Ward; Whitcombe, Darlison, Smith, Tyler, Foster, Traill.

Wigan: Ryan; Ratcliffe, Ward, Ashcroft, Hilton; Mountford, Bradshaw; Gee, Egan, Barton, White, Blan, Hudson.

Referee: Mr G S Phillips (Widnes).

*The 1948 Challenge Cup Final programme.*

try. He was within a few yards of the line and the ball came across. Normally they'd miss him and pass it to somebody else, but this day they gave Dilorenzo the ball and he ran two or three yards and plopped over the line. It took two or three of them to pick him up! I think they signed him out of Lancashire somewhere.'

### Peacetime glory

The stalwarts who bravely held faith with the 13-a-side cause at the turn of the century were rewarded for their courage, commitment and foresight, after almost four decades of struggle, with the most successful period in the club's history following the end of the Second World War.

The building process begun by Harry Hornby in the 1930s and continued through the war years bore fruit in the late 1940s and early 1950s as Northern's exploits shone like a beacon

*King George VI meets Northern's players prior to the 1948 Challenge Cup Final.*

through the gloom of post-war austerity.

Bradford continued the improvement of the immediate pre-war years, establishing themselves in the higher echelons at a time when the competition in the 'single league' professional game was generally even.

The reigning champions finished fourth in the first peace-time campaign and slipped to a relatively modest tenth the following season but there was ample consolation as the side became the first to make three successive appearances in a Challenge Cup Final in the Wembley era. Wembley became almost a secondary home for Bradford Northern, with appearances in 1947, 1948 and 1949.

Importantly, Northern achieved their successes in great style, with many of the players signed prior to the war to the fore.

Ernest Ward, captain in each of the three finals, set a stylistic lead in the centre helped by an armoury which included a deceptive change of pace, a masterly dummy and a priceless ability to protect his winger, while a glittering array of back talent was led by the incomparable Welsh maestro Willie Davies.

Davies was a creative player of the highest class, belying the general experience of converted Rugby Union stand offs throughout the game's history. That attribute, combined with a neat turn of pace, helped create numerous tries for his three-quarters as he tested his opposite numbers on the outside to pull in opposing centres.

Winger Eric Batten, of the famous dynasty, had inherited his uncle Billy's habit of leaping over opponents in an age when the tactic remained within the laws of the game – and there was no better example of the ploy than in a league match at Leeds in May 1947, played before the Loiners' record crowd of 40,175, when he hurdled over his brother Bob.

The trio were to be joined on Great Britain's 1946 tour Down Under by centre Jack Kitching, another major threat to beleaguered defences, while other quality backs in a great side included scrum-half Donald Ward (brother of Ernest) and full-back George Carmichael.

No back line, of whatever quality, can prosper without a solid platform up front and there was no pack more imposing than Bradford's, led by the remarkable heavyweight prop Frank Whitcombe.

The Welshman, although weighing in at around 18 stones, was remarkably light on his feet and his imposing presence was stylishly supported by the likes of influential loose forward Ken Traill and rangy second row Trevor Foster who remembered: 'The war was over and everybody was getting back to normality. Our great coach Dai Rees, a fine player and tourist himself, was our manager throughout all those successful seasons. He worked out great tactics and made us into a very formidable team. We had a fine pack, with the great Billy Davies at halfback – a real gem of a player – Ernest Ward in the centre with Jack Kitching, and Eric Batten and Emlyn Walters on the wings.

'Our big prop Frank Whitcombe was outstanding, on and off the field. He was always ready for a laugh and he was a tremendous forward and dictated play from the scrum. Scrimmaging in those days was very important and very hard; there was tremendous, excellent football from the scrum onwards.

'The great thing was to get the ball away from the scrums out to the backs. The wing three-quarters are the fast men and they were the people who were expected to score the tries. The forwards held back because hard scrimmaging in muddy weather took a lot out of you. It was the backs who were expected to perform and score the tries, that was the great thing about the game in that era.

'Eric Batten was a giant of a winger. He would jump over defenders and it was good to watch.

'We also signed Alan Edwards just after the war. He had been a truly great winger with Salford and he came to us towards the end of his career and proved a very, very good buy. He scored a try in the defeat by Wigan in the 1948 Challenge Cup Final.

'Jack Kitching, our 6ft 4in centre, could blaze down the middle really well, but Willie Davies was the kingpin. He augmented all the moves from the scrum and put people into the gap. He was a great man to follow; I scored a number of tries through Willie making openings near the try line. He was born class, with wonderful hands and great speed.'

Davies, a Welsh Rugby Union international who turned professional for a £1,000 fee, played for Bradford from 1939 to 1950, making 237 appearances and scoring 55 tries. A key player in each of the 1947, 1948 and 1949 Challenge Cup Finals, he became the first Welshman to be awarded the Lance Todd Trophy with a scintillating performance in the 1947 victory over Leeds.

He had also been the last player to score a four-point drop goal in Rugby Union's international championship, also registering a try

*Northern prop Frank Whitcombe upends a Warrington player in the 1948 Championship Final at Maine Road, Manchester.*

in the 7-0 win over Ireland in 1939.

Davies, however, was particularly noted for his ball-playing abilities. Centre Jack Kitching said: 'If you received a pass from Willie you were heading for a gap – you knew he had done all the spadework.'

Bradford, with an abundance of such talent on board, wasted no time in getting into gear, recording a record away league victory with the 22-0 success at Oldham in early September 1945.

Only 14 days later, Northern enjoyed their biggest win since the 68-2 routing of Bramley in 1906 with a 54-3 verdict over Leeds at Headingley and the astonishing vein of rampant rugby continued when Liverpool Stanley were put to the sword 67-0 at Odsal in a game in which captain Ernest Ward set two new club records.

The centre's 34 points, with four tries and 11 goals, bettered the 25 set by Fred Cooper

## Charlie Ebbage

*'The best centre I ever saw was Ernest Ward. Stan McCormick – a fine winger with Broughton Rangers, Belle Vue and Warrington – once told me that if he'd heard that some players had made 75 yards, no one had been in front of them. If Ernest Ward had made 75 yards he knew he'd beaten several men.'*

against Swinton Church in the Challenge Cup in March 1897, while Ward's goal tally also represented a new high.

Northern quickly added a second trophy to the championship that had been secured in the final war-time campaign, disposing of Hunslet 8-0 and Dewsbury 7-2 en route to the Yorkshire Cup final victory at Thrum Hall, Halifax, over Wakefield Trinity.

**Six tourists**

Northern's successes ironically backfired on the club as the first post-war season came to a close.

The Australian Rugby League, eager to provide a hungry public with international competition, issued an invitation to the Rugby Football League for a Great Britain tour, which was readily accepted.

Six Bradford players, Foster, Whitcombe, Ernest Ward, Kitching, Batten and Davies, were selected and joined a Lions squad that sailed south from Plymouth on the aircraft carrier HMS Indomitable on 4 April 1946 – leaving Northern without several of their best players and with 10 league matches remaining.

Prior to the Lions' departure, Northern were on course to finish top of the table. Although the first three of their outstanding games were won, the task inevitably took its toll on Rees' weakened squad.

Four of the last seven games ended in defeat, with the result that Bradford finished in fourth spot – three positions ahead of fifth-placed Barrow, nine behind leaders Wigan and just one point adrift of third-placed Wakefield Trinity – and were therefore compelled to travel to Wigan in the Championship semi-final, which resulted in an 18-4 defeat.

It was, however, a different matter two seasons later when Bradford, having again finished fourth, were once more obliged to visit

Central Park for the right to contest the Championship Final at Maine Road, Manchester – and secured a victory that arguably ranks alongside any other in the club's history.

A year earlier, Dai Rees had helped Northern to their first victory at Wembley with a piece of typically shrewd opportunism and equally perceptive tactics, as Trevor Foster recounted: 'We played Leeds in the 1947 Challenge Cup Final. There was tremendous rivalry between the clubs, based in two great cities very close together.

'We went down to London on the Thursday afternoon ready for this great contest. On the Friday we went to Wembley to look around the ground, hoping to have a run out on the pitch. We got to the ground and our astute manager Dai Rees sought out the groundsman and asked if we could go on the field. He said, "no, no certainly not". Dai palmed him with a £5 note and we were allowed onto the ground. That was important, of great benefit to us. Running out onto the field at that great stadium was inspiring. We had a good hour on the field, which was very, very good.

'As we were coming off the Leeds team had arrived, but the groundsman would not let them

*The Mayor of Bradford takes a drink from the Challenge Cup in 1949. Northern captain Ernest Ward, together with his wife and son, share the enjoyment.*

# Charlie Ebbage

*'The coach driver didn't know the way to Wembley for the 1947 Cup Final. Frank Whitcombe, who was an HGV driver, took over the wheel and drove the team to the stadium. Another motorist thought that Frank had cut him up at a corner. He stopped the coach with the aim of taking the matter up with Frank. When he saw the size of him, though, he drove off!*

*'Frank always had a smile on his face. He had very small feet for a man of his size. He used to sneak out with Billy Davies' boots on. I don't know whether Billy wore Frank's!'*

*The 1949 Challenge Cup Final programme.*

play on the ground at 3 in the afternoon.

'The match was a titanic struggle. Dai Rees decided that our scrum-half Donald Ward would be acting half at the play the ball and would pass the ball wide, keeping it away from the very big Leeds forwards who were very, very strong in the tackle and would knock you pretty hard.

'The tactic put us in good stead. Emlyn Walters went over and scored a try, and they got two goals by the great New Zealand full-back Bert Cook, who could kick goals from all angles. But we broke away and scored a try and I was fortunate to be the one to score it. The ball was kicked up in the air into their 25 line, Bert Cook jumped for the ball, I went for it at the same time and it came into my hands. I strolled over for the try, we kicked the goal, and lo and behold we won.'

Northern, of course, were of sufficient quality to have prevailed against the Loiners regardless of Rees' persuasive methods. The Yorkshire League was won in 1947–48, and there were also Yorkshire Cup successes in 1948 and 1949, mainly with the players who had served Northern so well during the conflict and in the immediate post-war years.

Indifferent league form was put to one side at the beginning of the 1948–49 season as Bradford defied the critics to target the Yorkshire Cup, beating Dewsbury over two legs, Huddersfield and, in the semi-final, Hunslet 12-5 at Parkside after having been held to a 7-7 draw at Odsal.

The 1949–50 season opened with the launch of a new publication, the *Rugby Leaguer*. Its correspondent 'Liver', pondering the future of a Liverpool Stanley side which was struggling with

low attendances, sought inspiration from Northern's renaissance and wrote: 'Some people say that Liverpool is so soccer-minded that there will never be proper support for Stanley. How little these people know!

'Let's remove the scene to Bradford, where the team from the wool city created a new record by appearing in three consecutive Wembley finals.

'The remarkable rise of the Northern is indeed one of the romances of the professional handling code. Wasn't it enough to dampen enthusiasm when so many people decided to support the idea of a switch from the Northern Union game to soccer?

'And yet when the club was poverty-stricken at the small headquarters in Birch Lane, there

*Welsh second row forward Trevor Foster crashed over for six tries, equalling the Northern club record, in the 28-16 league win over Wakefield Trinity at Odsal on 10 April 1948. Northern's other two tries went to Alan Edwards and Emlyn Walters, with George Carmichael adding two goals.*

*Winger James Dechan had scored six tries against Widnes in January 1905 and had repeated the feat the following November in the 48-8 mauling of Brighouse.*

# A match to remember
## Challenge Cup Final

*Bradford Northern 12 Halifax 0*
*Wembley*
*7 May 1949*
*Winger Eric Batten, who had had a woeful time 12 months earlier, was the hero as Northern, making a record third successive appearance at Wembley, enjoyed a comfortable victory over their derby rivals before a highest-ever crowd of 95,050.*
*Batten, whose two errors had been instrumental in the 1948 defeat, laid the demons to rest with an inspiring performance after resolving to stay on the field despite having sustained a fractured shoulder in the opening minutes.*
*The flyer's courage was confirmed beyond any doubt shortly after that set back when Batten chased a kick by centre Ernest Ward to dive over for the game's first try, Ward converting from the touchline.*
*Hooker Vic Darlison and his pack ensured that Northern enjoyed the lion's share of possession throughout the first half and Bradford, although denied any further score before the break, duly extended their lead on the hour when Ward landed a penalty.*
*Scrum-half Don Ward, best known for his work around the scrum, added to his reputation when he worked a smart move with loose forward Ken Traill to send second row Trevor Foster over, Ernest Ward again improving to ensure that, with eight minutes left, the match was won.*

*Ernest Ward took the Lance Todd Trophy as Man of the Match for his creative contribution and valuable goals. Batten, however, was a key figure in choosing to stay on the field in an era in which substitutes were not allowed.*
*So, too, was coach Dai Rees who bravely selected 18 stone prop Frank Whitcombe, an absentee through injury since late January. His inclusion negated what would have otherwise have been a significant advantage by the heavier Halifax pack and the ploy worked, Northern winning 42 of the 55 scrums.*
*Bradford Northern thus became the first side to return to Wembley as a defeated team within 12 months and win while Halifax – who had finished the season in twenty-fifth spot to become the lowest-placed side to feature in a Challenge Cup final – acquired the dubious distinction of being the first side to fail to score at the Empire Stadium.*

*Bradford: Leake; Batten, Kitching, E Ward, Edwards; Davies, D Ward; Whitcombe, Darlison, Greaves, Tyler, Foster, Traill.*

*Halifax: Chalkey; Daniels, Reid, Price, MacDonald; Kenny, Kielty; Condon, Ackerley, Rothwell, Healy, Pansegrouw, Mawson.*

*Referee: Mr G S Phillips (Widnes).*

---

were the faithful few who would not let go of that tiny thread which kept the club together.

'Northern were the chopping blocks of most teams, season in, season out. Then the old Steam Pigs, as they were then known, leapt into the limelight overnight when they beat an Australian touring team.

'People could not believe their eyes when they read the result in the papers. "It's a misprint," they said. But no, Northern had won.

'Then came the steady rise to fame and the club which once had one of the smallest grounds in the league became licensees of what is one of the biggest sports enclosures in the British Isles – Hampden Park included.

'So there's a tale, a remarkable tale, which reads almost like one of Hans Andersen's and it's not without the bounds of possibility that Liverpool may follow Northern's example.'

The *Rugby Leaguer* also considered Bradford's immediate future and reflected: 'R.L. followers and also those 'exiles' in many parts of the country often wonder how Bradford's veterans keep on going while other clubs

*Parading the prize! The Northern side hoist Ernest Ward and the Challenge Cup.*

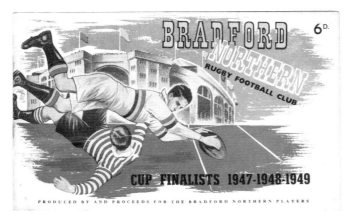

*Northern's players, proud of their achievement of having reached a third successive Challenge Cup Final, produced a souvenir brochure.*

concentrate on youth.

'But there is always a time when a player has to hang up his boots and therefore we are not likely to see Frank Whitcombe and George Carmichael out again.

'While Bradford will again be playing some of these veterans, there will be an enterprising policy of giving youth a chance.

But you can never tell. Bradford might be back at Wembley again with some of the old stars twinkling again.'

The *Rugby Leaguer* was wrong. Northern would not, in fact, return to the Empire Stadium for another 24 years but Rees' men nevertheless came close to securing a remarkable fourth successive appearance, reaching the semi-final in 1950 after victories over Oldham, Keighley and St Helens (by 11-0 in an Odsal replay following a scoreless draw at Knowsley Road).

## A legend remembers
### Trevor Foster

'We had a wonderful run after having won the Challenge Cup for the first time since 1906 and again reached the final in 1947–48.

'Unfortunately we never got going that day. That's sport, you win some, you lose some. Wigan were a great side with Joe Egan, Ken Gee, Martin Ryan – a fine full-back – all colleagues of mine on the 1946 Australian tour, great men and wonderful athletes.

'We came back and had another marvellous reception, but we had lost the Cup. It could be because we'd won it the year before. You don't go to lose, obviously, but we were perhaps too lackadaisical.

'But lo and behold the year after we were down to Wembley again, with 95,000 people there, playing Halifax in our third Challenge Cup Final on the trot.

'It was a great contest. Halifax and ourselves were great rivals, with a lot in common and we had great respect for each other as players.

'We were always in front in the game. I managed to score a try and it was another very happy time for our Bradford Northern club, making history with three successive trips to Wembley.'

Widnes, however, ended the dream with an 8-0 win at Wigan before a crowd of 25,390 – other than the 14,400 who watched the 1937 replay between Keighley and Wakefield, the lowest gate for a semi-final for 15 years. There were 69,898 at Odsal for the other semi-final between Leeds and Warrington.

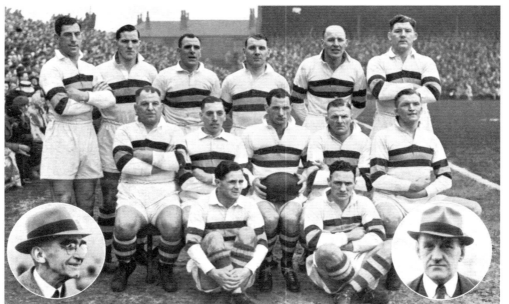

*Bradford Northern, 1949. Back row (left to right): Foster, Radford, Batten, Greaves, Kitching, Tyler. Middle row: Darlison, Leake, Ernest Ward, Edwards, Traill. Front row: Davies, Don Ward. Inset are managing director Harry Hornby and coach Dai Rees, two men who helped steer the club and the team to greatness.*

# 5.
# Gone Missing - 69,105 Spectators

Northern acquired a reputation in the late 1940s and early 1950s as non-players in the transfer market; a state of affairs that didn't please all of the supporters and shareholders.

The directors claimed that few if any men had become available who were better than those already at Odsal and that spending money solely in order to please the crowd would inevitably lead to a return to the doldrums of the 1910s, 1920s and early 1930s.

Harry Hornby and his colleagues could, in any event, point to a number of successful acquisitions, notably Alan Edwards who had been snapped up for £700 from Salford in 1946, despite concerns from some fans regarding his fitness. The winger had overcome a series of injuries to give four years of exceptional service and coach Dai Rees had also got the best out of captures such as utility back Bill Leake, from Huddersfield, second row Barry Tyler, loose forward Ken Traill, utility forward Ron Greaves and prop Brian Radford.

*Bradford Northern were believed to be the first football club in the north of England to stage a game under floodlights when they entertained New Zealand beneath the lamps in 1951. The programme celebrates the occasion.*

By 1949, however, and despite the fact that the club had featured in three successive Challenge Cup finals, the side was clearly ageing. Within two years such as Frank Whitcombe, Willie Davies, Donald Ward, Vic Darlison and George Carmichael had retired, while Eric Batten had become player-coach at Featherstone Rovers, who he would take to Wembley in 1952.

With little suitable talent believed to be on offer in the north of England, Rees was enlisted to scour the valleys of his native south Wales, while Hornby flew to New Zealand on what was to be a productive exercise.

Hornby had been tipped off by former player George Gilbert that a number of men could be available and he returned with five signatures. The first four comprised full-back Joe Phillips, centres Norman Hastings and Bill

*Northern in the early 1950s. The Odsal outfit, while unable to quite sustain the form and good fortune that had earned them three successive trips to Wembley in the late 1940s, remained a major power.*

*Barry Seabourne leads Bradford Northern out in the mid-70s. The Rugby Football League ruled in the early 1950s, following incidents in which match officials were manhandled, that the stairway be fenced off.*

Dickson and winger Bob Hawes, all delivered in late July 1950. And, early the following month, Bradford were able to announce that All Black winger Jack McLean had accepted the professional ticket.

The latter signing was hailed as a major coup and McLean duly gave magnificent service to Northern, as did Phillips, both on and off the field. The cost for the quintet was reported to be £10,000 – a huge amount, but money which would be amply repaid in the ensuing four or five years.

McLean settled quickly and established a new Northern record of tries in a season with 63 touchdowns in 46 appearances in 1951–52.

The flying Kiwi had eclipsed the previous best of 36 – recorded by Alan Edwards in 1947–48 – by Boxing Day when his brace at Keighley took him to the 37-try mark.

McLean went on to leave Edwards' total way behind, but he still didn't come top of the Rugby League list for that season. That accolade went to Huddersfield's Lionel Cooper, with 71 tries.

McLean's best display in 1951–52 was on 12 April when he raced over for five touchdowns in the 32-4 victory over York at Odsal. He bagged four tries in each of the home games against Castleford and Keighley, and in the 52-12 verdict at Cardiff. He netted six hat-tricks during the season, playing an important role as Northern took pole position in the table.

## Ebbing away

There are, Mark Twain insisted, lies, damn lies and statistics.

Even Twain, though, would probably have been taken aback by the bald figure of 69,105 – the difference between Bradford Northern's highest attendance for a home game, when 69,429 turned up on 14 March 1953 for the visit of Huddersfield in a Challenge Cup quarterfinal, and the 324 who drifted through the Odsal turnstiles a little over a decade later for the Division Two fixture with Barrow.

All Rugby League clubs – indeed all sports – had experienced a waning of interest as TV, the motor car and other diversions hit the traditional Saturday afternoon habit. But that factor does little to explain the painful, slow yet inexorable decline that hit Bradford Northern.

Bradford had, less than a year before

*Northern's Yorkshire Cup first round, two-leg tie with Featherstone Rovers in 1951 ended in chaos when the sides finished all square at the end of the second match. Bradford, who had lost 4-2 at Odsal, squared the issue by winning the return at Post Office Road 11-9. Previously the clubs would have arranged a replay. New rules introduced by the Rugby Football League at the beginning of the season, however, stipulated that from 1951–52 teams were required to play 15 minutes each way of extra time.*

*That was also understood by the referee who, when some of the players of both sides left the field after 80 minutes, assumed that they had gone to the changing rooms for refreshments and called a two-minute break. Northern and Rovers officials mistook his signal as an indication that the contest had ended and instructed the remaining players to retire to the dressing rooms.*

*By the time the issue had been resolved a number of players were in the bath. The RFL, far from happy with both clubs, fined each £50 and ordered a replay at Belle Vue, Wakefield, with neither Bradford or Featherstone being allowed a share of the receipts. Northern won the game 17-9.*

attracting that mammoth crowd, entertained 56,476 in the Championship semi-final, also against Huddersfield, but the descent had been swift after average gates of 17,310 and 17,169 respectively had been recorded in 1951–52 and 1952–53.

The mean attendance in 1953–54 – the year that 102,000, and more besides, turned up for the Challenge Cup final replay – was 12,182, a disconcerting 5,000 down on the previous two years although the two huge attendances against Huddersfield offered part of the explanation.

Four years later, that average had dropped to 4,675 and, three seasons further on, in 1960–61, to a desultory 1,859. An incredible transformation. And matters were to get worse.

The total gate in the 1962–63 season – the old club's last full campaign – was 23,888; slightly above a mere third of the attendance for that Huddersfield cup-tie a decade earlier.

The old Bradford Northern called a halt after a mere 324 hardy souls turned up for the visit of Barrow on 23 November 1963 – the day after President John F Kennedy's assassination.

The next and – under the then regime – last game at Odsal was on 7 December 1963 when Leigh, who were thought to have brought between 500 and 600 of their own supporters, attracted an 841 attendance.

With the bank insisting that it could no longer loan money to a patently sinking ship and the directors at the end of the road, the decision was made to go into liquidation.

*The Wardley Plan. A vision of a future Odsal, proposed in the early 1950s.*

---

# A match to remember
## Championship Final

*Bradford Northern 6 Wigan 13*
*Leeds Road, Huddersfield*
*10 May 1952*
*Bradford, who had come top of the table for the first time since 1904, were denied the title by a Wigan outfit which secured the championship for the fourth time in seven seasons.*
*Northern missed the leadership of Ernest Ward, who was ruled out with a shoulder injury, but could still have won but for a number of controversial decisions by the referee which irked their supporters in the 48,656 crowd – nearly 8,000 fewer than had witnessed their semi-final victory over Huddersfield at Odsal.*
*Mr Appleton earned the opprobrium of Northern's fans when he brought prop Brian Radford back from what would have been a certain try, ruling that loose forward Ken Traill's pass had been forward.*
*Northern, 5-4 down at half time after responding to a Nat Silcock try and Ken Gee goal with two Joe Phillips penalties, went close to taking the lead when centre Joe Mageen was tackled short of the line, winger Jack McLean subsequently being forced into touch after another raid.*
*Phillips, however, edged Bradford in front with his third penalty and what could have been a championship-clinching score went begging when Traill, with only full-back Martin Ryan to beat and support arriving, opted to kick and saw his effort sail into the crowd.*
*Wigan made the most of the escape, responding with a Gee penalty and Jack Cunliffe try. And, after sustained Northern pressure, a breakaway touchdown by Ryan sealed the Lancastrians' win.*

*Bradford: Phillips; Hawes, Mageen, Hastings, McLean; L Haley, G Jones; Shreeve, N Haley, Radford, Foster, Tyler, Traill.*

*Wigan: Ryan; Hilton, Broome, Roughley, Nordgren; Cunliffe, Alty; Gee, Mather, Woosey, Silcock, Large, Street.*

*Referee: Mr C Appleton (Warrington)*

*Leeds full-back Bert Cook is credited with the longest goal kicked at Odsal. Cook landed a penalty measured at 56 yards on 27 September 1951. The New Zealander was said to have sent the ball a total of 80 yards.*

The Rugby Football League was duly informed and the club's results for the 1962–63 season were expunged from the records.

## Amateur status

Len Haley would not have believed such a moment possible when he signed for Northern almost by default 13 years earlier. The culturally-gifted stand-off takes up the story.

'I was just coming out of the Army – this was 1950 – and I was playing Rugby Union with the Duke of Wellington's regiment with Geoff Butterfield, alongside Mike Hardy and Dennis Shuttleworth who were England half-backs. Geoff Butterfield asked me if I would go over to Cleckheaton and play with them, which I did.

'I got picked to play for Yorkshire at Ulster but somebody rang the Rugby Union and told them that I'd played Rugby League. I'd only played as an amateur, with Overthorpe Rangers who subsequently became Thornhill Trojans, but the outcome was that I was banned.

'Northern's coach Dai Rees had already asked me to go to Odsal but I'd turned him down because I wanted my Yorkshire cap. Anyway, Dai heard about me being banned and he came to see me, it was 10 or 11 o'clock at night. He said, "Now then Len, what are you going to do? You'll have to play for us now, won't you?" I said, "Well,

*Joe Mageen attempts to outflank Wigan in the 1952 Championship Final at Leeds Road, Huddersfield.*

I'll hang on a bit." He said that was pointless and he was right. I waited two or three weeks and nothing happened so I finally said I would sign. Northern had been offering me £1,000 whilst I was playing Rugby Union but that had changed. "No," he says, "you'll have to take £250 now." All through my career, though, he made it up to me in other ways. When I was injured he would always give me a wage packet, which wasn't the normal thing in those days. It was only losing pay but he didn't have to do it and I'd quite a few injuries over the years. I'd a broken nose, a dislocated elbow, both cartilages out and a broken foot. So he compensated me that way.'

## Challenge Cup history

Odsal was involved in three pieces of Challenge Cup history in 1953 and 1954.

The ground was chosen to host the first-ever televised Challenge Cup draw on 9 January 1953, which was also noteworthy as the first live broadcast on the BBC Newsreel. Northern were drawn at home to Batley – who had beaten Bradford in the 1898 Challenge Cup Final after twice having been paired with Leeds in rehearsals – and went on to attract a record attendance for any game in which one club had home advantage for the visit of Huddersfield in the third round.

The authorities were taken by surprise by the huge crowd that descended on Odsal a little over 12 months later, on the evening of 5 May 1954.

Indeed the Bradford Northern Manager himself, Harry Hornby, did not believe that the ground was ready to stage a Cup Final and felt that profits from the game should be allocated for future development of the stadium in accordance with the Wardley Plan.

It was noted, before the match, that the lower slopes had been completely terraced, although only with sleepers which could be treacherous in wet weather. The New Stand, completely seated, housed 4,800 spectators while there were 1,260 seats in the Old Stand and 3,000 track seats.

It was not felt, considering the dour nature of

*History was made on 31 October 1951 when Odsal staged what is understood to have been the first post-war floodlit game in any code of football.*

*The occasion was Bradford's fixture with the New Zealand tourists, played out under the glare of a series of high-powered lamps attached to the roof of the main stand, with other lights pinioned to poles around the pitch.*

*Northern added to the theatre by instructing both sets of players to enter the pitch in darkness, lining up ready for kick-off prior to the unannounced switch-on. The 29,072 fans, who paid £3,172, gasped as one in amazement at the spectacle and went home in a state of further delight after having witnessed a 13-8 win for Bradford.*

*Northern, perhaps because of opposition from other clubs who may have felt at a disadvantage, failed to build on the successful experiment. Bradford did not take part in the 1955 Independent Television Trophy, contested by Featherstone Rovers, Huddersfield, Hunslet, Leigh, Oldham, Wakefield Trinity, Warrington and Wigan on London soccer grounds, and missed out entirely on the BBC2 Floodlit Trophy, which ran from 1965–66 until 1979–80. Northern installed lights in that final season but did not enter the competition, switching on for the league game with St Helens on Tuesday 27 November 1979.*

*The defeat by Wigan at Leeds Road, Huddersfield in May 1952 marked Bradford's last appearance in a Championship Final until the advent of Super League in the mid-90s. Wigan second row Nat Silcock crosses for the Pie Eaters' crucial first try, with Northern's defence floundering.*

the Wembley clash between Halifax and Warrington, that Odsal's capacity was at risk – even though all stand tickets had been sold within seven days.

In the event, an estimated 60,000 people were in the ground an hour before the scheduled 7.00pm kick off, and more were still arriving at half time.

Those who got in late were lucky if they saw anything of the game as their view was blocked by a wall of spectators standing scores deep on the flat bank at the top of the Rooley Lane banking.

More latecomers broke down the stadium perimeter fencing near the speedway pits area, and the crowd was ten deep along the goal lines; others attempted to climb onto the roof of the new stand before being persuaded by the police to climb down.

Bradford supporter Harry Sheard was just one of the hordes of fans who struggled to get to the game and home again. 'We got a bus from

Cleckheaton for the match but got off at Low Moor because there was no chance, it was stood in the traffic.

'We ran up to the ground and into the clubhouse where we watched supporters coming in from a window. We could see it was going to be a terrific crowd so we said we'd better get down.

'We were just going past the back of the stand when all the fencing came down from the car park, on the slope of the hill. Ruddy hundreds charged down there, so of course we ran like hell and got right at the back and found a spot where we could see.

'There were over 102,000 there officially but how many got in for nowt I don't know.

'We walked home and of course I was in dead trouble when I got back. It was "where have you been?" '

## A gentleman steps down

Trevor Foster announced his retirement as a player in 1955. Among the glowing testimonials was one from Ces Mountford, the former Wigan and New Zealand half-back who had moved into management with Warrington. Wrote Mountford: 'From the Rugby League playing fields at the season's end there will be no Trevor Foster of Bradford Northern and to me the fact is as sad as it reads, for he is one of the greatest forwards of his position it has been my pleasure to watch and to play against.

'The best advice I could give to young forwards of today is go and watch Bradford and model your style on Trevor Foster, one of the greatest of our time. As a sportsman there is none better.

'Our game will be the worse for his retirement. Why he should retire I do not know for his display at Warrington last October was nothing short of the season's best.

'So well did he play that some of our younger players remarked. "He must have been good when he was younger." My reply was easy: "Yes, he was great."

'If Trevor can model a Bradford pack on his own style there will always be good football at Odsal.

'"Au revoir" to a great player and a gentleman.'

John Wilson, the long-serving former Secretary of the Rugby Football League, enthused: 'Rugby League followers in general and those of Bradford in particular will

*A huge 69,105 attendance – by some distance the largest for any Rugby League game not played on a neutral venue – turned up at Odsal in 1953 for the Challenge Cup quarter final tie with Huddersfield. The massive crowd provides a spectacular backdrop as New Zealand winger Jack McLean, with Ernest Ward in support, takes on the Fartown defence.*

*The crowd of 69,429 that witnessed the third round Challenge Cup tie against Huddersfield on 14 March 1953 remains the biggest for a Rugby League match not played on a neutral ground.*
*Odsal provided the highest attendance for any code of football that afternoon – and the gate for the clash with the competition's eventual winners dwarfed the healthy-enough figures at the other quarter-final games.*
*Leigh drew 32,051 for their tie with eventual runners-up St Helens, 25,423 gathered for the match between Warrington and Leeds, and an attendance of 20,455 was recorded for the fixture involving Wigan and Hull KR.*
*There was, too, competition in the city of Bradford from two other sporting events, both of which drew reasonable crowds.*
*Bradford Park Avenue hosted Hartlepools United before 6,000, while 9,000 passed through the turnstiles at Lidgett Green for the Rugby Union fixture between Yorkshire and the East Midlands. Twelve months earlier, Northern had entertained Huddersfield in the Championship Play-Off in front of 56,476, and there had been a crowd of 48,000 for a Challenge Cup replay with St Helens in March 1950. The highest crowd for a match involving Bradford at Odsal since the club was reformed in 1964 is 27,459 for a Challenge Cup tie with Wigan in April 1966.*
*Trevor Foster, who played in the 1953 game, said: 'It was a tremendous day, most unexpected. The place was absolutely agog. It was one of the biggest crowds at Odsal for a match of any description, apart from the great 102,000 for the 1954 Cup Final replay. I think it was Dick Cracknell who got a couple of tries, and we were beaten 17-7 unfortunately.'*

remember Trevor Foster, long after he has ceased to play, as one of the best second-row forwards who ever came from Wales.

'They will remember him not so much for his try-scoring feats, although he has got his share, but for his ability to hold the ball until he could part with it to advantage and to take the tackle if such was inevitable, rather than let a colleague do so.

'But most of all they and I will remember him as a man who played the game in the true spirit of Rugby; who did not consider that every knock that came his way was deliberate and intended, and consequently never retaliated.'

Foster's early rugby experience may have come in useful when in October the following

# A match to remember
## Yorkshire Cup Final

Bradford Northern 7 Hull 2
Headingley
31 October 1953
Bradford, who had beaten Hull 40-8 seven days earlier in a league fixture at Odsal, found the Airlie Birds an altogether tougher proposition when the sides renewed hostilities with a trophy directly at stake.
The powerful Hull pack dominated the early stages but were left without reward for want of essential support, and Northern took the lead against the run of play when full-back Joe Phillips, accepting a rare opportunity to come into the line, missed out centres Joe Mageen and Bill Seddon to send winger Bob Hawes in at the corner.
Phillips, who was unable to add the conversion, landed a couple of penalties to leave the Bradford fans in the 22,147 crowd reflecting on a 7-0 interval lead.
In a turgid second half, Northern were denied any further score but they had already done enough. Hull,
who had missed three penalty attempts, had the last word when full-back Colin Hutton kicked a penalty almost on the stroke of time.
The players duly climbed up into the Headingley stand to collect the Yorkshire Cup. Neither they nor their supporters were to know that a serious decline was imminent. It would be 12 long years before Bradford would lift another trophy; ironically, that trophy would be the Yorkshire Cup, and at the same venue, with a shock win over hot favourites Hunslet.

Bradford: Phillips; Hawes, Mageen, Seddon, McLean; Jenkins, Goddard; Tyler, N Haley, W Jones, Foster, Storey, Traill.

Hull: Hutton; Bowman, Riches, Turner, Watts; Conway, Tripp; Scott, Harris, Coverdale, Markham, A Bedford, J Whiteley.

year the Rugby Football League toyed with Rugby Union rules after a tackle.

Northern met Huddersfield in an exhibition game at Odsal in which play was restarted by the Union method.

The experiment, however, failed to last the full 80 minutes, RFL officials present instructing the teams to revert to League rules.

Bradford won the match 14-6 – both sets of players were reported to be delighted that Union rules would not be adopted.

There was less delight, though, a little less than three years later when Northern slumped to a surprise 11-2 home defeat in the Challenge Cup at the hands of Huddersfield.

Bradford, who went on to finish tenth in the 1958–59 table – their highest rating by some distance between 1956–57 and their demise in 1963 – had not succumbed at the opening stage since 1935, when York had prevailed 2-0 in a replay after a 12-12 draw at Wiggington Road. Huddersfield, themselves in a lull, lost 15-2 at Salford in the second round and closed the campaign in nineteenth position.

That defeat and a continuing decline brought a major casualty when Dai Rees, the legendary coach who had guided Northern to Wembley

*Captain Trevor Foster introduces his players to the Lord Mayor of Leeds prior to the Yorkshire Cup Final against Hull at Headingley in 1953.*

appearances in 1947, 1948 and 1949, parted company with the club after a quarter of a century's service following a stormy shareholders' meeting on 25 January 1961.

A proposal that Rees should have his directorship of the club revoked was carried by 53 votes to 36 and from that point the Welshman's days at Odsal were numbered.

Rees, together with Trevor Foster, had joined the Bradford board on the basis that neither would be put under financial pressure. Foster,

*Stand off Len Haley and second row Trevor Foster have matters under control against Halifax at Thrum Hall.*

who had replaced his fellow Welshman as first team coach the previous spring, had stepped down from both capacities in December when the club's bank requested personal guarantees from all directors.

That led to a special shareholders' meeting at which it was agreed that the bank's wishes should be complied with – following which Rees reminded those present that he and Foster had become directors on the understanding that they would both be free of financial constraints.

Although the subsequent vote went against him, Rees continued as stadium manager – a role bizarrely created for him following Foster's appointment, which had allegedly been made as a cost-cutting measure – before departing for

Halifax, for whom he had played in the 1920s and 1930s.

## Towards the end

Questions over the club's treatment of its loyal servants continued throughout the early sixties.

Len Haley recalls how even the great Ernest Ward had not been allowed to leave Odsal in a dignified manner. 'There was a lot of political in-fighting and all sorts of things going on. Ernest Ward hoped to coach but they wouldn't offer him anything at Bradford so he went to Castleford, where he wanted to be player-coach. Northern wouldn't allow it and Ernest was very disappointed by that, after all he'd done at Odsal. It went to a tribunal and he finally got permission to turn out at Wheldon Road.

'The management at Odsal had started to change. Harry Hornby had gone, otherwise many of the things that happened wouldn't, I'm sure, have taken place. I don't know what it was, money or what, but they started to sell their best players.

'Veterans like myself used to wonder who was coming in next. Players you'd never heard of would arrive and they'd be straight in the team on the Saturday. It was difficult to see what the management was doing but we never got involved, we just got on with playing and we didn't question any decision at all, we just took it as it was.

---

# A legend remembers
## Trevor Foster

*'I played for Bradford Northern for 17 seasons. My last match, officially, was against Hunslet at Odsal and they included one of my greatest rivals and one of the finest forwards I ever played against, the Australian Arthur Clues, the former Leeds player. 'He knocked some stuffing out of me many, many times but we were great friends. In that particular match, which was billed as Trevor Foster's last before retiring, he carried me off on his shoulders. He was one of the greatest forwards I've ever played against, without a shadow of a doubt, and he became a great friend of the Bradford Northern club and in particular of Frank Whitcombe. They were boozing pals – Frank kept a pub in Bradford and Arthur had his sports business and used to go over and stop with Frank on occasion. They'd spend all night in the cellar drinking beer – great friends.'*

*Twelve months after the retirement of Trevor Foster, Joe Phillips and Jack McLean announced that they, too, were to hang up their boots. Phillips left the north of England to run a hotel in Cornwall while McLean returned to New Zealand.*

*The side had risen from seventeenth in 1954–55 to eighth but, apart from something of a false dawn in 1958–59 when Northern closed at tenth, harrowing times were ahead.*

*One result during the 1955–56 campaign can, with hindsight, be seen as seminal; a harbinger of things to come.*

*Bradford should have travelled to St Helens on 24 March 1956 for a third round Challenge Cup tie in reasonably confident mood. St Helens, the holders, presented a serious challenge and one that could have been viewed as daunting after having posted a 15-6 win over Warrington and a 48-5 crushing of lowly Castleford. Northern, though, had reached the quarter-finals by virtue of a 10-9 victory at Hunslet – who had been semi-finalists in each of the previous two seasons – and a 5-2 success at Rochdale Hornets. No one could have predicted that Bradford Northern would lose by a record margin for a professional side in a quarter-final tie.*

*Saints were rampant in a sensational 53-6 thrashing – a scoreline which left Bradford reeling and which may have been a factor in the continuing decline in Northern's gates.*

'They were selling all the players they could get money for. They wanted to sell me to Halifax when I was coming up to 10 years' service, and I wouldn't go because I was due a benefit. They said, "Well if you don't go, we won't play you in the first team." And for three seasons I was mostly in the second team but I still played 288 times for Bradford.'

Against that background it was hardly surprising that Bradford Northern slumped to the heaviest and worst defeat in the club's history with the capitulation at Wakefield Trinity in the first round of the 1960–61 Yorkshire Cup.

Trinity, who were to go close to winning All Four Cups that season – securing the Challenge Cup, Yorkshire Cup and Yorkshire League but missing out to Huddersfield at the final hurdle, the Championship final – inflicted a 73-5 thrashing which represented the biggest losing margin ever experienced by Northern.

Wakefield fell just short of the total recorded by Leeds in September 1931, when Bradford lost 75-18, and the *Telegraph & Argus* headline of 'Feeble, Pathetic – Northern just gave it up!' summed up the sorry display.

Bradford Northern's team, a fairly full-strength selection, was: Hatte; Nunns, Penketh, Sutcliffe, Brook; D Davies, Broadbent; McLean, Welsh, Marston, Hemingway, T Robbins, Winnard.

Bradford Northern took the unhappy step, in December 1963, of withdrawing from their remaining fixtures – exactly a century, ironically, after the formation of the first Bradford club – as the downwards spiral reached its inevitable conclusion.

Northern, who had finished bottom of the table in the previous two seasons, were again adrift at the foot of Division Two in the second year of an aborted divisional experiment and attendances were at a demoralising low.

Debts totalling £8,099 were accepted as being too high to maintain and the announcement was made, in mid season, that Bradford Northern were at an end after 56 years of very mixed fortunes. The club's last result was the 33-5 home defeat by Leigh on 7 December 1963, winger Enslin Dlambulo scoring the last try. Bradford Northern's final victory was the

*Bill Seddon forces his way over against Hunslet. Loose forward Ken Traill, who joined Northern from the Parksiders, is suitably impressed.*

*The true image of the world record attendance (officially 102,569 but in reality many thousands more) at Bradford for the 1954 Challenge Cup Final replay between Halifax and Warrington. The gaps in the crowd, caused by the steep Odsal bankings, have been 'filled in' in some subsequent photographs. The dressing rooms are clearly shown at the top of the photograph, highlighting the long walk to the pitch facing both teams.*

surprise 27-6 verdict over Salford at Odsal on 14 September 1963 – a result that ended a run of 24 games without a win.

The club's results were duly expunged from the tables for the 1962–63 season, the RFL officially announcing the end on 18 March 1964 after a consortium led by Trevor Foster had spent the winter embroiled in talks with the existing directors, the council, the RFL, shareholders, creditors and anyone else considered able or willing to help.

The episode, however, was to lead to a new dawn amid a heated debate as to whether Northern's demise could be attributed to the experiment with two divisions after six decades of a single league.

*Rugby League Magazine*, in its April 1964 issue, argued: 'For many years the majority of Rugby League clubs set their faces sternly against Two Divisions. When, in June 1961, they did finally have a change of heart it was probably largely out of desperation – an "any change must be for the better" sort of feeling.

'One of the things which was held against Two Divisions for so long was that it was blamed for several clubs going out of existence in the early

*The sale of Malcolm Davies to Leeds for £3,000 early in 1957 was of particular significance during an era in which Bradford Northern's directors were under fire for regularly selling the club's best players.*

*On the face of it the deal represented good business as Davies had been signed from Leigh just five months earlier for only £750.*

*There were, however, other factors in play which clouded the issue. The fans were furious that a player who had quickly become a firm favourite was leaving so quickly and supporters voted with their feet at the next game, when the gate was almost 2,000 lower than usual.*

*More pertinently, a key factor behind Davies' sale was that Bradford's directors were unhappy that the player, who ran the club's successful pools scheme, was taking commission. However, his departure precipitated the scheme's subsequent collapse, ending a vital source of income and leading inevitably to the club's eventual demise.*

*Other transfers that attracted the ire of loyal supporters included those of Ken Traill and Jack Scroby to Halifax, Milan Kosanovic to Wakefield Trinity, for £2,000 in June 1961, Derek Davies to Leeds for £5,750 in November 1961, and Terry Robbins to Bramley for £6,000 in January 1962.*

1900s. In the years to come the recent Two Divisions experiment will, no doubt, be held responsible for the Odsal crisis and the subsequent ending of Bradford Northern.

'But was it Two Divisions that killed Northern? Wasn't the writing on the wall for years before the League was split into two? The decline in the fortunes of the club following the breaking-up of the great Odsal teams of the 1940–1950 era was reflected in a big drop in attendances. The following figures show how the average Bradford Northern attendances dwindled during the subsequent years:

| | | | |
|---|---|---|---|
| 1951-52 | 17,791 | 1956-57 | 4,791 |
| 1952-53 | 16,862 | 1957-58 | 4,645 |
| 1953-54 | 12,134 | 1958-59 | 3,747 |
| 1954-55 | 8,577 | 1959-60 | 2,960 |
| 1955-56 | 6,911 | 1960-61 | 1,858 |

'Then the falling off of the club's pools scheme throttled its economic lifeline and the end became inevitable. It was these factors, not the Two Divisions experiment that forced the directors of Bradford Northern to say they could not go on.

'News of the possibility of a new Bradford club is welcome. The sponsors will be well aware of the many problems which face them, but everyone will wish them well. We need Bradford on the Rugby League map.

'The scrapping of Two Divisions will not, in itself, solve the problems of poor "gates". It merely adds the need to find an adequate substitute. And when we've decided on a "top sixteen," or whatever gets the vote, two big needs still remain – a higher standard of play and the introduction of more personalities into the Code.'

Ironically, the call for 'more personalities' came during a period that boasted more than most, including a host of characters among the refereeing fraternity. Long-standing supporter Harry Sheard recalls: 'Half a dozen of us used to meet in the corner near the bottom of the steps,

## A legend remembers
### Trevor Foster

"It was a time of indecision, you might say, in the late 1950s and early 1960s. Things were not going well, the team was of a very mixed calibre, and we had quite a rough time.

'It is a sad part of the history of Bradford Northern, particularly as far as I was concerned with all the wonderful years I'd had. The gates went down abominably, in fact we played Barrow and there were only 350 people or something of that nature there, which was absolutely appalling.

'The club was faltering and the directors at that time could not get a grip of the situation for one reason or another. Once you're down in professional sport you've got a very, very hard task to recover.

'The club collapsed. It was unbelievable, something you couldn't put your finger on, those huge terraces with very few people aboard. It was a minor disaster. All that wonderful talent, wonderful attributes that were connected with Odsal stadium, all fell away.'

where the players ran onto the field after the long walk down from the pavilion. It was all sludge and we'd dug into it with our heels over the months and the years and made a level stand there. We all knew where we'd be and we'd make room for one another there.

'In the last 10 minutes of a match half a dozen policemen would come and stand at each side of this long walk and when the referee came off they all went round him and took him up to the top. I remember Eric Clay, they called him the Sergeant Major. He was very strict; we used to right enjoy getting there and giving him a right "you lousy so and so". He'd probably had a good game but if he gave something against Northern that we didn't agree with we'd give him hell. And there were little Thorpey, a bit of a humpy backed chap, he was a good referee.'

Such diversions, however, offered scant

*Fourteen years of service rewarded. Ernest Ward's Testimonial Brochure.*

*Heading for oblivion – a Bradford Northern line-up shortly before the club's collapse in 1963.*

consolation for Northern's poor form, summed up in *Rugby League Magazine* which pointed out that in the 1962–63 Divisional programme Hunslet had been the only team to win all their home matches and Bradford the only side never to win away from home.

A factor in that sorry story was Northern's poor defence, which left them adrift at the foot of the Mackeson table.

Len Haley remembers, clearly, the end. 'I'd just retired when Bradford Northern folded in 1963. I'd finally got a benefit, the match they gave me was the Leeds match and they presented me with a cheque for £250, which they said was the takings for the match. I think the gate was about 3,500.

'I played up to the end of the 1962–63 season and then thought that I might as well call it a day. I'd been there for 13 years and I could see that nothing was happening, in fact things were just getting worse all the time, and I'd done my other cartilage.

'They went five or six matches the following season and then it just folded which wasn't surprising because there were no gates and no pools money.

'That was one of the big things that doesn't get mentioned. A player, Malcolm Davies, was running the pools on his own for the club and was bringing in a fair amount of money. He was taking a percentage, I don't know how much, but the directors didn't like that and they transferred him. They thought they'd try to run it

themselves but they couldn't run the club properly so they weren't going to be able to run the pools. It involved a lot of work going around the public houses. So the pools collapsed and that was the final straw that brought the club down.'

---

**The season that never was**

*Bradford Northern's results for 1963–64, subsequently expunged from the records, were:*

| Date | Opponents | Result |
|------|-----------|--------|
| *August* | | |
| 24 | Dewsbury (h) | L 12-15 |
| 31 | Barrow (a) | L 9-29 |
| *September* | | |
| 4 | Doncaster (h) | L 8-16 |
| 7 | Featherstone (h) Yorks Cup | L 10-24 |
| 9 | Wakefield (h) Eastern Div | L 14-25 |
| 14 | Salford (h) | W 27-6 |
| 21 | Liverpool City (a) | L 7-17 |
| 28 | Leigh (a) | L 0-43 |
| *October* | | |
| 5 | Huddersfield (h) Eastern Div | L 7-30 |
| 12 | Batley (h) | L 9-12 |
| 19 | Doncaster (a) | L 3-25 |
| *November* | | |
| 2 | Liverpool City (h) | L 2-6 |
| 9 | Rochdale Hornets (h) | L 17-27 |
| 16 | Batley (a) | L 10-26 |
| 23 | Barrow (h) | L 0-29 |
| *December* | | |
| 7 | Leigh (h) | L 5-33 |

# 6.
# Rebirth – 1963-70

**Revival**

The battle to reform Bradford Northern began, crucially, while the old empire was still in its death throes.

Trevor Foster's consortium, which now included his old playing colleague Joe Phillips, had worked tirelessly but unsuccessfully towards a rescue plan during the dark winter of 1963–64 but at a meeting on 12 February had formed a working committee which agreed that a new club could be formed.

*A piquant moment. Bradford Northern's new signings line up on the Odsal terraces following the club's reformation.*

That decision, importantly, was made on the basis that the existing club's membership of the Rugby Football League be terminated and was vital in that it kept public interest in a 'new Northern' alive.

On 19 March 1964, within 24 hours of the demise of the old club, Bradford Council confirmed to Foster and his colleagues that Odsal would be available should a new club be formed.

Moving with the pace which had characterised his play, Foster applied to the Rugby Football League, on 23 March 1964, for membership and the consortium announced

that a public meeting would be held at St George's Hall on 14 April.

Over 1,500 people gathered on that historic occasion to hear former players such as Ernest and Donald Ward, Eric Batten and Vic Darlison announce their support.

Dai Rees sent a telegram, stating, 'It's a long way from Birch Lane to Wembley, it can be done again!'

Joe Phillips, with Foster a real mainstay behind the new drive, told the gathering that £5,000 was needed and that the sum could be raised by the issue of £1 shares. Some cash had already been raised and pledges had been made for more.

The response, that evening, was immediate and positive. £1,000 was raised and the 'new' Bradford Northern was past the embryonic stage. Support intensified from the people of Bradford and a new company – Bradford Northern (1964) Ltd – was formed on 20 April 1964.

Heart-warmingly, the wider Rugby League public also got behind the venture, with clubs throughout the game offering – and giving – their active backing.

The groundswell was unstoppable. By mid-May, the £5,000 target had been passed, and the Rugby Football League, at its meeting on 22 May 1964, rubber-stamped the application for membership. Bradford Northern were back in business – with a spring in their step rather than the stoop which, previously, had been the inevitable consequence of many years of decline.

*The 1964 Leeds 7s Trophy, won by the 'new' Bradford Northern within weeks of the club being reformed.*

Trevor Foster remembers: 'We were backed by everybody. Bradford had a great history in the game of Rugby League Football, from Birch Lane onwards.

'Joe Phillips did a marvellous job, his name will always be on top of the Town Hall of Bradford. He was a delightful person, with a great imagination, and he went round various clubs asking for players on loan etc. He had a great response from everybody, a great response. And lo and behold we got reinstated. Members of the Rugby Football League came over and said "We'll give you every help we possibly can." And there we were, in 1964, back on the field of play, taking on Hull KR in our first match – thanks to those particular people who started off the meetings all around the city of Bradford, particularly Joe Phillips. They did a wonderful, wonderful job for this city.'

*The dawning of an era. The Lord Mayor of Bradford meets the players prior to reborn Northern's first game, against Hull KR, in August 1964.*

### Building

The timing of the new club's launch could, perhaps, hardly have been better. The spring-time birth gave Joe Phillips, Trevor Foster and their colleagues the chance to build a squad for the 1964–65 season and the first consideration – which players from the old team should be retained – was resolved when Goeli Abed, Carr, George Gomersal, Trevor Schofield, Eric Sutcliffe and Gary Thornton were re-signed.

Few of those, however, had been established first team regulars and Northern moved quickly to snap up additional talent.

---

# A legend remembers
## Trevor Foster

'The wonderful story as far as I'm concerned, and as far as my career is concerned, but most important for the people of Bradford and supporters of Rugby League football in the city, is how the club rose from out of the depths right into the sky. It was a question of hard work and of people putting their hands in their pockets towards various expenses.

'A group of people met every week in one of the local hotels and we built up meetings week in, week out at various spots around the city. We established a very good working team to get the club back into its rightful place.

'We decided we would go public into the great St George's Hall and see what sort of reaction we would get. We had no qualms at all about taking this on and a meeting was arranged at St George's Hall at 7.30 on the Monday night.

'At ten to seven there was hardly anybody there. At half past seven that night the Hall was full, people came at the last minute.

'We'd done our homework very much and I got hold of Joe Phillips, the full-back who had left Bradford and finished his career at Keighley, and asked him to chair the meeting.

'Joe was a man with great foresight, a really excellent character. He said "Yes", and he took over the running of the club after that night, when £1,000 was raised. Lots of people donated money, gave money and bought £1 shares. We were back and the flags were flying.

'I wrote a letter that night to the Rugby Football League, posting it at midnight, asking for permission to be re-introduced. The RFL's Bill Fallowfield, a man of great foresight, agreed and we were registered back into the game. It was a great success and something that will never be forgotten in this city.'

---

In a remarkable illustration of goodwill, many clubs either waived transfer fees or allowed Bradford to take players at bargain-basement prices. Wakefield Trinity set the standard, charging nothing for prop Jack Wilkinson, who joined Northern as their first player-coach, and other clubs began to contact Bradford with their own offers of help. And, by late July, a decent-looking squad had been assembled for the sum of £15,250.

Incredibly, Northern collected a trophy

*The 1964 team lines up with the club's directors.*

before the 1964–65 season got under way. With the squad in patent need of some kind of match practice, the decision was made to enter the inaugural Leeds Sevens. Few expected Bradford to make much of an impact but the pundits were way off the mark. Northern's representatives confirmed their footballing abilities with a series of stunning performances, beating Dewsbury and Halifax in the opening rounds before disposing of Leeds 8-5 in the semi-final.

Huddersfield, the only remaining hurdle, were unable to halt the procession, Bradford prevailing 16-7. Sevens Rugby League may not have been the real thing, and everyone at Odsal was fully aware of that. The competition, however, was still there to be won and that target had been achieved. Bradford Northern had announced their arrival.

Northern had to wait until 2 September for their first win. An opening-day reverse at the hands of Hull KR was followed by defeats at Hunslet and Featherstone Rovers, before Jack Wilkinson's charges got off the mark with a 20-12 success against Salford's Red Devils at Odsal.

The side, however, was to lose 10 of its next 11 games, sliding to the nether regions of the table.

New signings were, however, being made with

*Australian winger Lionel Williamson squeezes in for a vital try in the 1965 Yorkshire Cup Final success against Hunslet.*

# Spirit of the age...

*From the Leigh v Oldham programme of 27 April 1964.*

'The new Bradford Northern:
'The work of the Committee dedicated to create a new Bradford Northern Club got off to an enthusiastic start when there was a splendid turn-up at a public meeting in Bradford on April 14th. Nearly £1,000 was contributed by the supporters who attended the meeting and it looks as if the target of £5,000 has every chance of being achieved before the club's application for membership of the Northern Rugby Football League is considered. There must be many supporters in the game who would dearly like to take part in the birth of a new club; their assistance would also be an extra insurance that the target figure would be reached in time.
'Subscriptions in units of £1 should be sent to Trevor Foster ... In return for this money the equivalent in £1 shares will be issued to the subscriber when the Company is formed. If the plans to form a new club fail to materialise, the money will be returned on or before the 31st July 1964. Please show your support in a practical way and send a subscription for shares.'

# Spirit of the age...

*Rugby League Magazine, August 1964.*
**'WHAT ABOUT IT, NORTHERN?**

It is fairly reasonable to assume that, having found out how their own particular favourites have gone on, most R.L. followers will be looking to see how Bradford Northern have fared in the early weeks of the season. This will be a vital period for Odsal, for a good start will provide a great fillip for the months ahead.
'Team building has gone on extensively during the close season and a glance at the names of the new signings suggests that if the players can strike the right blend from the start they will be a force to be reckoned with. That must be one of the first aims of player-coach Jack Wilkinson, who is an experienced campaigner in the game.
'Rugby League in Bradford – at Greenfield, Birch Lane and Odsal – has known its ups and downs. They have plumbed the depths and they have scaled the heights. It will be good for the game if the new club is a successful one. YOU can help, by going along to Odsal to see them make the effort.'

# A match to remember

## Northern Rugby League

*Bradford Northern 20 Hull KR 34*
*Odsal*
*22 August 1964*

*If ever a scoreline didn't particularly matter, it was on the occasion of Northern's first full match of the new era.*

*A crowd of 14,542 – 42 times the miserable gate for the Barrow fixture almost 12 months earlier – gathered for the historic game, Hull KR providing the opposition on a day in which Rugby League reverted to a single league, aborting a three-year experiment with two divisions after only a couple of seasons.*

*The Robins, as Challenge Cup runners-up the previous season, presented a troublesome challenge but the fledgling Bradford side repaid their supporters' encouragement with a brave performance. Northern, in fact, led 10-7 in the early stages but Rovers' inevitably superior teamwork began to tell in the second half.*

*Bradford, for their part, served an entertaining brand of football which, again inevitably, often lacked cohesion.*

*The supporters, however, were more than satisfied and applauded the team off after witnessing two tries for centre Brian Lord, touchdowns to winger Joe Levula and stand off Ian Brooke, and four goals by full back Keith Williams.*

*Hull KR's scorers comprised winger Chris Young, second row Eric Palmer and hooker Alan Holdstock, with a brace apiece, stand off Alan Burwell and winger Bob Harris, with full back Cyril Kellett adding five goals.*

*Lord and Holdstock helped reignite Odsal by being sent off, after a minor skirmish, in the second half.*

*Bradford: Williams; Levula, Lord, Todd, Walker; Brooke, Jones; Wilkinson, Ackerley, Tonkinson, Fisher, Ashton, Rae.*

*Hull KR: Kellett; C Young, Moore, Blackmore, Harris; Burwell, Hatch; Tyson, A Holdstock, Taylor, Bonner, Palmer, Poole.*

*Referee: Mr E Clay (Leeds)*

**Two Rugby League 'greats' re-unite. Ernest Ward with former Salford, Workington and Great Britain skipper Gus Risman, who was appointed Northern's Manager in the mid-sixties.**

such as Garth Budge, Terry Clawson, Alan Hepworth, Alan Rhodes, Tommy Smales, Errol Stock and David Stockwell joining the crusade.

A healthier-looking squad had, however, not come without cost and eyebrows were raised when a loss was announced for the season of £20,550, a figure that was inevitably compared to the total deficit of £8,099 that had caused the former club to collapse.

The legendary Gus Risman, who had steered Workington to great heights when the Cumbrian club had been formed at the close of the Second World War, was appointed coach, Wilkinson stepping down from his temporary role. *Rugby League Magazine* reflected: 'After a few years in the "wilderness" Mr A J Risman returns to the Rugby League game in an official capacity as team manager at Odsal. In his first week or two he will have been weighing up the prospects before him and the factors that are for or against the new Northern.

'On the credit side are the enthusiasm of the Odsal officials, the promise of support from the public, and the ability of the players who have been signed. On the debit side is the disappointing playing record to date, and the fact that, individually skilful though many of the players are, they have not yet "clicked" as a team. When they do, it will be a vastly different story at Odsal.

'When Gus Risman took over, Northern had won two games (against Salford and Batley) and lost seven. They had scored 111 points and had 143 scored against them, figures which suggest that there is material worth working on, for the margin of points is not a wide one considering the number of defeats.

'Following a great playing career with Salford and Workington Town, Gus did not have the best of luck as manager with Salford and Oldham. This Odsal job could wipe out the memory of those disappointments.'

*Rugby League Magazine* was also delighted to announce that, 'after 302 games and 116 tries in nine years at Huddersfield Tommy Smales has moved to Odsal and is hoping to play an important part in the Bradford revival'.

Smales reveals that he himself harboured private doubts as to the wisdom of his move. 'I went from Huddersfield, with whom I'd won a Championship medal in 1962 and played at Wembley the same year, to Bradford in late 1964. Huddersfield were a wonderful club but they had made a promise to me which they had kept all those years but which they broke when I was at the back end of my career.

'I was due my benefit and I didn't want to go, the people there were smashing, but this had happened and it was a point of principle.

'So I told Huddersfield coach Dave Valentine, and Bradford came to see me. Jack Fricker and Harry Womersley. I could tell they were people that really wanted to go places and that they really, really meant it, they weren't just in it for a laugh. So I signed for them. They'd played about 15 games and they hadn't won one. I remember going to my first training session and thinking, "Tommy, just on principle, what have you done? Have you signed your life and career away?"'

*Return to glory! Tommy Smales collects the silverware after Northern's notable win over Hunslet in the 1965 Yorkshire Cup Final.*

## Atmosphere

The veteran scrum-half quickly realised, however, that he had made a significant move. He recalls: 'The atmosphere at Bradford Northern at that time was very unusual. Even opposing supporters had sympathy for them. They wanted Bradford back, you can't let clubs like that go out of the league.

'When Bradford went to buy a player clubs used to let them have them cheaper than anybody else, to help Northern rebuild their side. I think that's what happened with me.

'It was very exciting actually because we started winning. We played Dewsbury at home and beat them in the mud, then we went to Whitehaven and drew, and the next game was against Leeds at home. I was having a bit of hamstring trouble and we'd only been playing

# A match to remember

## Yorkshire Cup Final

*Bradford Northern 17 Hunslet 8*
*Headingley, Leeds*
*16 October 1965*

*Only two years earlier, when Northern were losing 25-3 at Doncaster and were – unknown to them at the time – only five games away from oblivion, the concept of winning any trophy was beyond imagining.*

*That, however, became the happy reality when, against all the odds, the red-hot favourites were disposed of in a match that encapsulates rugby romance at its best.*

*Hunslet, a major power, had featured in the classic Challenge Cup Final against Wigan only five months earlier and had in their ranks several internationals and a host of county caps.*

*Bradford, by contrast, were a mixed bag of cast-offs, veterans and young hopefuls, a hotchpotch of a side that was endearing itself to a wider Rugby League public eager for Northern to succeed.*

*The acquisition of the marvellous scrum-half Tommy Smales, still in his pomp, from Huddersfield served evidence that Northern were serious and with Gus Risman as manager the side had strong men at the helm.*

*Smales' old side had been disposed of after a replay in the semi-final but Hunslet, with the likes of Billy Langton, John Griffiths, Geoff Shelton, Geoff Gunney, Bill Ramsey, Dennis Hartley and Ken Eyre in their ranks, presented a different proposition entirely.*

*Bradford were unfazed and took the lead, after having withstood tremendous pressure by the big Hunslet pack, when former Wakefield centre Ian Brooke left several defenders sprawling with a sensational try from 75 yards.*

*One-time Featherstone prop Terry Clawson added the conversion and a penalty but Hunslet forced their way back into contention when Shelton crossed in reply. But, in a repeat of the first half pattern, Bradford established a real grip on the contest when, following another pounding on their own line, stand off Dave Stockwell created a real try to remember. The former Halifax man was not blessed with sizzling pace but somehow, from his own 25, he launched a 60-yard raid, a series of intelligent dummies and feints bamboozling would-be tacklers until the way was clear for Australian winger Lionel Williamson to race over unopposed. Hunslet once more hit back, this time through winger Tommy Thompson, who would subsequently move to Odsal. But the wily Smales settled the issue, scuttling round the blind side of a scrum to send Williamson in for his second score to set the stage for highly emotional scenes on the final whistle as fans raced onto the pitch to chair the conquering heroes.*

*Bradford: Scattergood; Williamson, Brooke, Rhodes, Walker; Stockwell, Smales; Tonkinson, Morgan, Hill, Ashton, Clawson, Rae.*

*Hunslet: Langton; Lee, Shelton, Render, Thompson; Preece, Marchant; Hartley, Prior, Eyre, Ramsey, Gunney, Ward.*

*Referee: Mr E Lawrinson (Warrington)*

**The Lord Mayor of Bradford contributes to Northern's 1965 Yorkshire Cup win. Ian Brooke and Tommy Smales take care of the trophy and its contents. Joe Phillips, on the far right, simply beams with delight.**

*An amazing capture. The Yorkshire Cup is shown off by the directors and the 1965–66 squad*

half an hour when it went. I stayed on, as there were no substitutes in those days, and we beat them.

'We started climbing the table and the following season we won the Yorkshire Cup when we beat Hunslet at Headingley. Dave Stockwell had a very good game. I think he was under-rated. Although people recognised him as a good player he was a lot better than many thought.

'It was so heart-warming at Odsal. Supporters were eager to talk to you after games in the clubhouse, they were all caught up in the atmosphere. Committee, players and supporters all pulled together. It was unusual, I've never seen it before and I haven't seen it since. That's

*Chairman Harry Womersley was a driving force as Northern consolidated. He is pictured presenting a long-service award to tea-lady Dorothy Ellis, with Stan Fearnley in attendance.*

why I think Bradford survived. The Board were very good, they mixed with players. It's the only time I've ever known that.

'Joe Phillips, the New Zealander, was Chairman. He'd had a wonderful career and he was ideal. So were Harry Womersley and Jack Fricker, they were like "All pals at the Pally" but you had to play well to get in the team.

'Opposing supporters were great as well. Later, when Bradford started building a good side and they were a force to be reckoned with, people outside the club probably changed their attitude a little bit. But early on, although obviously Featherstone wanted Featherstone to win and Castleford wanted Cas to win and what have you, everybody wanted Bradford back because they were a club that had a wonderful history, the same as a lot of other clubs, and it's horrible to see any club go out of the game.'

**Yorkshire Cup**

Bradford staged a rousing assault on the 1965–66 Yorkshire Cup, against a background of six league wins in nine outings and a 28-15 victory over the touring New Zealand side.

Keighley were beaten 19-2 in the first round at Lawkholme Lane, and Hull KR's hopes were ended at Odsal with a 12-6 verdict.

Huddersfield, the only remaining barrier as the final loomed, forced a 7-7 draw at Odsal in the semi-final and that result appeared to have ended Northern's hopes. But, 24 hours later, Bradford produced perhaps their finest performance since their revival, winning 7-4 in a closely fought affair at Fartown.

Northern went even better in the final, beating red-hot favourites Hunslet at Headingley. As Trevor Foster recalls: 'That victory over Hunslet was most important. That was a wonderful occasion and it put us back on

*Full back Terry Price. The big-money signing from Welsh Rugby Union was a phenomenal kicker.*

the map; it was a day that those who were there and the players will never forget. Bradford Northern were back out of very, very difficult circumstances and back to glory.

'Crowds of up to 10,000 were coming to Odsal, the feeling towards Bradford Northern had been revitalised, and a new wave of success was about to happen.

'We were innovative. We started to make the match day a happy day and a good day, something to remember, and cheerleaders were introduced. That brought families and young people into the ground and they had a close relationship with the team. They idolised the players, there was no doubt about that, and that was one of the finest things that happened.'

Bradford, setting a lead in so many ways, were also in the vanguard of an early move towards summer rugby. *Rugby League Magazine*, in February 1966, revealed: 'Mr George Lunn, secretary and director of the Blackpool Borough club, has put forward a plan for summer Rugby League football.

'The plan is for a season of forty weeks, extending from mid-February to mid-November and, unlike the present League system, each club would meet every other team at least once. A club would play all other clubs in its own county league (28 matches), three clubs from the other county home and away (6 matches) and the other twelve once only, six at home and six away.

'The RL Challenge Cup Competition (to start in March and finish at Wembley in May as at present) and the County Cups (starting in

September) would give a minimum of 48 games in a season.

'Two clubs in particular – Bradford Northern and Featherstone Rovers – have previously circularised clubs with a view to the adoption of summer football, but there has never been a great deal of enthusiastic response to their ideas. Will it be any different this time?'

It wasn't, but Northern were proving themselves as innovators, in some respects decades ahead of the rest of the game. Tommy Smales remembers: 'Bradford were the first to have cheerleaders, in fact I suggested it. I got on to Harry Womersley about it. I said: "Why don't you go and get somebody to market it for you, get a salesman, get some of these lasses that throw pom poms around?" What they did, they got two pom pom girls and obviously years later the Bulls took it up.'

Miss Diane Rhodes became Rugby League's

*Olympic relay sprinter Berwyn Jones, a former Welsh Rugby Union schoolboy, was a successful convert to Rugby League and gave Northern fine service after switching from Wakefield Trinity.*

*Terry Clawson, a goal-kicking prop forward blessed with all the skills – and an abiding knowledge of Rugby League's more prosaic arts.*

first majorette early in 1966. In a romantic twist she married Northern's Australian winger Lionel Williamson and later returned with him to his homeland.

While the victory over Hunslet was a real catalyst in Bradford's revival, Tommy Smales has even fonder memories of the 7-6 Challenge Cup win at Widnes – winners in 1964 – later that season. 'They had a really, really good side. Vince Karalius was in charge of the Chemics at the time, but we went there and beat them despite having a man sent off in the first 10 minutes.

'Frank Myler was playing for them and so was Karalius. It was a real win, was that, in fact those ding-dongers are the best matches to win, it's about character and standing up and being counted. But if you're in one and you lose it's not much cop.'

If some clubs in the 1960s had had their way, some of those 'ding-dongers' would have remained something of a well-kept secret. TV coverage was seen as a major cause of declining attendances and Wigan, upset by a gate of only 26,809 for the Third Ashes Test of 1959 – 20,000 short of capacity and the lowest attendance of the series – were among the leading protesters.

Bradford Northern were caught up in the wrangle when, after having earned a home quarter-final tie with Wigan, the Pie Eaters refused the BBC entry to Odsal.

Wigan ended Northern's Wembley hopes with a 15-6 win, going on to reach Wembley where, with hooker Colin Clarke suspended, they lost 21-2 to neighbours St Helens. The Saints skipper Alex Murphy allegedly instructed his players to stray offside at every opportunity in

*All teams need a little luck somewhere along the way to win silverware, particularly in knockout football. Bradford Northern discovered that a touch of fortune is also necessary once trophies are in a club's possession.*

*The Yorkshire Cup, secured in such exhilarating fashion with the victory over Hunslet, went missing twice while in Northern's keeping.*

*On each occasion, officials and players were relieved to come across the undamaged old trophy.*

*The valuable piece of silver first went astray when the squad attended a function at the Queens Hall, Bradford, a month after the famous win. Coach Gus Risman took the cup in his car which was broken into during the event. The police were called and the mood lifted when the cup was found, after a search, behind a wall in Wilton Street.*

*Northern were just as lucky the following August; Leeds less so.*

*Bradford, who had regained the WH & O Wills Sevens Trophy with victory at Headingley in the 1966 Sevens, gave the Supporters' Club permission to show off their silverware at a presentation night at the Admiral Nelson.*

*The Supporters' Secretary kept both trophies in his car when he returned home, leaving the Yorkshire Cup in the boot and the Sevens Trophy on the back seat.*

*His early-morning cornflakes, though, were ruined when he discovered that his garage had been broken into and his car stolen.*

*The vehicle was recovered later that day with the boot unlocked and the Yorkshire cup safe. Leeds' Sevens Trophy, though, had gone – and it has never been recovered.*

the knowledge that the resultant scrum from the kick to touch would be won; a ploy that led to the reintroduction in 1966–67 of the tap penalty.

Bradford also made two pieces of history at the beginning of that campaign. The side opened with eight away games, including the preseason friendly at Castleford and the Yorkshire Cup clash at Huddersfield, because of delays in completing structural work at Odsal and remedial work to the pitch, which had suffered from drainage problems for many years.

Incredibly, Northern won each league game (slipping 8-4 at Fartown) and after losing their opening home match with Workington 26-13 extended their away league run to seven successes with a 37-10 verdict at Doncaster.

Bradford, four points clear at the head of the table, subsequently stumbled a shade in the league and closed the campaign in fifth spot before going out to Warrington 12-6 in the first round of the Championship play-offs, which had been extended to 16 sides – more than half the 30 teams in the competition – when the RFL reverted to a single league in 1964–65. The game's governing body had aborted a three-year experiment with two divisions one season early because of reduced attendances in the lower tier.

Northern continued to ring the changes in an

*Albert Fearnley, an astute coach who later became club secretary.*

*Rugby League Magazine August 1967.*
*'Old habits die hard and for a lot of people Saturday afternoon is still the "right" time for a football match, but many in official RL circles are looking forward to the time when the "ice will be broken" so far as Sunday play is concerned in first team matches.*
*'Bradford Northern and Dewsbury would have paved the way by playing their Yorkshire cup-tie on Sunday, September 3rd, but the Yorkshire County Committee felt unable to accept the legal responsibility involved in gate admission at a Sunday game and they refused permission.'*

effort to bring crowd-pleasers to Odsal. The transfer back to Wakefield of Ian Brooke for £8,000 helped fund the acquisition of star players such as Trinty's former Olympic sprinter and Great Britain international Berwyn Jones and Lions centre Geoff Wriglesworth. Captain Tommy Smales, meanwhile, headed to Australia and North Sydney, whose faith in the Bradford board's honesty in fulfilling their financial part of the bargain – George Ambrum arrived at Odsal in return – proved to be amply justified.

There were, though, also changes at boardroom level. Difficulties which would prove to be long-running surfaced in late 1966 when it was proposed at a special meeting of shareholders that the number of directors be reduced from 12 to seven.

A vote in favour of the motion led to five directors resigning on the basis that they could not accept the result.

Headlines of a more positive nature were made the following summer. Northern hit both the back and front pages on 26 July 1967 with the capture of Terry Price, the Wales Rugby Union full-back. Bradford beat off strong competition for Price's services with the help of a huge offer of £8,000 – a new record for the club.

That was quickly repaid. Almost a thousand supporters turned up to watch Price's early training sessions and crowds rose by up to 2,000.

A phenomenal kicker, the Welshman headed the club's points-scoring list in 1967–68 with 215, from 97 goals and seven tries, while the ball-playing forward Terry Ramshaw was another major influence.

Price enjoyed a four-year stint with Northern, switching to American Football club Buffalo Bills in August 1971.

Trevor Foster remembers: 'Terry Price was a great personality. He came from Llanelli Rugby

Union and made a great impact. It struck all the national newspapers because he was a Welsh Rugby Union international and it was a wonderful capture by the directors. A lot of people came to the ground to see him. He was a big, strong man and could kick the ball over great distances, almost the length of the field.

'He was what you might call a stay-at-home old fashioned Rugby League full-back, he never ran much with the ball but his kicking was phenomenal, in fact unique.'

While the acquisition of such as Price was welcome, the supporters, perhaps more aware than fans elsewhere of the need to be solvent following the events of 1963, grew increasingly anxious about Northern's rising debts as the 1960s drew to a close.

The figure had, by January 1968, increased to £28,000 but the board countered that £70,000 had been spent on players since 1964 with the aim – declared from the outset – of giving the Bradford public the team it deserved. The directors also stressed that the old club, in 1963, had no assets despite being only £8,000 in the red. By contrast Northern circa 1968 had star players to sell, if need be, to more than cover any deficit on the balance sheet. And the acquisition of trophies with as strong a side as the board could muster would correct the situation.

Captures such as Welsh forward Jim Mills from Salford in July 1968, and the legendary Neil Fox, bought from Wakefield Trinity for £5,500 in August 1969, failed to stem a slide in the rankings from sixth in 1967–68 to twenty-seventh of the thirty-team pile in 1970–71.

Northern went down to a record home defeat of 42-3 at the hands of St Helens in mid-August and that miserable experience was eclipsed on 5 September when Leeds won 49-10 at Odsal.

The mood of the fans wasn't helped when hard-bitten Welsh hooker Tony Fisher, a member of Great Britain's Ashes-winning side in Australia during the summer, went to Headingley for £7,000 in another move aimed at balancing the books.

*Bradford Northern became, with Leigh, the first British club to stage a game on the Sabbath when they entertained York on 17 December 1967. The Rugby Football League had sanctioned Sunday matches earlier in the year and Northern took a different view to the likes of Barrow, Batley, Huddersfield, Hunslet, Leeds and Whitehaven, all of whom stated that their players objected 'on religious, moral or social grounds'. Northern had no such compunction. Nor did the club fear the Lord's Day Observance Society, which insisted that it would ensure that all sports clubs abide by the law of the land. Bradford got around legislation prohibiting any charge for admission by allowing spectators in for free on production of a programme or handbill, bought outside Odsal for four shillings. 10,377 fans took up the offer, and Northern won 33-8.*
*Leigh, meanwhile, beat Dewsbury 15-10 at Hilton Park before a 6,000 crowd.*
*The initiative wasn't Bradford's first taste of Sunday rugby. Northern had played on the Sabbath 19 years earlier when, in the second fixture of a two-match tour of France, they beat Carcassonne 16-10. The opening game, a 21-17 victory at Toulouse Olympique on 15 May 1948, was Bradford Northern's first outing on foreign soil.*

The 1970s, however, were to realise an upturn in the club's playing fortunes although the financial situation would continue to deteriorate.

**BRADFORD NORTHERN**
Rugby League Football Club (1964) Ltd.

**OFFICIAL HANDBOOK**
Season 1969/70     Price 2/-

*The Bradford Northern Handbook, from the 1969–70 season.*

# 7.
# Platform Shoes and Platform for Glory

The 1970s – dubbed the decade that style forgot – hardly started well for Bradford Northern.

Arguably Rugby League's answer to the 'Fab Four' during the heady revivalist days of the mid-sixties, Northern looked in danger of turning into the equivalent of a group struggling to book a turn at the nearest working men's club as the desultory rating of twenty-seventh in the table in 1970–71 was followed by a 12-4 defeat by Doncaster at Odsal in the first round of the following season's Yorkshire Cup.

The poor opening, however, was followed by a consolidating spell of two wins and two draws in six games which suggested that a side including three players signed the previous year – Welsh second row Stuart Gallacher, Barrow full-back Eddie Tees and Bernard Watson – was beginning to gel as a unit.

A transformation in fortunes led to Bradford heading the table for a short spell and although that status was not maintained the capture from Leeds for a mere £3,000 of international scrum-half schemer Barry Seabourne proved to be a masterstroke.

Tees' form was crucial, also, as Northern rose to second spot in the table. The Lancastrian eased past the previous goals- and points-in-a-season records held by Joe Phillips of 138 (totalled in 1952–53) and 305 (1951–52) with 364 points from 173 goals and six tries to confirm that any fears over the departure of Terry Price had been misplaced.

Tees only failed to score in one game – the Challenge Cup defeat at Bramley – with his highest total being the 10 goals recorded in the home victory over Whitehaven.

Bradford's assault on the championship, however, ended with the 14-10 defeat at Odsal at the hands of St Helens at the penultimate stage of the championship play-offs. Northern had crushed Warrington 37-0 in the first round and accounted for Castleford 22-12 in the quarter-finals to suggest an appearance in the final could be on the agenda.

**Empty pay packets and a return to Wembley**
That Challenge Cup defeat against Bramley at least had the saving grace of confirming that the players had faith in themselves. Bradford's players, though, certainly took the wrong option

*Powerful packman Stuart Gallacher gave Northern grand service in the early 1970s. Signed from Llanelli Rugby Union club, he was transferred to Keighley during the 1974–75 season.*

# A match to remember
## Challenge Cup Final

Bradford Northern 14 Featherstone Rovers 33
Wembley
12 May 1973
'It's a long way from Birch Lane to Wembley'.
Dai Rees' telegram, sent to the famous public meeting at the St George's Hall on 14 April 1964, proved to be prophetic.
The former Northern coach had ended his message with the exhortation 'it can be done again!' and, less than a decade later, his vision became reality.
That impressive achievement for a club relaunched from the very depths has, perhaps, been too often overlooked in the light of a heavy defeat in a game in which a new high was set for the aggregate score in a Challenge Cup Final.
Featherstone full-back Cyril Kellett, who had been limited to one goal in Hull KR's defeat in 1964 by Widnes, enjoyed much better fortunes on his return to the Empire Stadium and landed eight goals from eight attempts to have a major say in the outcome.
So did Rovers' prop Vince Farrar. The highly-experienced member of the redoubtable Featherstone pack hardly needed any incentive to give his all for his hometown club but if any extra motivation was required it was provided by Bradford counterpart Kel Earl who, perhaps rashly, relayed to the media in the build-up exactly what he would do to the veteran.
The tables were, emphatically, turned, leading to Earl's early substitution by coach Ian Brooke. By then, with

Northern 17-0 down and a quarter of the match gone, it was too late.
Featherstone's Peter Fox, making his name as an astute and motivational coach which would lead to two spells at Odsal, ensured that Rovers maintained their grip despite second half tries by Bradford winger David Redfearn and loose forward Stan Fearnley, with full-back Eddie Tees kicking his fourth goal after three first half penalties.
Rovers guaranteed that there would be no way back for Bradford, adding a long-range try by centre Mike Smith – featured for many years in the introduction to the BBC's Saturday afternoon Grandstand sports programme – and a David Hartley touchdown to two first half tries by John Newlove and a try by that man Farrar.
Northern, however, had at least been on centre stage; an achievement that would have been unthinkable 10 years earlier.

Bradford: Tees; Lamb, Stockwell, Watson, Redfearn; Blacker, Seabourne; Hogan, Dunn, Earl, Joyce, Pattinson, Fearnley. Subs: Treasure, Fearnley.

Featherstone: C Kellett; Coventry, Smith, Newlove, K Kellett; Mason, Nash; Tonks, Bridges, Farrar, Rhodes, Thompson, Stone. Subs: Hartley, Hollis.

Referee: Mr M J Naughton (Widnes).

after they had been called upon to travel to McLaren Field at the second round stage in 1971–72.

Senior members of the first team squad reckoned that the board hadn't offered enough winning pay. A compromise was reached, with the players put on a higher rate for victory, and nothing if they lost.

Bramley, at that time, were languishing in their perennial position in the lower reaches of the table but it was no secret within the game that the Villagers, with the likes of loose forward Johnny Wolford, second row Graham Idle, powerhouse

*Half back David Treasure is unable to mask his disappointment after Bradford had succumbed to Featherstone at Wembley in 1973.*

winger Jack Austin – all of whom would feature with Northern at the end of the decade – and enterprising stand off Trevor Briggs in their ranks, were on the rise.

The west Leeds club was to qualify for the top flight when the RFL reverted to two divisions a year later, and would also win the BBC2 Floodlit Trophy in glorious fashion in late 1973 with a sensational victory at Widnes.

The judgment of Bradford's players had, therefore, to be questioned – if not their underlying confidence – when

# A match to remember
## Player's No 6 Trophy Final

*Bradford Northern 3 Widnes 2*
*Wilderspool, Warrington*
*25 January 1975*

*Bradford put the disappointment of the Yorkshire Cup semi-final exit behind them in emphatic fashion, going on to win the Player's No 6 Trophy in its fourth season and collect the £5,000 victors' cheque.*

*Northern accounted for Dewsbury at home in the first round, disposed of Oldham at the Watersheddings at the next stage, and pulled off one of their best results in years with a 17-7 quarter-final success at home to a Leeds side that had prevailed in the previous 12 games between the clubs.*

*Whitehaven formed the last hurdle, at their compact Recreation Ground base, and in typically Cumbrian fashion pushed Bradford all the way before Northern, who had been ahead only 5-3 at half time, forced their way to the final with an 18-8 scoreline.*

*That set up a clash with Widnes (who would go on to win the Challenge Cup that year) at a mud-bound Warrington hit by gale force winds.*

*Bradford, with scrum-half Barry Seabourne in vintage form in collecting the Man of the Match award, took the spoils with the only try of the game, second row forward Dennis Trotter and stand-off Mick Blacker setting up the position from which Seabourne sent full-back Stuart Carlton over with an artful one-handed pass round the back of a defender. Seabourne, however, facing the wind, missed the conversion attempt and the Chemics got back into contention when full-back Ray Dutton landed a penalty. Widnes could, maybe should, have taken a match-winning lead when a Dutton effort in the second half was blown backwards by the strong wind towards uncovered winger Chris Anderson, who would go on to be a successful coach with Halifax and Australia. There was no joy this time, though, for the Aussie who fumbled before crossing for what would otherwise have been the winning try.*

*Bradford: Carlton; Francis, Ward, Gant, Redfearn; Blacker, Seabourne; Earl, Jarvis, Jackson, Joyce, Trotter, Fearnley. Subs: Kelly, Pattinson.*

*Widnes: Dutton; Prescott, O'Neill, Aspey, Anderson; Hughes, Bowden; Mills, Elwell, Sheridan, Adams, Blackwood, Laughton. Subs: Karalius, Peek.*

*Referee: Mr G F Lindop (Wakefield).*

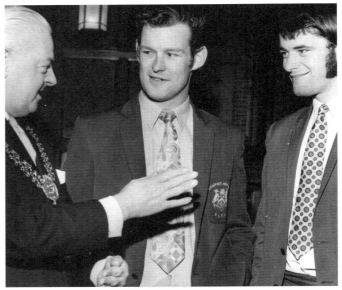

**Full back Eddie Tees and centre Bernard Watson consider the finer points of the game with the Mayor of Bradford.**

they accepted their directors' offer.

An 8-5 defeat, albeit after having scored the only try of the game through David Redfearn, left the first team squad with egg on their faces; and, pertinently, perhaps with firmer resolve for the following year's competition.

Ian Brooke's men gravitated through the opening rounds of the 1972–73 Challenge Cup in almost furtive fashion against a background of mediocre league form that would condemn them to Division Two when the Rugby Football League reverted to a divisional structure for 1973–74.

Northern closed the campaign in twenty-third place after having been a mere two points behind the leaders in mid-September. Several real hammerings were sustained along the way, including a 58-12 defeat at Castleford which eclipsed the previous worst league reverse of 57-

**Rugby League had a reputation as a hard game in the 1970s. Stuart Carlton, temporarily oblivious to the world, probably wouldn't argue.**

2 at Hunslet in 1933–34.

The team, however, confirmed its true abilities with its exploits en route to a first appearance at Wembley since the third successive outing in 1949.

All four victims finished the season in the top 16, thereby securing top flight status the following year. But Bradford, helped by home advantage in each of the matches up to the semi-final, were suitably unfazed.

Cumbrians Whitehaven discovered that their Odsal hoodoo of 1957, when they were denied victory over Leeds in the Challenge Cup semi-final by a late drop goal by Loiners scrum-half Jeff Stevenson, was still intact as Northern eased to a 17-4 first round win.

Hull KR, the previous season's Yorkshire Cup winners, were seen off 13-8 at the next stage and Wigan – who had emulated the Robins with victory 12 months earlier in the Lancashire Cup – were left adrift 11-7 in the quarter-finals.

There appeared, though, to be little prospect of progress past Dewsbury in the Headingley semi-final. The men from Crown Flatt would complete the season as champions for the first time in their history – at Odsal, with an outstanding win over Leeds – and with players such as centre Nigel Stephenson, hooker Mick Stephenson, brothers Alan and John Bates and stand-off Allan Agar in their ranks were a class outfit and hot favourites.

Dewsbury, however, were to be denied a return to Wembley since appearing in the first final at the great stadium in 1929 by a superb performance by Northern who limited their opponents to a Mick Stephenson try and goals by Agar and Nigel Stephenson. Bradford, meanwhile, were on their way back to Wembley after a 24-year wait through two David Treasure touchdowns, a David Redfearn try, and five goals from Eddie Tees, with Barry Seabourne and Bernard Watson each adding a goal.

Northern's standing as seventh-from-bottom in the league was the lowest of any Challenge Cup finalist since 1949 – their opponents Halifax, on that occasion, having come twenty-fifth of the 29 teams then in membership of the RFL.

## A legend remembers
### Peter Fox

'When I joined Bradford the first time it was wet and damp and I was walking round the field by myself, just looking about me. I thought, "Foxy – good solid player but no international – now coach for Bradford Northern in this famous stadium."

'I'd been to watch the first floodlit game at Odsal; that's the picture in my mind of Bradford, the lights low down in Odsal stadium. Then I went to the 1954 Cup Final replay, when we could hardly see.

'It wasn't a posh ground but it was a fantastic stadium because it was an impressive bowl that could hold so many people. And I thought, "I'm now coach of the team that plays at Odsal, the most famous rugby ground in the world."

'I remembered the 1940s when Trevor Foster and Vic Darlison played with Frank Whitcombe and Ken Traill. Darlison was a big mate of my dad's, he was a Featherstone lad. When I was a kid I'd got my cut-out books and Bradford was one of the first teams in them. When I walked round Odsal I thought, "I'm in this great stadium, Odsal is phenomenal." I could never have thought, "I'm going to Park Avenue."'

*An historic image. Keith Mumby crosses for a try on his debut against Doncaster on 4 November 1973. The 16-year-old full back went on to become one of Bradford's greatest players and servants.*

*The fans join in the celebrations after a try in the 1974 Challenge Cup round two win over Swinton at Station Road.*

## A title – and a 'great' emerges

The stigma of having finished bottom of Division Two in 1962–63 and of having not seen out the following season was assuaged, to some degree at least, with the Division Two championship success of 1973–74.

Northern came top of the pile in an era in which there was relatively little between the leading sides in the country and the so-called 'lesser lights' – as illustrated by Northern's appearance in the previous May's Challenge Cup final from twenty-third spot – and were hot favourites from the outset to secure the title.

Their bid was boosted by the midsummer signing of scrum-half Ken Kelly from St Helens for what was described as a club record fee but, oddly, remained undisclosed.

And another player was to emerge during the campaign who was to become a legend at Odsal.

Keith Mumby, at 16 years of age, was drafted into the side for the home game against Doncaster on 4 November 1973 and went on to become one of the best full-backs in the history of the game.

The youngster made an immediate impact, scoring 27 points with a try and 12 goals in the 72-9 victory as Northern bettered their previous best win, the 68-2 verdict over Bramley in the 1906–07 Yorkshire Cup.

The youngster's total was the highest recorded by a player on debut in the British game and suggested that Bradford had unearthed an adequate replacement for Eddie Tees, whose

shock retirement had paved the way for Mumby's sudden elevation.

Bradford, as titleholders, went on to enter the ill-fated Club Championship at the end of the season alongside Division One sides, beating Salford 17-8 at Odsal after a 16-16 draw at Weaste before losing at Wilderspool to eventual competition winners Warrington 15-9.

Northern's season wasn't without its early controversy, however, as the players failed to turn out for both the Wigan Sevens in the summer of 1974 and the pre-season friendly at Castleford.

*Centre Peter Roe bypasses Widnes full back David Eckersley on his way to a try in the 1977–78 Premiership Final. Jim Mills and Bill Ramsey, each of whom had spells with Bradford, watch in dismay.*

# A match to remember
## Premiership Trophy Final

*Bradford Northern 17 Widnes 8*
*Station Road, Swinton*
*20 May 1978*
*Northern bounced back from a powerful opening by the Chemics to capture the Premiership Trophy for the first time.*
*Loose forward Bob Haigh, the official Man of the Match, was a key figure as Bradford, 5-0 down after 11 minutes after a period of sustained pressure deep in their own half, went on to dominate the remainder of the game.*
*Fortunate not to have been two points behind in the opening seconds, when Widnes were wide with a penalty attempt, Peter Fox's men rallied with a touchdown for Haigh, who cruised over off Alan Redfearn's astute pass.*
*Full-back Keith Mumby tagged on the goal and Northern secured a lead they were not destined to lose when Haigh and prop Ian Van Bellen linked up to send rangy centre Peter Roe scything through from 30 metres.*
*Mumby was unable to land the touchline goal but the damage to the Chemics' cause had clearly been done, judging by the heated exchanges between their players. Veteran stand off Johnny Wolford stretched the lead to four points with a well-taken and well-timed drop goal*
*on the stroke of half time and that one-pointer came in handy when Widnes responded midway through the second half with centre Mal Aspey's second try, Paul Woods failing on this occasion with the conversion. Bradford went on to add a touchdown on the hour for winger David Redfearn, Mumby improving from out wide, after a quality move from their own goal line sparked by Alan Redfearn and continued by winger David Barends, Haigh, Wolford, second row Dennis Trotter and centre Jack Austin.*
*David Redfearn prevented Widnes from forcing their way back into contention, kicking the ball dead to quell a threatening raid, and the clinching score came six minutes from time through Barends, who clattered over from dummy half after Graham Joyce had been hauled down short.*

*Bradford: Mumby; Barends, Roe, Austin, D Redfearn; Wolford, A Redfearn; Van Bellen, Raistrick, Thompson, Trotter, Joyce, Haigh. Subs: Fox, Forsyth.*

*Widnes: Eckersley; Wright, Hughes, Aspey, Woods; Gill, Bowden; Mills, Elwell, Shaw, Adams, Hull, Laughton. Subs: Ramsey, George.*

*Referee: Mr J E Jackson (Pudsey).*

The strike was called when the directors, concerned with costs, withdrew the clause from the club's standard contract whereby bonuses were linked to the size of the crowd.

Matters came to a head as the first match of the season proper, at York, drew closer. But with the board pondering on whether to field a side of A-teamers and juniors a compromise deal was agreed at the eleventh hour.

Northern went down 21-12 at Wiggington Road but recovered from that setback with four successive victories, reaching the semi-finals of the Yorkshire Cup before losing to Hull KR after a replay. And they also came away from the match at York with prop Colin Forsyth, signed on the spot for £5,000 after impressing for the Minstermen.

Suitably strengthened, and with the Players No 6 Trophy on the Odsal sideboard, Northern ended two lengthy losing sequences in Lancashire. The side won 9-7 at Salford in March 1975 to come home with winning pay from the Willows for the first time since August 1958. And St Helens, unbeaten against Bradford at Knowsley Road since the Challenge Cup game in 1951, were toppled 17-7 in October 1976.

That win helped Northern to contest, with Leeds, the right for eighth position in the First Division and a subsequent berth in the end-of-season Premiership play-offs. Bradford eventually took the spot but not in the way they would have wanted. The Loiners, needing to win at Salford in their last game to knock Northern off their perch, were 5-2 ahead when young half back Chris Sanderson went down in a tackle and failed to rise. The York product was pronounced dead after being carried to the dressing rooms, the match was abandoned, and the fixture expunged from the records. Bradford were beaten 13-2 at Featherstone Rovers in the first round.

*Threequarter David Redfearn strides over for a derby try against Halifax.*

## Brooke, Francis and the wily Fox

Coach Ian Brooke, the man who had guided Bradford to a first Challenge Cup final in 24 years and had steered the club to success in the 1974–75 Player's No 6 Trophy, stepped down in September 1975 after abuse from a section of the Odsal crowd became too personal for comfort.

Brooke, who had scored the try that sent Northern on the way to Yorkshire Cup Final success over Hunslet nine years earlier, found that memories can be short in sport when he needed a police escort to the dressing rooms after the 22-2 home defeat by Leeds in the same competition.

A fortnight later, after Wakefield Trinity had wrested the Players No 6 Trophy from Bradford at the first stage with a 32-12 verdict, a repeat of that unsavoury episode led the Northern coach to tender his immediate resignation.

Within four days, Bradford had appointed Roy Francis, the coach who had made Leeds into one of the most attractive sides in the game in the late 1960s but who had enjoyed rather less success after his return from North Sydney.

Francis managed to steer Northern, who were five points shy of safety at one stage, out of relegation trouble, helped by the captures of such as centre Peter Roe, who moved from Keighley at the turn of the year in a £6,500 deal, Johnny Wolford (Bramley, for £5,000) and Terry Clawson.

That trio helped Bradford register eight wins and a draw in their last 11 games to avoid the

*Roy Francis coached Northern for a period in the mid-70s. Given the long walk back to the changing rooms at Odsal, half time pep talks were conducted in full view of the stand.*

grim reality of the drop. Francis, however, did not stay long, departing Odsal at the end of the following season. He was replaced by Peter Fox, the man who had masterminded Featherstone Rovers' Challenge Cup Final success over Northern in 1973; and the man who would steer the club to unprecedented championship success.

The coach with the trademark trilby set about moulding Bradford into a team that would be very difficult to beat, epitomised by the ending of an unhappy record at Wigan.

It was, in fact, thirteenth time lucky when Northern travelled to Central Park in the second round of the Challenge Cup in 1977–78.

Bradford won 22-10, ending a sequence of 12 successive defeats at the famous ground. The Pie Eaters had, in the previous quarter of a century, won 10 and drawn two of the matches played at Wigan – and one of those draws had been in a friendly.

Although Northern slipped 16-8 at Leeds in the third round, league form continued to be satisfactory and Bradford closed the campaign as runners-up, edging St Helens with a little help from the players at Featherstone Rovers, who had gone on strike.

Bradford and Saints went into their last league games of the season with Northern, on 44 points, needing to win their scheduled fixture at Post Office Road to have any chance of overhauling St Helens, who had totalled 45 points and were due to meet Hull KR.

The Saints duly won 23-13 but it did them little good. The RFL, unhappy with Featherstone, opted to determine final placings on a percentage basis. Northern took second spot with 75.86 per cent, with St Helens on 74.99 per cent.

The outcome, other than the acquisition of runners-up medals, was largely academic. Bradford had home advantage in the first round of the Premiership play-offs anyway, having finished in the top four, and duly beat a Leeds side preparing to defend the Challenge Cup at Wembley 18-10. Ironically, St Helens provided the opposition in the semi-final, which was

## A match to remember
### Yorkshire Cup Final

*Bradford Northern 18 York 8*
*Headingley, Leeds*
*28 October 1978*

*Ball-handling maestro and field-kicker extraordinaire Johnny Wolford flew 7,000 miles from business in Singapore to help guide Northern to victory over a never-say-die Division Two side making its first appearance in a major final since the 1957 Yorkshire Cup decider.*

*The veteran, introduced as a substitute at half time, made an immediate impact with a 40-yard kick to touch which was rewarded with a heel at the subsequent scrum by hooker Tony Fisher.*

*Wolford made the most of the possession, sending loose forward Bob Haigh over to give second row Neil Fox a simple conversion and stretch Northern's advantage to five points after the sides had gone in at the break at 5-5.*

*A further touchdown for Les Gant, who nipped over in the corner off a pass by his co-centre Derek Parker, ensured that Wolford's expansive approach reaped more reward.*

*Gant prevented York from getting back into the game with a try-saving tackle and more Minstermen pressure was rebuffed by Parker who pulled off an interception to race away over 80 yards for a killer score, improved by Fox who had kicked a first-half penalty after being unable to convert Alan Redfearn's early solo try.*

*Brave York had the last word with a late touchdown by full-back Gary Smith. Stand off Barry Banks had kicked two first half goals, Barry Hollis adding a drop goal.*

*Haigh, meanwhile, had extra cause for satisfaction. The loose forward collected the White Rose Trophy as Man of the Match to add to the Harry Sunderland Trophy in the previous May's Premiership final.*

*Bradford: Mumby; Barends, Gant, D Parker, D Redfearn; Slater, A Redfearn; Thompson, Fisher, Forsyth, Fox, Trotter, Haigh. Subs: Wolford, Joyce.*

*York: G Smith; T Morgan, Day, Foster, Nicholson; Banks, Harkin; Dunkerley, Wileman, Harris, Rhodes, Hollis, Cooper. Subs: Crossley, Ramshaw.*

*Referee: Mr M J Naughton (Widnes).*

*Stan Fearnley and Mick Blacker revel in the acquisition of the 1975 Player's No 6 Trophy.*

played on a two-legged basis. Northern went down 14-10 at Knowsley Road in the opener but recovered at Odsal with a 19-12 success to set up a meeting with Widnes at Station Road, Swinton, in the final.

The Chemics were beaten 17-8, a win that particularly delighted Keith Mumby. 'I enjoyed beating Widnes that day. They always did us in the Cups but we got our own back that year.

'It was my first major final. We'd got to semi-finals but Widnes always knocked us out. There was one game, at Odsal, when we were winning and it was close to full time. They kicked through and I ran across and went down sideways, to try and cover the ball, but one of their players – Stuart Wright or Mal Aspey, I'm not sure who – kicked it forward. Our winger Dave Barends was behind and he fell over me, with me going down for the ball, and the referee gave a penalty.

'They kicked it and drew with us and we had to go to their place where they beat us. The referee said I was lucky he hadn't given a penalty try. I couldn't believe it.'

Fox, despite having secured the Premiership, was not prepared to rest on his laurels. The foundations for the dual championships of 1979–80 and 1980–81 were laid in the summer of 1978 and during the following season as Northern's boss embarked on a well-considered rebuilding programme.

Fox started the process by snaring Jeff Grayshon as his on-field lieutenant from Dewsbury for a club record £14,000 and then enticed hooker Tony Fisher back from Castleford, together with Paul Starbuck from Oldham.

Centre Nigel Stephenson followed Grayshon from Crown Flatt to Odsal in the November, with Johnny Wolford and Jack Austin heading in the opposite direction.

Pragmatic loose forward Len Casey was lured from Hull KR as the transfer record was again stretched in a £23,000 deal funded in part by the sales of Dean Raistrick to Halifax and Graham Joyce and Ian Slater to Leeds, with scrum-half Paul Harkin moving to Craven Park in exchange.

The new record didn't last too long, Fox heading to his old club Featherstone in the spring to return with hooker Keith Bridges, Bradford forking out £23,000 and Tony Smith in a £24,500 package.

One player that Fox didn't want to lose was Johnny Wolford, a hugely talented performer who many rate as one of the most creative men of the post-war era.

Fox recalls: 'Johnny Wolford was at Bradford when I went there and we had a very good season. He then wanted to go to Dewsbury – I don't know why – and he blames me for transferring him but it wasn't me. He's told that ever since, when we've met, and I say, "No, Johnny I didn't, and what's more tha took away

## A legend remembers
### Keith Mumby

*'Peter Fox was a real coach, a motivator. He'd tell you straight to your face what he wanted of you and what he expected of you. He knew what he was talking about and he never forgot anything.*

*'He used to say that his Championship-winning side was his "Grandads team" but they did it, didn't they? He could transform players who didn't look particularly special. He'd motivate them, and it was nearly always a forward game with us.'*

*Working to instructions. Bob Haigh and Peter Fox reflect on the background to the 1978 Premiership Trophy success.*

## Injury crisis and mounting debts

After having been in contention for the title, an indifferent close to the 1978–79 campaign – with seven defeats in the last 11 games – led to Bradford sliding to eighth spot in the table. The situation wasn't helped by an injury crisis which compelled Northern's board to postpone the fixtures with Wigan and St Helens on 22 April and 24 April respectively, a move which invoked a £200 fine by the Rugby Football League.

Northern, though, put those troubles behind them by reaching the Premiership Final for the second successive year. Bradford won 18-17 in the first round at Hull KR after having trailed 13-0 at half time and followed up that victory with a 14-11 verdict at Warrington in the semi-final.

The pressure of having played 10 games in 22 days told, however, in the decider against Leeds at Fartown, Huddersfield, where an early Steve Ferres goal flattered to deceive in the 24-2 defeat before a 19,489 crowd.

Off the field Northern's financial situation, as the 1970s drew to a close, mirrored that of many

another lad that I wanted at Bradford, tha took Jackie Austin." Jackie was a mate of mine, but they were big mates.

'Wolford was an exceptional player. He wasn't the fastest and when I came to Bradford he was playing loose forward. The first thing I did was move him back to stand-off half, out of the ruck. I said: "Tha's a creative player. Tha can play at loose forward but I may as well have another workhorse there. I want a clever player like thee in the middle of park so I can control the backs and control inside the forwards." "I'm not fast enough now," he said. "Tha's fast enough for me Johnny, tha's a creative player."

'Johnny went to Dewsbury but I got Nigel Stephenson in exchange. Nigel wasn't a speed merchant but he was another thinking, planning footballer, a player that could do things.'

Bradford, meanwhile, were not diverted from the immediate action on the pitch and duly added the 1978–79 Yorkshire Cup to the previous season's Premiership.

The trophy, moreover, was won the hard way, with three tough ties on route to a final (against Division Two side York) that was much more closely fought than anticipated.

Leeds were overcome 24-23 at Odsal in the first round in a game in which Northern had trailed 15-9 at the interval, and that success was followed by a 28-17 verdict over Hull KR, also at Odsal, in round two.

Hull were overcome, again at home, 12-7 in the semi-final to set up what, on paper, appeared to be the simplest task of the tournament. Northern, however, had to work hard before overcoming the Minstermen.

*Neil Fox kicking for goal in the 1978–79 season. Fox, best known as a Wakefield Trinity player, passed Jim Sullivan's existing career record while with Northern, for whom he scored 12 tries and kicked 85 goals and a drop goal in 70 appearances. His final total of 6,220 points, amassed between 1955 and 1980, is unlikely to be surpassed.*

*The Northern side help star man Johnny Wolford celebrate the 1978–79 Yorkshire Cup Final victory over York.*

other Rugby League clubs.

The total deficit at Odsal, prior to 1978–79, was £51,959. Despite, or possibly because of, the side's success a loss was made on that campaign alone of £53,721; all but doubling Bradford's debts.

Peter Fox defends his role in the equation. 'When I spent money, I made money on players I sold. I didn't take money out of the kitty to buy. I did swaps, and I was never ambitious enough to go for the top players. One or two players that I did sign that I thought were important were such as Deryck Fox, who played a tremendous part in Bradford's success. In my second year I bought Paul Newlove, who was a big buy, but Northern got their money back for him. So what money I spent we got back again.'

One of Fox's best players, Keith Mumby, moved up through the junior ranks and was almost lost to Rugby League before he had started. 'I wasn't really interested in rugby,' he recalls. 'I was playing for Bradford Boys rugby but I was playing for Bradford Boys football as well.

'I didn't think I was getting anywhere in football and I hated the training; I thought it was hard. I just carried on with the rugby. I enjoyed it more than I did the football, although the training ended up just the same!

'I was lucky with my debut. I scored 12 goals and a try but I did wonder whether it would go against me. Some people who start well just fall away. But all the players got behind me and helped me out; it just went better and better.'

Meanwhile, a player was moving up through the Colts who would, like Mumby, have a major impact on Bradford Northern. The youngster was Brian Noble, who recalls: 'I made my debut for the Colts at the age of 15, under Garth Budge. He was a very good coach indeed. I only got a few minutes off the bench but it was quite intimidating. Colts rugby was very, very strong so it was tough and a big lesson. There were a lot of good players around me. Ian Slater was the stand-off, Paul Harkin was at scrum-half and big Eddie Okulicz was in the pack. I went on to play for the first team, as did John Pitts and the late Steve Johnson, so there were plenty of big lads and I was well looked after. You did need that because the game was probably a little bit more violent than in the Super League era. There were players around that would knock you off the ball, people who didn't mind sending one through as they say, often from the second row to liven you up a bit. It was obligatory and there was a real art to the hooking game.

'I progressed to the second team when I was 17, then I probably went about my apprenticeship. I remember Ronnie Barritt giving me a lift to training – I used to get the bus everywhere – and he asked me what my ambitions were. I said, "I want to play No. 9 for Bradford Northern." He said, "Well you've got to change your goals straight away son, you want to play No. 9 for Great Britain!" You never know what you're going to achieve but things worked out for me in that respect.'

## A legend remembers
### Keith Mumby

*'I nearly went to Leeds, although I didn't know it. They came in for me but I never got told. Sid Hynes was their coach at the time and we were chatting at a dinner once, years later, and he just happened to say he came in for me one season and Bradford just said "No." I'd never heard of it till that day.'*

# 8.
# Double Trouble – 1979-80 & 1980-81

Bradford Northern became only the third club to win the Rugby League championship in consecutive seasons when they retained the title in 1980–81.

In becoming the first team to achieve the feat since the re-introduction of two divisions in 1973–74, Northern joined Huddersfield (1911–12 and 1912–13) and Swinton (1962–63 and 1963–64) in the pantheon of greats.

Bradford's success in the 1979–80 championship was achieved against a background of significant progress in each of the knockout competitions.

Northern exited the Yorkshire Cup in the second round, slipping 30-5 at home to Wakefield Trinity after having won at Huddersfield in the opening stage. The side had a real tilt at the Challenge Cup, going out to Hull 3-0 in an epic quarter-final at Odsal after having beaten St Helens 11-10 at Knowsley Road in round two and Blackpool in the first round.

And the John Player Trophy was won after a

*Cultured stand off or centre Nigel Stephenson gets a try in the 1979 Challenge Cup semi-final against Widnes at Station Road, Swinton. The Chemics went to Wembley with a 14-11 win but Stephenson and his Odsal teammates were to be mollified by consecutive championship successes.*

typically dour decider with Widnes before Bradford were denied by the Chemics 19-5 in the Premiership final.

There was ample consolation for the latter setback with the championship. Northern finished top of the pile for the first time since 1951–52, when Wigan had prevailed in the top-four final at Leeds Road, Huddersfield. But their right to the title was not to be denied, on this occasion, by the vagaries of knockout football.

The championship was regained for the first time since the war-time success of 1944–45 on the simple basis of Bradford having topped a table in which each team played every other side once at home and once away.

Northern set the agenda for the rest of the league with five opening wins, including notable successes at St Helens (21-10, in a first win at Knowsley Road since 1949) and Hull (6-4) before faltering at the turn of October with a 10-8 reverse at Warrington, followed by a 17-15 home defeat by Leigh.

Bradford lost two more games in the run-up to Christmas, 11-6 at Castleford and 14-5 at home to Hull KR, on 9 December.

Between-times, though, York, St Helens and

*In forthright mood. Peter Fox, the master coach behind consecutive championships, gets his point across.*

# The long Walk

*Odsal was possibly unique among football grounds for the long, often dramatic and occasionally painful entry to and exit from the pitch required of the players and the match officials.*

*From the mid-1930s until 1985 the two teams, the referee and his touch judges changed in dressing rooms high on the hill at the Rooley Lane end of the ground before wending their way behind the crowd and down the steps by the side of the main stand prior to emerging onto the pitch.*

*The walk, measured at around 250 yards, provided pure drama, particularly at floodlit games, with the anticipation of the crowd intensifying from the moment the players came out of the dressing rooms until they entered the field of play.*

*There was also theatre at half time, with teams invariably opting to remain on the pitch for their interval pep talk. And there was, often, added spice at full time when opposing players felt the wrath of Northern fans for any indiscretions, real or perceived. So, from time to time, did the referee. Bradford – who had been disciplined by the authorities for incidents at Birch Lane in the 1910s and 1920s – occasionally fell foul of the Rugby Football League, notably in September 1952 when Northern, who had finished top of the league the previous May, lost at home to newly-formed Doncaster in the second leg of a Yorkshire Cup first round tie.*

*The south Yorkshire side, who had triumphed 12-11 at Tatters Field, stunned Bradford and the majority of the 15,700 crowd with an 11-9 win which many home supporters felt owed much to the predilections of the referee. The hapless whistler, while making his way up the steps, was spat upon, punched and knocked to the ground, losing his whistle and watch in the process, before being helped to the safety of the dressing rooms by home officials and police.*

*Bradford Northern, held by the RFL to have failed to provide sufficient protection, were instructed to post warning notices and provide changing facilities closer to the main stand for the match officials; an instruction which appeared to be forgotten with the passage of time.*

*Northern 'great' Keith Mumby recalls of the long ascent: 'If you'd lost, it was a long way up because you were down in the dumps. But if you'd won you just seemed to get carried up there by supporters'.*

*Scrum half Alan Redfearn, central to Northern's tactical approach in the Fox years, breaks from a scrum.*

Wigan – at Central Park, for the first time in 27 years – had been accounted for. And the reverse at the hands of the Robins was to be the last until 2 March, when Wakefield Trinity edged an 18-15 thriller at Belle Vue.

That defeat, which ended a run of seven successive league victories, was followed by the third round Challenge Cup exit at the hands of Hull, which may have effectively aided Northern's bid for the title. A thoroughly focused Bradford carved out crucial away wins in the space of four days at Workington and, after having been 10-1 down at half time, Widnes (ending a 14-year barren run at Naughton Park) before completing 'doubles' over Salford and Wigan.

Leeds, too, were left with nothing to show for their efforts against Bradford in league football when Northern won 7-2 at Headingley but it was

*A winner! Derek Parker grabs the try that polished off Widnes in the 1980 John Player Special Trophy Final.*

**1979–80: First Division (leading six)**

| | P | W | D | L | F | A | Pts |
|---|---|---|---|---|---|---|---|
| Bradford Northern | 30 | 23 | 0 | 7 | 448 | 272 | 46 |
| Widnes | 30 | 22 | 1 | 7 | 546 | 293 | 45 |
| Hull | 30 | 18 | 3 | 9 | 454 | 326 | 39 |
| Salford | 30 | 19 | 1 | 10 | 495 | 374 | 39 |
| Leeds | 30 | 19 | 0 | 11 | 590 | 390 | 38 |
| Leigh | 30 | 16 | 1 | 13 | 451 | 354 | 33 |

altogether tougher at Borough Park where Blackpool, already relegated, were rock solid before losing 15-14.

The hard earned win, followed by a disappointing home defeat by Warrington, left Bradford a point ahead of Widnes. And with three games to play the Chemics' scheduled visit to Oldham for the final game of the season was emerging as a real winner-takes-all clash.

It didn't work out that way. Comfortable victories over Workington and Hunslet ensured that Northern went into the Widnes match resting on an unassailable three-point cushion. And a below-strength side, selected with the forthcoming Premiership competition in mind, slipped to a relatively meaningless 21-5 defeat which could do nothing to dampen celebrations, and helped earn Fox recognition as Coach of the Year.

**And again**

The title had been won, moreover, without the presence of loose forward Len Casey. Just 14 days after the fine John Player Special Trophy Final win in January, the Great Britain international had left Odsal after a 13-month sojourn, returning to Hull KR. Quite apart from having benefited from the impact of the pragmatic packman at his peak, Bradford could argue that the two transfers represented excellent business, Casey having been bought for £23,000 and sold back for £38,000.

Leading sportsmen will testify that while it may be hard to win a major honour it's much more difficult to stage an immediate repeat. Bradford, however, did just that; admittedly with a touch of unwilling help from those around them.

A closing sequence of seven straight wins and a falling off of form by several rivals helped Northern pull off what, at one stage, had appeared to be the impossible dream of retaining the title in 1980–81.

Bradford, by mid-March, had suffered nine defeats and one draw in their 23 league games. And a sequence of three successive reverses – at Hull and Leigh and, in the first round of the

**How the title was won - 1979–80**

| Sept | 2 | Hunslet | (a) W 13 - 5 |
|---|---|---|---|
| | 9 | Wakefield T | (h) W 27 - 3 |
| | 23 | St Helens | (a) W 21 - 10 |
| Oct | 7 | York | (h) W 23 - 12 |
| | 14 | Hull | (a) W 6 - 4 |
| | 28 | Warrington | (a) L 8 - 10 |
| Nov | 4 | Leigh | (h) L 15 - 17 |
| | 11 | York | (a) W 23 - 10 |
| | 25 | Castleford | (a) L 6 - 11 |
| | 27 | St Helens | (h) W 13 - 9 |
| Dec | 4 | Wigan | (a) W 13 - 2 |
| | 9 | Hull KR | (h) L 5 - 14 |
| | 16 | Leeds | (h) W 7 - 5 |
| | 23 | Salford | (a) W 14 - 11 |
| | 26 | Blackpool B | (h) W 28 - 0 |
| Jan | 27 | Hull KR | (a) W 10 - 9 |
| Feb | 12 | Hull | (h) W 12 - 5 |
| | 17 | Leigh | (a) W 11 - 8 |
| | 27 | Castleford | (h) W 12 - 3 |
| March | 2 | Wakefield T | (a) L 15 - 18 |
| | 16 | Workington | (a) W 20 - 13 |
| | 19 | Widnes | (a) W 11 - 10 |
| | 23 | Salford | (h) W 15 - 0 |
| | 30 | Wigan | (h) W 16 - 5 |
| April | 4 | Leeds | (a) W 7 - 2 |
| | 6 | Blackpool B | (a) W 15 - 14 |
| | 9 | Warrington | (h) L 4 - 10 |
| | 13 | Workington | (h) W 32 - 15 |
| | 16 | Hunslet | (h) W 41 - 16 |
| | 20 | Widnes | (h) L 5 - 21 |

# A match to remember
## John Player Special Trophy Final

*Bradford Northern 6 Widnes 0*
*Headingley, Leeds*
*5 January 1980*
*Superb defence – the factor that had prompted Peter Fox to acquire the services of such as Len Casey, Jimmy Thompson, Graham Idle and Jeff Grayshon – helped Northern to an epic victory over a Widnes outfit that enjoyed the majority of possession with a 17-12 scrum advantage.*

*Keith Bridges was, for once, outhooked – on this occasion by the redoubtable Keith Elwell – but the Bradford rearguard was up to the task in a game notable for a series of high tackles.*

*Full-back Keith Mumby put Northern ahead with a penalty in the ninth minute and Northern twice went close when scrum-half Alan Redfearn orchestrated raids from which Derek Parker and David Redfearn almost profited.*

*Bradford's try came courtesy of Bridges who, after winger David Barends had been bundled into touch after yet another attack inspired by Alan Redfearn, won a scrum deep in the Widnes 25.*

*David Redfearn's long pass sent Parker in at the corner to forge a 5-0 interval lead and the only score of the second half went to Nigel Stephenson who landed a drop goal in the forty-third minute.*

*Widnes, though, could still have snatched the issue but were twice confounded in the closing stages when David Redfearn pulled off timely interceptions.*

*Casey, who defied tonsillitis to play, collected the Man of the Match award.*

*The side had an extra hurdle to face, however; their own ecstatic fans, who formed an almost impenetrable barrier to the dressing rooms. Captain Jimmy Thompson reflected: 'It was a tough match but the hardest part was getting back through our own supporters'.*

*Bradford: Mumby; Barends, D Redfearn, D Parker, Gant; Stephenson, A Redfearn; Thompson, Bridges, Forsyth, Grayshon, G Van Bellen, Casey. Subs: I Van Bellen, Ferres.*

*Widnes: Eckersley; S Wright, Aspey, George, Burke; Hughes, Bowden; Hogan, Elwell, Shaw, L Gorley, Hull, Adams.*

*Referee: Mr W H Thompson (Huddersfield).*

*Captain Jimmy Thompson and his players celebrate the 1979–80 John Player Special Trophy success.*

Challenge Cup, by 17-13 at a Salford outfit destined to be relegated – hardly suggested that Northern were in the mood to mount a serious challenge.

There was, though, a chink of light; the leaders, Warrington, were only three points ahead of Bradford in a highly competitive season.

Northern, though, had played more games than any of their rivals and, in reality, appeared to have little to contest other than the Premiership. And the side was by no means certain of making eighth spot.

The Cup defeat at Salford, while dispiriting, turned out to be the catalyst; aided and abetted by a poor closing furlong by Bradford's competitors.

Northern, in stark terms, had to win all seven of their remaining fixtures and hope that results elsewhere went their way.

They took firmer control of their own destiny with victories at home to Castleford, Warrington and Widnes and successes at Workington, Featherstone Rovers and Leeds.

The last day of the season arrived with Warrington ahead of Northern on point's difference. The Wire's last fixture was at a Leigh side coached by their former player-coach Alex Murphy, while Bradford were hosting Hull.

Leigh, with nothing to play for in the 'no man's land' above the relegation zone, confirmed that simple pride is an important factor in Rugby League by beating Warrington to help set up their own championship success of the following season.

*1979-80 Champions Bradford Northern display their trophy haul.*

Bradford, meanwhile, were nerve-free in a 38-18 stroll against the Airlie Birds to send their supporters in the 8,565 crowd into raptures as news came through of Leigh's gesture.

Northern had won the title with 41 points, a figure that was to remain the lowest totalled by a championship side until 1987–88 when Widnes (albeit from 26 games compared to Bradford's 30) topped Division One with 40 points. Wigan emulated Widnes' record in 1989–90.

**Work ethic**

The Odsal side's main attribute, arguably, was strong defence allied to an indomitable work ethic. No one epitomised that more than the less than aptly named Graham Idle. The workaholic back row forward became, in 1980–81, the thirty-fifth player to have collected a championship medal after appearing in all his side's league games. Idle, who made 30 outings (including one as substitute) had initially made his name as a full-back with Bramley, going on to Wakefield Trinity with whom he appeared at Wembley in 1979. Primarily a defensive forward of the highest calibre, Idle scored one try in the title run and made 36 appearances in total during a season which ended with a remarkable event in London.

Northern agreed to meet RFL 'new boys' Fulham at Craven Cottage, in a £5,000 challenge game, on the eve of the 1981 Challenge Cup Final.

Fulham, who were coached by the inspirational former Widnes scrum-half Reg Bowden, had

secured promotion from Division Two in their first season and had a real folk hero in one-time Bradford prop Ian Van Bellen.

A comment made on the radio by Northern Chairman, Jack Bates, that the Londoners would struggle in the top flight led to Fulham throwing down the gauntlet – and 11,926 turned up for the test of wills.

Fulham proved themselves on the night, winning a match between two full-strength teams 20-8. Bates, however, was vindicated 12 months later. The Craven Cottage team were indeed relegated, going down as the fourth-from-bottom side. And in a bizarre twist it was to be Northern, with an 8-5 victory at Odsal in late April 1982, who sealed their fate.

A player who, like Idle, symbolised the honest, no-frills approach that most appealed to Peter Fox was Alan Redfearn, a scrum-half who very nearly moved to Halifax before his Odsal career got into gear.

Fox remembers: 'The first time I saw Alan Redfearn was at training. I was standing on the steps at Odsal, the players were running round the top and I asked, "Who's that kid leading the

| 1980–81: First Division (leading six) | | | | | | | |
|---|---|---|---|---|---|---|---|
| | P | W | D | L | F | A | Pts |
| Bradford Northern | 30 | 20 | 1 | 9 | 447 | 345 | 41 |
| Warrington | 30 | 19 | 1 | 10 | 459 | 330 | 39 |
| Hull KR | 30 | 18 | 2 | 10 | 509 | 408 | 38 |
| Wakefield Trinity | 30 | 18 | 2 | 10 | 544 | 454 | 38 |
| Castleford | 30 | 18 | 2 | 10 | 526 | 459 | 38 |
| Widnes | 30 | 16 | 2 | 12 | 428 | 356 | 34 |

*Prolific winger David Barends sets out in pursuit of another try.*

| How the title was won - 1980–81 | | | |
|---|---|---|---|
| Aug | 31 | St Helens | (a) L 6 - 16 |
| Sept | 7 | Oldham | (h) W 21 - 10 |
| | 14 | Barrow | (a) W 12 - 10 |
| | 21 | Leigh | (h) W 22 - 2 |
| | 28 | Wakefield T | (a) D 15 - 15 |
| Oct | 5 | Leeds | (h) W 11 - 5 |
| | 12 | Hull KR | (a) L 14 - 28 |
| | 19 | Salford | (h) W 27 - 5 |
| | 26 | Warrington | (a) W 10 - 7 |
| Nov | 9 | Barrow | (h) W 13 - 5 |
| | 16 | Oldham | (a) L 2 - 9 |
| | 30 | Hull KR | (h) L 7 - 26 |
| Dec | 14 | Salford | (a) L 9 - 18 |
| | 21 | St Helens | (h) W 11 - 0 |
| | 26 | Halifax | (a) W 10 - 5 |
| | 28 | Halifax | (h) W 19 - 10 |
| Jan | 1 | Castleford | (a) L 18 - 19 |
| | 4 | Workington | (h) W 15 - 10 |
| | 11 | Widnes | (a) L 2 - 10 |
| | 18 | Wakefield | (h) W 7 - 6 |
| Feb | 1 | Featherstone | (h) W 21 - 19 |
| | 8 | Hull | (a) L 9 - 10 |
| Mar | 8 | Leigh | (a) L 14 - 18 |
| | 15 | Castleford | (h) W 13 - 3 |
| | 22 | Workington | (a) W 14 - 13 |
| | 29 | Warrington | (h) W 26 - 7 |
| April | 5 | Featherstone | (a) W 22 - 18 |
| | 12 | Widnes | (h) W 13 - 5 |
| | 17 | Leeds | (a) W 26 - 18 |
| | 20 | Hull | (h) W 38 - 18 |

chase?" It was Alan Redfearn. I said, "Well, he keeps fit and he trains."

'Albert Fearnley, who had gone to coach Halifax, wanted him and Alan came to me in the bath one night and asked, "Pete, do you think I'm ever going to get a chance at Bradford, because I feel like signing for Halifax?"

'I said: "I can't promise anything. If Barry Seabourne gets injured tha'll get thee chance and if tha does well, it's up to you. Don't go just yet. Give me a few weeks and we'll see how it goes."

'Anyway, something happened, I picked Alan, and he played well. Barry decided he wanted to go coaching and Alan Redfearn went from being a solid A-teamer to a Great Britain scrum-half under our system, because he could play behind a winning pack. He used to do exactly as I told him. He wasn't a speed merchant, but he could tackle, he could do the first priorities; everybody's got to be able to tackle because at some time or other they'll have to.

'I'd got players that'd tackle their hearts out all day and that saved work for others. I used to play players in the right positions to benefit the whole team; you've got to have teamwork and each player has to believe in the fella next to him. I've had many a team where a player's complained about another, "He won't do this Foxy, he won't do that." I once told Jeff Grayshon: "Look, he's the best I've got so instead of playing hell with him all the time, give him a little bit of encouragement. Put your arm round him." He said: "I can't do that!" I said: "Tha can." And he did that for me, did Grayshon, and he come back

to me a few weeks later and said "Tha were right about him".

'Having a player like Grayshon in your team was wonderful because he'd do that for me. He could pass things on. It was the same with Jimmy Thompson and Vince Farrar at Featherstone, they were wonderful players for me.

'The first thing I did when I went to Bradford was to try to sign Vince Farrar. We talked to him, offered him money and all sorts and he said: "I can't leave Featherstone, my wife works here, I work here, my kids go to school here, I can't go."

'Jimmy Thompson was on tour in Australia and when he got back he said, "Yes, I'll come. I want to prove myself." So he came to Bradford and it was the best signing I ever made. Shortly after that Vince Farrar, Charlie Stone and John Newlove all went to Hull and they could have come to me in the early days. I was grieved about that because Hull went to the top of the league.

'I went to Bradford initially because in 1977, when I was coaching Bramley, Harry Womersley – who was Chairman of the Rugby Football League as well as of Bradford – appointed me to the England job. I always say I coached England to two successive defeats!

'I'd told Bramley that I'd gone to help them out and that I'd clearly be looking to move on after a year to a bigger club. I took them from near the bottom of the table to promotion and Harry Womersley took me to Bradford Northern in '78.

'We won 11 or 12 matches and Harry, a smashing bloke, thought we weren't going to get beat. We did very well to win the championship

---

## A legend remembers
### Peter Fox

*'I'd sooner have had Keith Mumby at the back of my team defending me than the Eighth Army. He was brilliant. We were playing at Fartown one day and I put my hand to my head, another try to Huddersfield; but the next thing Mumby went flying over the field and took him out at the corner flag. He was the best defensive full-back there's ever been and he was more than just a defensive player.*

*'You hadn't to teach him anything about defence but when he went on the tour to Australia they did him down. He missed one or two tackles, he didn't get in the Test team, and he got slaughtered for it. I was sloughened for Mumby because he was the best full-back that Bradford's ever had and one of the best full-backs in the league, no question. He was a right lad as well.*

*'That's another thing, my players had to be right lads. If he wasn't a right lad he could go, because he'd upset everybody.'*

---

## A legend remembers
### Peter Fox

*'We were in the dressing room after we'd won the Championship in 1979–80 and Trevor Foster came in. "Peter, can I say a few words?" he asked. "Being you, Trevor, you can." "Listen lads," he said, "all I want to say is you've given me the thrill of my life winning the Championship and I want to say this to you. I rate Peter Fox as the best manager–coach since Dai Rees, I rate Peter as good as him." Now, that was the last success they'd had until I came on the scene. And to hear a player like Trevor Foster, with his experience, say that Peter Fox was as good a manager and coach as Dai Rees! "Well," I thought, "that's nice of you, Trevor."*

in '79–'80. When I took them over they were limited in a lot of senses, Bob Haigh was there, he was a veteran but a very good player. Bradford had been a very exciting team but they couldn't win anything. They played good football but they used to win with scores like 32-24.

'The first man I would have signed at Bradford was at Castleford. When I coached England I had him at loose forward. He was Steve 'Knocker' Norton. They wouldn't sell him, but a few weeks later they sold him to Hull. I was annoyed about that because Knocker said he only wanted to play for me, and he was the best club loose forward in Rugby League there's ever

**Coach Garth Budge, the man who moulded much of the young talent at Odsal.**

## A legend remembers
### Peter Fox

'I was proud to be coach of Bradford and what we did it was magnificent, but I had a rugby chairman there, Harry Womersley, who was brilliant. He wouldn't say a bad thing about anybody and he was the best football chairman I've ever had. Harry, though, used to listen to anybody and he would come to me and say, "Peter" – because he was on the international scene – "what about so and so?" I'd say, "Harry, he's not for me, I don't want him. This is Foxy. No." But then I'd go to him and say I wanted such and such a player and, as with Knocker Norton, he would say we couldn't afford him. But Harry would listen and I couldn't go wrong, and it was the same with Ken Windus, the financial chairman, Ronnie Firth and all those fellas. I had a good rapport generally with that group of directors.'

## A legend remembers
### Brian Noble

'When Fulham started up they were after a hooker. I was a young bloke ready for tapping up and I think I walked around with the transfer request in my back pocket for three months, not daring to put it in; not just because of Peter Fox but because of the other people around me. I had a lot of good advice from Keith Bridges, he was probably the main mentor I had, but Tiger Handford helped and I managed to get great guidance from people like Jimmy Thompson as well.
'Len Casey played his part, Jeff Grayshon was superb as I went through the ranks and there were some substantial, solid people with good character that helped me along the way in my playing career.'

been. Although at international level, while he was a good player, he never quite did what he did with his club.

'I couldn't get Vince Farrar so I signed Jimmy Thompson and he made the weakest tackler – Colin Forsyth – into a good tackler, just by being alongside him. Colin was a very good prop forward but he never tackled. When he played with Thompson he had to, they all did, because Jimmy led by example.'

*Len Casey. Northern had excellent service from the Great Britain loose forward and also made a tidy profit on his purchase from, and resale to, Hull KR.*

### No favourites

Peter Fox can lay claim to possessing man-management skills unsurpassed in Rugby League and, possibly, in any other sport. He explains: 'I had no favourites. The player with the least ability was the best, and I didn't give the best player time off or anything extra.

'Jeff Grayshon once said to me at Bradford: "How come you're always talking to this player and that player but you never talk to me about what I've to do or what I haven't to do?" I said: "Jeff, they are the players in our team with the least ability, so they need more instruction from me than you do. When tha's not doing what tha's supposed to be doing, I'll tell thee! I only have to tell you better players once and it's right. Lesser players need more time and more instruction to gather it all together."

'I trusted my players. I used to trust every player I'd got and I'd get them to trust in me.

'The worst thing was when I got a player – only one or two, not a lot – that I thought wouldn't be able to get into my team and stay in. I knew I'd have to transfer him and I used to try and get other clubs interested, so that the lad

*Peter Fox, the supreme motivator, occasionally incurred the wrath of the authorities. The referee exchanges views during a match against Leeds.*

*Champions Bradford and Challenge Cup winners Widnes at the end of the 1980–81 season with an array of silverware.*

had somewhere to go. It was the hardest thing, having to tell a player: "I'm sorry, you're not going to make it with me so I'm advising you we'll get another club". And I did that. That's why very few players have ever had anything detrimental to say about me. I never did treat players badly, not ever.'

Grayshon, the archetypal Peter Fox player, was arguably as fine a captain as Bradford, or any other club, has had.

A hard-driving forward who would never take a backwards step, he developed under Peter Fox from the hard-running back row forward who was a key component of Dewsbury's surprise and still-revered Championship success of 1972–73 into a pragmatic and composed ball-handling prop.

Grayshon was a player whose abilities could be taken for granted but were noticeable in his absence, when his leadership qualities were also sorely missed.

His loyalty was unquestioned and that quality was confirmed when, after seven years at Odsal, he followed his mentor Fox to Headingley in late October 1985.

The front row man duly returned to Bradford 18 months later, after Fox's departure from Leeds. He played his last game for Northern against Hull KR at Odsal on 25 October 1987, when a fractured ankle threatened to end his career, before moving to Featherstone Rovers and subsequently Batley. While at Leeds he became the oldest player, at the age of 36, to be

*The 1980–81 Bradford squad, with their prize.*

*Happy Days! Dennis Trotter, Dave Redfearn and Alan Redfearn share a joke at a civic reception.*

capped by Great Britain when, after a three-year absence from the international scene, he was selected for the last two Tests in the 1985 tied home series with New Zealand.

### No stars

For all his internationals, however, a striking feature of Peter Fox's coaching record is the way his teams seemed to be greater than the sum of their parts, achieving more success than perhaps could have been expected from the players involved. His philosophy was simple: 'I didn't want a team of world-beaters, because they tend to please themselves what they do. That's what I got when I went into the England and Great Britain camps, when I wasn't allowed to select the team – it was picked by committee.

'I refused the Yorkshire job until they told me I could pick my own team. We had eight wins out of eight, it's never been better than that.

'It's when you pick your own team that there's trust between players. I used to tell them what they had to do, what their jobs were. I didn't want a team of stars because they just do what they want. But with my teams I had probably three or four exceptionally good players, and I had them spread through the side, in the three-quarters, at halfback, in the forwards, whatever. The rest would be workmanlike players who I knew could do their jobs.'

*Job completed. Coach Peter Fox with evidence of Northern's superiority.*

# 9.
# A Force to Be Reckoned With – 1980s to 1995

Bradford entered the 1980s as the best team in the country on the only analysis of any real relevance – as champions in successive seasons in 1979–80 and 1980–81.

Although unable to maintain that status, the side remained a power in the period prior to the launch of Super League.

Together with every other club in the game Northern were unable to match on a consistent basis the super-rich Wigan outfit that from the mid-eighties onwards acquired many of the best players and made them even better by turning them into full time professionals.

Although Bradford would not finish higher than fourth in the 1980s (in 1987–88) and would peak at second in 1993–94 as the Super League era beckoned, significant progress was made in the various knock out competitions.

Wembley may have stayed tantalisingly out of reach but Northern generally made an impact on the Challenge Cup, failing to reach the quarter-finals on only three occasions and going out at the penultimate stage in 1983 (to Featherstone Rovers, who went on to beat Hull in one of the biggest of Wembley upsets), 1992 and 1993.

There were, however, plenty of successes on which to ponder, particularly in the Yorkshire Cup. Bradford reached the final four times in the 1980s and 1990s, before the competition was culled at the end of 1992–93, winning the 1987–88 competition after a replay with Castleford.

The side, as champions, were among the favourites to lift the 1981–82 Yorkshire Cup and justified that rating with three impressive wins to book a berth in the final for the first time since 1978.

Halifax, of Division Two, were scuttled 33-5 on their own Thrum Hall patch in the first round and the more daunting visit to Headingley left Fox's favourites unfazed with an 11-5 verdict.

That win handed Bradford the 'reward' of a visit to Hull KR at the penultimate stage. The Robins looked to have ended Northern's hopes when they established a nine-point lead shortly

*Skipper Jeff Grayshon, believing his players were not receiving adequate protection from the referee, withdraws his troops from the fray at Hull KR in May 1982.*

after half time. But Fox weaved his magic to coax his players to a remarkable recovery, Bradford leaving Craven Park with a 12-11 victory to earn a meeting with Castleford in the decider.

## Walk-off

There was a less happy finish for Northern a few months later at the same venue.

The league campaign closed with Bradford, on 41 points – the same as in their championship season 12 months earlier – taking fifth spot, not enough to secure a home game in the Premiership play-offs.

Northern were compelled to travel to Hull KR in a match that was destined to enter sporting folklore.

An abrasive contest ended in the 56th minute when Northern skipper Jeff Grayshon was dismissed by Widnes referee Robin Whitfield for dissent with Hull KR 17-8 ahead.

Five players had already walked, with John Millington (Hull KR) and Northern's Gary Van Bellen catching early red cards, followed by Rovers' Steve Hartley and Dean Carroll (Bradford).

# A match to remember
## Yorkshire Cup Final

*Bradford Northern 5 Castleford 10*
*Headingley, Leeds*
*3 October 1981*
*Bradford, with youngsters Brian Noble – drafted in at hooker in place of the injured Tony 'Tiger' Handforth – and Ellery Hanley in the side, were unable to contain a speedy Castleford outfit that despite being without unfit player-coach Mal Reilly adapted better to the poor conditions.*

*Prop Barry Johnson, taking over the leadership role from Reilly, was an authoritative figure and earned the White Rose Trophy as Man of the Match for his part in the Glassblowers' clinching try.*

*Johnson was involved in six of Castleford's preceding eight moves, his contribution varying from directing from dummy half; to making ground with powerful runs; to finding touch with a raking kick; to creating opportunities with a deft range of passes.*

*That potent combination presaged a move, on the hour, in which scrum-half Bob Beardmore completed a run-round before sending stand off John Joyner over the whitewash, back row David Finch adding his second goal of the game.*

*The score extended Castleford's lead to eight points following a converted first half try for centre Gary Hyde, who benefited from incisive approach work by full-back George Claughton, who had raced 40 yards off a Joyner pass before slipping a telling ball.*

*Hyde's touchdown wiped out an early Hanley penalty but Bradford, despite Noble's impressive 16-14 pull in the scrums, were unable to reduce the deficit until 12 minutes from time when, with Hanley having been moved to the wing after a heavy knock, David Redfearn and Alan Redfearn combined to send Alan Parker over. Les Gant raised late hopes with a dangerous attack but Bradford's bid petered out before a desultory 5,852 crowd, the BBC's edited highlights policy having forced a 2.15pm kick off.*

*Bradford: Mumby; Barends, Hale, A Parker, Gant; Hanley, A Redfearn; Grayshon, Noble, Sanderson, G Van Bellen, Idle, Rathbone. Subs: D Redfearn, D Jasiewicz.*

*Castleford: Claughton; Richardson, Fenton, Hyde, Morris; Joyner, R Beardmore; Hardy, Spurr, Johnson, Finch, Ward, Timson.*

*Referee: Mr R Whitfield (Widnes).*

The home side's Ian Ellis had also received his marching orders before Grayshon was sent off for querying a decision. Grayshon then allegedly ordered his team to follow him off the field – a claim he was later reported to have denied – and Northern Chairman Ronnie Firth refused to allow them to return on the basis that he feared for their safety.

The match was abandoned, the RFL awarded the game to Hull KR, and Northern were fined £4,000 and banned from all cup competitions other than the Yorkshire Cup the following season.

An appeal, supported by a 12,000-name petition, led to the cup ban being suspended for three years and the stipulation that Firth resign, which he did.

*Two immortals. Ernest Ward makes a suitable presentation after Keith Mumby establishes three new career records for Bradford, eclipsing Joe Phillips each time. His two goals against Halifax at Christmas helped him bypass Phillips' 1,463 career points, while his try in the same game edged him ahead of the New Zealander's total of 46 touchdowns. In addition, his four goals at Workington in the Challenge Cup in March took him past Phillips' record of 661 successes with the boot.*

*Northern made the national news with the signing of Wales Rugby Union international Terry Holmes. The scrum half's debut at Swinton ended unhappily, his suspect shoulder giving way under a tackle and leading to an early departure.*

The fine stood, as did Grayshon's four-game suspension, one of which was the first round Yorkshire Cup game against the Robins at Odsal the following season when a weakened Northern battled back from 14-5 down early in the second half to win 15-14 in the shock of the round.

Division Two side York proved a tough nut at the next stage, going ahead with a long range try for Paul McDermott before losing 8-5, and it was hard at Post Office Road in the semi-final where, after a scoreless first half, Bradford won 11-0 with Carroll kicking three goals and two drop goals and Gary Hale scoring a late try to reach their second consecutive final.

**Tactics**

If that victory owed something to Peter Fox's tactical acumen, there was a more vivid illustration of his lateral approach a couple of months later. Fox, the master strategist, devised a ploy that led to Northern almost pulling something off that was beyond the Great Britain victory over the 1982 Australians. He reveals the background: 'Young John Green was our full-back and I told him, "When they kick the ball to you they'll come racing down the field. Kick it back, no hesitation, as far as tha can."

'My thinking was that their full-back might get to it but he wouldn't have his armoury of support with him. So we tackled him down there, their team had to get back, and they used two or three play-the balls with no men. We kept them hemmed in a bit; that was a simple strategy to stop them.

"It doesn't work all the time because they eventually tumble to it. But they were like that – as soon as they got the ball they'd kick deep into your half and all the side would chase you down. They'd tackle you so much you couldn't get out of your 25. And if you didn't do that, you couldn't score.

'It was only in the last few minutes that they scored a try, it was 7-6 for long enough.

'We always had strategies, you've got to try things. We had one move in particular. From the touchline side, what can you do with the ball? You can spread it across the field but their line will come up and tackle you, so you lose ground. So you take one drive in, two drives in, three drives in, and you get beyond the middle of the field. And then you immediately switch play, because all their tacklers are moving with your players. We scored no end of tries just from that.'

Brian Noble, meanwhile, had forced his way through as the regular hooker, building on 12 appearances in 1979–80 and 15 the following season, then 24 and up to 39 in 1982–83. He reflects: 'I was in the frame in the 1980–81 championship season. I was the third choice hooker at the club for three years but I actually played more games than the two above me. We had Keith Bridges, 'Tiger' Handford, Dean Raistrick and David Dyson when I first started but for two years running I played plenty of games; more, I think, than my counterparts together. So whilst I was third choice and Peter Fox always used to remind me of that, I think that after a third year of consistent football he suggested that he was going to give me a shot.'

*The 1987 Yorkshire Cup Final against Castleford was a rousing affair. Tempers fray, not for the first time in a torrid clash.*

### Ellery Hanley

A player who was always going to 'get a shot' was Ellery Hanley, fast making a mark as a junior player in the Yorkshire League. Peter Fox remembers: 'The coach at Leeds junior side Corpus Christie rang Harry Womersley to tell him that he'd got this young player and we needed to have a look at him. The player in question was Ellery Hanley. Harry picked me up with Eric Hawley and we went to watch Ellery playing in Wakefield. Harry asked me what I thought and I said, "He's a good, solid player, he's worth signing on." I also signed two players from Wakefield. One, the stand-off half, became a referee – Russell Smith – and I signed the loose forward Ian Fleming, and I signed Ellery.

'There was a question over where to play Ellery at first. He'd played centre as an amateur; I played him at stand-off and I always thought he'd make a loose forward because he was tough. He was one of those players who wasn't a clever ball handler but with the ball in his hands he could do anything.

'He could beat men. We used to have planned moves but I always said to my players, "If Ellery Hanley ever calls you, he's the only man that can break a planned move up. If he asks for the ball, give him it." It worked a treat.

'Ellery scored over 50 tries. He won £17,000: £7,000 for being the player of the year and £10,000 for scoring over 50 tries. It was the first time it had ever been put up. Nobody ever thought a Bradford Northern back could win that, because we were supposed to be a forward-oriented team. They'd no idea. I couldn't help us being good tacklers; all my lads were solid.'

### Manningham at Odsal

The Bradford fire disaster of 11 May 1985, when 56 people died as flames engulfed the main stand at Bradford City's home game with Lincoln, led to Northern inviting the beleaguered soccer club – the direct descendant of their old rivals Manningham – to Odsal until the rebuilding of Valley Parade was completed in December 1986.

City's first game at Odsal was on 8 October 1985 when a 5,638 crowd turned up for the Milk Cup tie with Brighton & Hove Albion.

The period of tenancy was fraught with problems, caused mainly by the disparate philosophies of rugby supporters and football fans. Soccer supporters felt that Odsal lacked atmosphere and there were concerns over the condition of the pitch and the impact on football games of the famous raised corners caused by the speedway track.

Rugby League supporters, in turn, were

uneasy over the barriers necessarily erected around the ground to separate home and away fans. Local publicans were obliged to close on soccer match days because of trouble and there was a serious incident during the fixture between City and Leeds United in October 1986 when United fans encroached into the Bradford section, above the changing rooms. A mobile fish and chip kiosk was set on fire before being rolled down onto the spectators below, who were able to escape onto the pitch.

**A quality signing**

Northern's supporters were able to focus on some silky Rugby League skills, meanwhile, when the club paid a record £65,000 fee for Leigh stand-off John Woods in August 1985.

The cultured maestro, who had captained Leigh to the club's second championship in 1981–82, was seen as the ideal partner for the robustly elusive Ellery Hanley.

New coach Barry Seabourne's rebuilding plans were thrown into some disarray, however, by the departures of captain Jeff Grayshon and Hanley, who was reported to have demanded a contract worth around £100,000 a year. The sum, Chairman Jack Bates insisted, represented a third of Northern's annual gate receipts and Hanley moved on to Wigan in September in a deal reported to be worth £150,000, comprising a cash sum and backs Phil Ford and Steve Donlan.

Woods wasted no time in showing his qualities, totalling 36 points in his tenth game for Bradford with five tries and eight goals as Northern swamped Swinton 48-20. His total surpassed the 34 registered by Ernest Ward, who had scored four tries and 11 goals in the 67-0 lashing of Liverpool Stanley 40 years earlier.

Another famous name joined Bradford later that autumn – one which made national headlines. The mournful tones in which BBC Newscaster John Humphreys announced to the nation on the evening of 3 December 1985 that Northern had signed Cardiff and Wales Rugby

# A match to remember
## Yorkshire Cup Final

*Bradford Northern 7 Hull 18*
*Headingley, Leeds*
*2 October 1982*
*Northern, who had belied mediocre league form to earn a second successive Yorkshire Cup final appearance, again had to be content with runners-up medals in a game in which full-back Keith Mumby was awarded the White Rose Trophy as the Man of the Match.*
*Bradford, denied several first choice men through injury or internal dispute, were always likely to struggle against a side that could afford to leave Great Britain loose forward Steve Norton on the bench but an 11,755 crowd – the best for a Yorkshire Cup Final for 14 years – was treated to a committed display in which Northern were only 8-7 down on the hour.*
*Norton's introduction at that stage, however, scuppered Peter Fox's hopes although Bradford loose forward Gary Hale – who had faced another quality performer in Mick Crane throughout the first 40 minutes – was a strong contender for the Man of the Match award.*
*Hooker Brian Noble was also in the frame for mastering his one-time Odsal mentor Keith Bridges in the loose and in the tight, where he won the scrums 10-8.*
*Northern, six points adrift after Hull second row Paul Rose (another stand out performer) and winger Paul Prendiville had crossed for tries that Lee Crooks failed to convert, drew level when Dean Carroll landed a drop goal and then kicked the conversion for a Keith Whiteman touchdown that had been cleverly created by Hale.*
*Crooks restored Hull's lead with a couple of drop goals, Carroll hitting back with his own one-pointer. But the fresh Norton proved to be the match-winner, sending Rose over for his second score and, after Crooks had landed a penalty, creating a late touchdown for winger Steve Evans.*

*Bradford: Mumby; Barends, Gant, A Parker, Pullen; Whiteman, Carroll; Grayshon, Noble, G Van Bellen, Idle, Jasiewicz, Hale. Subs: D Smith, Sanderson.*

*Hull: Kemble; Evans, Day, Leuluai, Prendiville; Topliss, Harkin; Skerrett, Bridges, Stone, Rose, Crooks, Crane. Sub: Norton.*

*Referee: Mr S Wall (Leigh).*

# A legend remembers
## Keith Mumby

*Keith Mumby, rated as one of the finest full-backs in the history of the game, shared with another Bradford 'great', Trevor Foster, the distinction of never having been sent off or even cautioned.*
*'I just did my job and my career passed by OK. I was never in a fight, there was just the game at Hull KR when Jeff Grayshon brought us off. It was ridiculous, every time there was a tackle there were knees and fists going in. When we tried to do it back, the referee penalised us.*
*'That's why Jeff took us off. They were getting away with murder.'*

Union scrum-half Terry Holmes was in marked contrast to the joy in the Yorkshire TV studios, where the deal was completed before the cameras in an atmosphere of positive excitement.

The Wales captain had switched codes for a reported £80,000 over three years but the delight quickly turned to dismay as concerns in some quarters over a suspected weak shoulder were confirmed in his first match.

The national media descended on Station Road, Swinton, for what would otherwise have been a comparatively low-key league fixture. And the debutant's involvement was short and less than sweet.

After having been involved in several early moves, Holmes was tackled to the ground, the impact forcing his left shoulder out of its joint. Led from the field after just 12 minutes by physio Ronnie Barritt, his Rugby League career appeared to be in jeopardy before it had begun.

It wasn't – despite a recurrence of the injury when the Welshman returned to action with the A team against Batley in January 1986. The medics opted for a remedial operation in which muscle and sinew from his arm was wrapped around his collar bone.

The initiative was a success. Holmes was ready for a return to action at the start of the 1986–87 season and played 32 games without mishap, scoring eight tries. He was, however, obliged to retire the following season after sustaining a career-ending knee injury. He had

*Celebration time. Paul Harkin keeps a safe hold on the Yorkshire Cup after the victory over Castleford in 1987. Brendan Hill and Kelvin Skerrett keep a grip on the Mayor, while their team mates are poised for any slips.*

*Hooker Brian Noble, centre Steve McGowan and winger Phil Ford. All happy after another success against Leeds.*

played 37 first team games, only one of which had been made in his first season, which had started in high-octane fashion for Bradford with 11 games won and only two lost.

That opening, though, became a frustrating memory after Northern were brushed aside 38-0 by the 1986 Australian touring side.

Bradford, in fine form until the game against the Kangaroos on 18 November, had been fancied in many quarters to stage an upset but the 10,663 crowd were treated, inasmuch as the fog that descended upon Odsal would allow, to a feast of expansive football by the Green & Golds.

Aussie skipper Wally Lewis, who had been linked with Northern two or three years earlier, gave Terry Holmes an object lesson in Rugby League skills and the Kangaroos rattled up seven tries, having been held to 16 points at the interval. Bradford's misery was only partly eased by the fact that two other Yorkshire sides (Hull and Leeds) were also nilled on the tour but the defeat certainly appeared to have a long-term impact.

Northern's subsequent form, apart from a brief run in the John Player Special Trophy, dipped alarmingly. Not one of the next 11 games was won (with Wigan inflicting a 60-6 defeat at Central Park, the highest since the 63-3 reverse at Hull in 1933 and made more painful by five

tries by former Bradford favourite Ellery Hanley).

The supporters, despite reported interest in Wales Rugby Union stand-off Jonathan Davies, began to vote with their feet. Only 1,669 turned up for the home draw with Hull on 11 March and there were just five more fans present when Hull KR arrived seven days later.

Those five, though, had their faith rewarded with a 24-6 victory in which the team had agreed to play for nothing as a gesture to the supporters. The result precipitated another remarkable transformation in fortunes, helped by the return

*Keith Mumby set three new records with Northern in the early 1980s. His try at Halifax on Boxing Day 1980 was his forty-seventh – a new record for a full-back, beating the 46 scored by Joe Phillips.*
*Another Phillips record, that of 1,463 points amassed between 1950 and 1956 was eclipsed in, ironically, another Yuletide fixture with neighbours Halifax. Mumby landed two goals in the 10-6 win on 28 December 1982 to reach the 1,464 mark. The full-back went on, in the same season, to become Northern's all-time leading goalkicker, his four goals in the 17-0 Challenge Cup win over Workington Town taking him to the 662 mark, beyond Phillips' 661.*

*Unhappy returns. Former Northern star Ellery Hanley, back at Odsal as captain of Wigan, gets his marching orders from referee Robin Whitfield.*

Council and with them we put together a package which resulted in us finding a way forward. We didn't get any money off the council; we just got an advance on monies that were due. With that, we managed to work through the trading deficit and we straightened things up. I think we did that within 18 months, which was quite an achievement.

'I became Chairman in 1989, as I recall. There were some hard-working people on the Board at the time but it was difficult to see the way forward because we didn't have anybody with any significant amount of money.

'Like a lot of clubs we have still never had a fairy godmother come along and pour millions; not even

of Jeff Grayshon from Leeds and the signing of the artful scrum half Paul Harkin from Hull KR.

Bradford closed the campaign with six victories from eight league games to emphatically end fears of relegation and force their way into the Premiership play-offs. St Helens, however, proved to be too high a hurdle, winning 46-14 at Knowsley Road.

**Of visionary men**

A man who was to become a significant figure at Odsal, and throughout the game, arrived on the scene as Terry Holmes departed. That man was Leeds-based solicitor Chris Caisley who, within two years, would become Chairman and would later oversee an astonishing change of image which would help steer the club to the heights of Super League.

He looks back: 'I joined in 1987 and it became apparent that finances were not that great. I remember there was a £500,000 cash shortfall at the club. We then got involved with Bradford

*Only a last-minute penalty miss from near the half way line by Ellery Hanley, who had already landed 12 goals, prevented Bradford from recording what would have been a highest-ever total in the league game with Hunslet at Odsal on 7 October 1984.*

*The wide attempt left Northern with a 72-12 win; the home tally equalling the score against Doncaster in November 1973.*

*Hanley totalled 55 tries (the most by any player in the English game since St Helens winger Tom Van Vollenhoven scored 61 in 1960–61) in the 1984–85 season.*

*Hanley owed his impressive total to intelligent support play, natural athleticism, an indomitable spirit and a muscular physique honed during many hours of solitary weight training.*

*The stand-off scored 40 of his tries in league games. His tally was the highest ever recorded by a non-winger and was all the more remarkable for having been amassed during a relatively indifferent season for Northern, who finished eighth in the league.*

*Fifty-two of Hanley's touchdowns were scored with Bradford. He also crossed twice for Great Britain in the 50-4 win over France at Headingley (captaining his country in the return match) and once for England.*

*He became only the second Bradford Northern player to pass the half-century mark in a season, emulating prolific New Zealand winger Jack McLean who had achieved the feat on no less than four occasions in the early 1950s.*

hundreds of thousands of pounds, or even in some cases tens of thousands of pounds, into the club. What we've achieved since '89 has been done on the back of our own abilities. It would be nice to have a Roman Abramovich around, but I think it makes success all the more rewarding when you get it.

'When you look at how Odsal was in 1989, it was crumbling and falling apart. We generated crowds on the back of one of the worst stadiums in the game in terms of facilities. We didn't have any corporate facilities whatsoever; the very minimal corporate entertaining that we did was done in a portakabin at the back of the main stand where we could get maybe 20-30 people in. So there were a lot of challenges in 1989, before Rupert Murdoch started to put his money in. We had to move forward from a very shaky base.'

As Caisley took the helm, another man arrived at Odsal who has since remained with Bradford.

*Northern and Peter Fox parted company at the end of the 1984–85 season.*
*Fox, who was replaced by Barry Seabourne, left Odsal for Leeds after having been informed at the beginning of February that his contract would not be renewed.*
*The directors' controversial announcement, which split the supporters and did not receive the backing of the players, followed a relative lack of success since the consecutive championships of four years earlier and reflected concerns over what was perceived as a 'defence-focused' style of play.*
*Club captain Jeff Grayshon, a strong believer in a coach regarded by many fans as something of a Messiah and by Grayshon himself as the best around, resigned his position over the issue.*
*Fox's last season in his initial, eight-year, period at the club saw Northern drop from joint top in late October to eighth by the close of the season.*

Great Britain second row Paul Medley had made his name as a rampaging runner and hard-hitting tackler and his abilities had become indelibly printed on the consciousness of most Northern fans when he came on as a substitute for Leeds in a game at Headingley and swung a game that

*A family 'dream-come-true' turned sour when former Bradford legend Jeff Grayshon, now at Featherstone, played against his son Paul. Grayshon senior shows parental concern as his son is led off with an injury.*

*Indefatigable and courageous, Jon Hamer typified Northern's forwards of the 80s and 90s.*

had appeared to be in Bradford's pocket with three tries in 18 minutes.

He says: 'I'd been devastated, as a home-grown lad, to leave Leeds for Halifax. It wasn't the happiest of times. Halifax got relegated and I was going to stand by them, because I'd a contract to honour, when Bradford came in at the eleventh hour. Halifax owed Bradford some money for Brendan Hill and they were in some financial difficulties at the time. The £110,000 they got for me paid off a few debts and sorted their problems, so that was realistically why the deal happened.

'This was in August 1989, and I was on honeymoon. The headlines were "Medley signs by fax from Fax!" I jumped at the chance of joining Bradford. It would have been the first time I'd have been playing at a lower level. I wanted to stay at the top and coming to Odsal was the best move that ever happened to me. The fans took to me and I took to them. I can honestly say that I didn't ever think, when I left Leeds, that I'd get the feeling back for the game.

But I actually enjoyed it more at Odsal than I did at Headingley, and I wouldn't have thought that possible.'

Medley and his team mates certainly enjoyed themselves in the Division One clash with Wigan in the early stages of the 1990–91 season. Ellery Hanley, now captain of the Pie Eaters, found himself sent off for the first time in his career in circumstances that captured the headlines.

Hanley, who was given his marching orders for dissent by referee Robin Whitfield as the teams walked from the field, was given the full backing of his Chairman, Maurice Lindsay, who was also a member of the Rugby Football League Board of Directors.

Said Lindsay: 'The captain is entitled to approach the referee to ask for clarification on

> *The 26-18 home defeat by Leigh in January 1987 ended prematurely when the visitors' timekeeper light-heartedly moved his hand towards the action button as the game drew to close, joking to Northern counterpart Trevor Foster that he would 'press this now, to make sure we get a win for a change!' The hapless official, however, caught the button in error, the hooter sounded, and the referee blew for time when over three minutes were left for play. Embarrassed Leigh officials were highly apologetic afterwards but Northern, who had no realistic chance of rescuing the game, accepted the incident as a genuine mistake and took the issue no further.*

the interpretation of the rules.

'On this occasion the match official had gone into the dressing rooms before the game to say that new scrum instructions had been received from Fred Lindop, the Controller of Referees, and that he would be enforcing them in a certain way.

'Our players felt that wasn't happening on the field. The standing instructions at Wigan are that only the captain is allowed to speak to the referee so they asked Ellery to approach him.

# A match to remember
## Yorkshire Cup Final

*Bradford Northern 12 Castleford 12*
*Headingley, Leeds*
*17 October 1987*
*Scrum-half Paul Harkin's midfield maestro performance, which earned him the White Rose Trophy as Man of the Match, wasn't enough to secure victory for Northern in a game which turned out to be the last of Welshman Terry Holmes' brief Rugby League career. A Martin Ketteridge penalty 15 minutes from time helped Castleford force a replay after Bradford, with Neil Roebuck on at the interval for Holmes and David Hobbs substituted for Jeff Grayshon, had hit back from 10-4 down to take the lead with a try for Karl Fairbank and two Hobbs goals.*
*Full-back Keith Mumby scored two first half goals before the 10,947 crowd, while Castleford had established their lead with touchdowns by winger David Plange and Aussie Test loose forward Bob Lindner, one of which Ketteridge improved.*
*Cas, who ignored a number of opportunities to drop a goal in the closing stages, were left regretting that failure when the replay – the first in the Yorkshire Cup final for 32 years – was arranged for two weeks later at Hunslet's Elland Road ground because of fixture problems caused by the tour by Papua New Guinea and the British Coal Nines. The date clashed with Castleford's lucrative home league game with Wigan and Wheldon Road Chairman David Poulter even threatened at one stage to pull out of the Yorkshire Cup to fulfil that fixture.*

*Bradford: Mercer; Ford, McGowan, Simpson, Francis; Mumby, Harkin; Grayshon, Noble, Hill, Skerrett, Fairbank, Holmes. Subs: Roebuck, Hobbs.*

*Castleford: Roockley; Plange, Marchant, Beattie, Hyde; Joyner, R Southernwood; Shillito, K Beardmore, Ward, Ketteridge, Fifita, Lindner. Subs: B Beardmore, Sampson.*

*Referee: Mr K Allatt (Southport).*

'There was a scrum penalty awarded against us just before half time. Ellery sought clarification and was dismissed.'

Bradford, ahead 17-6 at the time of Hanley's dismissal, had to withstand a strong Wigan rally in the second half before winning 31-30 with the help of a 'pushover' try for substitute David Croft at a scrum on the visitors' line.

### Fox returns

Peter Fox, meanwhile, returned to Odsal in 1991–92 on a matter of principle involving his former club Featherstone Rovers. 'I left,' he explains, 'because they wouldn't re-sign Jeff Grayshon at 40 years of age. They said he was too old.

'Age has got nothing to do with it. I said, "If he's 100 and he's good enough, he plays." But age can be a thing with rugby, if you get to 30 you are looked on as over the hill.

'I didn't abide by things like that. Grayshon came up to me at Featherstone and asked me what was happening. I asked him what he meant and he said that they hadn't re-signed him. So I left word with Rovers that they must sign Grayshon before I come back from holiday. They didn't, so I told them that if they didn't sign him I would leave. I don't know whether they believed me or not but a few weeks later they still hadn't signed him, so I went. Then Bradford came for me and that's when I went to Odsal the second time.

'Northern were second from the bottom of the league, eight points adrift of the third-from-bottom club, when I joined. Featherstone, who I'd left, were in the top eight.

'Bradford got out of the bottom two, winning at Hull Kingston Rovers to make sure, while Featherstone went to Wakefield in one of their last matches and got beat. Rovers were relegated and we survived. I saved Bradford from relegation and they've never been back.'

Northern, in fact, came close to winning the championship in 1993–94, missing out only on points difference to Wigan. Brian Noble has painful memories of the campaign, in more ways than one.

'I dislocated a shoulder twice in my last season with Bradford Northern. I damaged it against Castleford in the first team, then again in a second team game at Warrington. That was one of the most painful nights of my life. I was on

# A match to remember
## Yorkshire Cup Final

*Bradford Northern 11 Castleford 2*
*Elland Road, Leeds*
*31 October 1987*

*A mass brawl on the stroke of half time warmed the 8,175 crowd as Northern secured what was to prove their last Yorkshire Cup success before the competition was ditched by the RFL five years later. Prop Brendan Hill, whose father Dave had played in the 1965 victory over fancied Hunslet, grabbed the first try and also picked up the White Rose Trophy for a powerful all-round performance which justified his decision to slim down to a new playing weight of 18 stones.*

*Castleford hit back with a Martin Ketteridge goal before a 12-man brawl, sparked by a tackle by Castleford loose forward John Joyner on his Northern opposite Wayne Heron, led to referee Kevin Allatt sin-binning Bradford's Karl Fairbank and Joyner before the second half began.*

*Prop David Hobbs added to Hill's try with a drop goal eight minutes into the second period. And a piece of magic by enigmatic winger Phil Ford, who was obliged to collect his own wild pass before sending Heron through a bamboozled defence, put Northern firmly in the driving seat after Hobbs' conversion.*

*That wasn't the end of the action, Bradford prop Kelvin Skerrett getting himself sin-binned on the hour and Cas back row man John Fifita being yellow-carded at the close, while Keith Mumby, back at full-back after having played at stand off in the first game, denied a Castleford rally with a couple of try-saving tackles. Jeff Grayshon – out with a broken leg – and Terry Holmes, who had played his last-ever game after sustaining a knee injury in the first match, were both awarded winners' medals.*

*Bradford: Mumby; Ford, McGowan, Mercer, Simpson; Stewart, Harkin; Hobbs, Noble, Hill, Skerrett, Fairbank, Heron. Subs: Roebuck, D Redfearn.*

*Castleford: Roockley; Plange, Marchant, Beattie, Hyde; R Southernwood, B Beardmore; Ward, Hill, Fifita, Ketteridge, England, Joyner. Subs: Boothroyd, Sampson.*

*Referee: Mr K Allatt (Southport).*

oxygen because the hospital was dealing with a major accident, and they couldn't get my shoulder back in. I remember laying on an emergency bed thinking "Christ this is bad, I'm in agony, I'm never going to get better from this."

'I ended up having a shoulder reconstruction and got back playing with the second team. Peter Fox said he thought my playing days were over and it was at that time there was a scandal.

'We could have won the championship in 1994. I was out injured with my dislocated shoulder and we went to Hull one Wednesday night and although we were top of the league there was laughing and joking on the bus.

'I think the staff got a bit disappointed with that and decided to have a witch hunt and I was a bit upset to be dragged into it. I wasn't even there.

*Second row Karl Fairbank, an inspiration in the Bradford pack, supported by scrum half Deryck Fox and hooker Brian Noble.*

'I think I played the following week for the second team and then for the first team. When I went to training the following Tuesday I was told that my contract had been terminated. That was professional sport. The Board and the coach, Peter Fox, decided that the alleged troublemakers were Steve McGowan, Dave Hobbs, Gerald Cordle, a couple of others and myself, and I got the bullet.

'I was very upset because I'd given my life to Bradford Northern. I learnt a lesson, though, about what you should and shouldn't do to people who have substance and have given a lot to clubs.

'A few days later I got a phone call from Peter Fox and Nigel Stephenson saying 'We've had a bit of a rethink, do you want to come back in and do a bit of coaching?' But David Hobbs, who had also got the bullet, had got the Wakefield job so I decided that although I'd Bradford in my heart it was a bit of a hard one to take, and I went to Wakefield for a year.'

**Pressure**

While Noble was away, Northern slipped under a welter of indifferent results that left Peter Fox under mounting pressure.

The players accepted collective responsibility for defeat in six out of seven games as the 1994–95 season entered the finishing straight and a section of the crowd began calling for the coach's blood. Fox, who responded with a 'V' sign, later explained: 'It was directed at one person who was acting in an abusive manner in front of women and children.

'I don't like that and I don't expect it just because we have not done as well as we have in the last two seasons.'

Differences at board room level over a number of issues, including Fox, had led to the resignation of director Philip Hobkirk who, in a statement, said: 'My resignation was entirely due to an unworkable relationship over many months between myself and Chris Caisley over many issues, none more so than the decision to extend the contract of Peter Fox.

'I am not, and never have been, in the business of rewarding failure.'

Northern occupied seventh spot, their lowest for two years, gates had slumped and gossip was growing regarding a possible takeover at Odsal. Fox, who also had to contend with difficulties over post-match drugs-testing of his players, remained resilient and said: 'I have had to place on the back burner for the past two months progress to sign three, or maybe four or five, quality players who are shortly out of contract and wanted to join me. Our finances wouldn't allow them to move.

'I hope people remember last season when making comparisons. Who scored more points

## Chris Caisley

'We brought Peter Fox in halfway through the 1991–92 season. He was probably the only coach in the game who could have saved us. What Peter had, in addition to all his other abilities, was tremendous motivational powers and that's what we needed at that time.

'We were a long way adrift at the bottom of the table but we won a hell of a lot of the last games and stayed up by the skin of our teeth. We'd reached a Premiership Final at Old Trafford against Widnes under David Hobbs and although we got slaughtered we had at least reached a final. We had Yorkshire Cup wins and we got to Regal Trophy finals, so from 1989 to the Super League era we'd probably over-achieved. We'd got a good pack but we lacked flair in the backs, we could never finish anything off. Ellery Hanley had gone, so we'd no real flash standout explosive player. Then Peter Fox came, and we got Paul Newlove who was probably the first real star back that we'd had. We'd had the likes of Phil Ford, good players, but in world-class terms Newlove was probably the first that we got pre-Super League. Then St Helens came in for him, which was probably the making of the club. That deal worked tremendously well because we got great service out of Paul Loughlin and Bernard Dwyer in particular.'

*Second row Karl Fairbank supports Brian Noble. Fairbank, a loyal servant, waived his right to a testimonial season.*

than Wigan, the team of the year? It is our defence, again, this season that is letting us down. But I feel strongly that we will finish the season with a flourish and give the fans something to cheer about.

'The board has two choices: either to stick with me or show me the door. But there is no way I'm retiring. I've got too much to offer this game yet.'

The end, though, was nigh and Fox now reflects: 'I told our Chairman Chris Caisley that we'd have to go back to Australia a second time, for a couple of forwards that could play the game. I told him I wanted an imposing forward, Paul Sironen or Paul Harragon. He came back with Robbie Paul and a New Zealand lad.

'Robbie turned out to be a good acquisition eventually but the next season was the one before Super League. We didn't have a team to play the game, so we were average, and that's when I left.

'I'd been given a contract extension, but when Caisley came back from Australia he'd done a deal with the big man, Murdoch. He brought one of Murdoch's men, Smithy, so when he came back he had to get rid of me. They paid me some compensation, a fraction of my salary. That put me out of the game and I've never been in it since.'

### Super League arrives

Times, meanwhile, were changing. The decision of the club chairmen who met at Central Park, Wigan on Saturday 8 April 1995 to form an elite 'Super League' – with many clubs set to merge as part of the 'master plan' – raised hackles throughout the game and led to protests by fans and calls for resignations at the following day's matches.

Northern Chairman Chris Caisley, however, was 100 per cent in favour and said: 'One cannot fail to be delighted by this monumental forward-thinking decision by the league's member clubs. It can only be the saviour of the game, opening the way to long-term expansion and a worldwide

## A legend remembers
### Brian Noble

*'I came into a strong team and subsequently we've always concentrated on having a great pack with the likes of David Hobbs, Kelvin Skerrett, Johnny Hamer and Brendan Hill. Back rowers like Karl Fairbank and Paul Medley came from Leeds. I had the privilege of playing with a lot of good players; some moved on and some stayed.*

*'I happened to stay as a player for almost all my career because I worked as a policeman. It was great to be in the community in Bradford but it meant that realistically I was tied to Northern.*

*'We were always in the frame and we were probably more successful against Wigan, who were the only full-time team at that stage, than were most other teams. We could never get them in the big one though, we lost about three Challenge Cup semi-finals, certainly two to Wigan and one to Featherstone in 1983 when Ellery Hanley scored a great try.*

*'The only thing I didn't do was play at Wembley but I had a glittering career. I still take great pride in my medals. As a coach I talk to my players about medals and final appearances; they stick with you a lot longer than any financial rewards that you get. That doesn't change as a coach, you like to play in finals and be part of the big occasion.'*

audience that will be drawn to Rugby League.

'Being realistic, it was a case for many clubs to accept or go out of business, such was the financial state of many of them.'

Caisley revealed that he had been talking with Halifax officials for several weeks about a possible merger, believing that the catchment area would support a powerful single team. But Halifax opted out and Caisley was considering moving in with Huddersfield. He didn't feel that a merger with Keighley, some 15 miles from Odsal and the harbinger, with match day razzmatazz, of much that followed in Super League, was a possibility.

## A legend remembers
### Brian Noble

*'I think the psychologists will tell you that pain and pleasure are what make you remember things. I certainly remember breaking my leg against Hull at Odsal and playing on. It sounds dramatic but it wasn't, it was a non-supporting bone, but I knew I was in a lot of pain. I sat down to get it looked at and the referee Colin Morris walked over, stood on my hand and broke that as well! So then I had to go off. Sky had started showing the games then and I remember giving him a gob full, which I think was unfortunately caught on their cameras, for that piece of misfortune.'*

### Alias Smith and Deakin

In the event Bradford probably made the right decision (and one which was emulated by all clubs, other than Huddersfield and Sheffield) to go it alone. The club was on the cusp of its finest hour and two men in particular would drive the whole enterprise forward in the early years of Super League.

They were Brian Smith and Peter Deakin.

Smith was confirmed as the new coach, quitting St George because of 'disillusionment' with the game in Australia, and particularly over the power struggle between the ARL and the Rupert Murdoch Super League. Prior to his departure from Australia, Smith had been fined 10,000 dollars for remarks made to a referee during a game.

The one-time Hull FC coach had initially turned the job down but an improved cash offer, with Smith also guaranteed full control on football issues, swung the deal.

Smith was joined at Odsal by new Marketing Executive Peter Deakin who declared: 'Just watch us go!'

Deakin said: 'The opportunity came out of the blue and I had no hesitation in accepting it in view of the mega changes which are coming within the game.

'There are exciting times ahead – and especially for Bradford, who have the fourth largest market after London, Paris and Leeds. There is a huge population base and a good spectator base.

'Rugby League is a tradition in the city and the potential at Odsal is limitless. We have appointed a coach who I believe will be a wonderful cutting edge for the sport. He is a man with ideas which I share; it is the dawn of a new era for Northern.'

Deakin added: 'Bradford has had to relaunch itself a couple of times in the past. We want to keep traditions alive while looking to the future.'

A former BARLA Great Britain international, Deakin was a product of the Oldham St Annes club and had spent two years as a professional with Oldham.

Former coach Peter Fox, meanwhile, reflected: 'The spectators were brilliant with me the first time, they used to come waving their arms and bowing at me. I used to say, "Just a minute, you need a bit of luck to go to Wembley."

'The second time it was OK for a while but then Super League was coming along, Murdoch was controlling the issues, and Bradford parted company with me. I wasn't pleased but I thought, "If they're not happy with what I've done for them in the years I've been with them,

## A legend remembers
### Peter Fox

*'I brought Len Casey to Bradford from Hull KR. He was a horrendous player to deal with – not in my case, we're big mates now – but he was a difficult man for the directors to handle over travelling and money.*

*'But I never had a minute's trouble with him while he was at Odsal and I didn't want him to go. He was magnificent.*

*'It was the same with Alan "Baz" Rathbone, who had been sent off no end of times. He got sent off once with us but he was a great lad, not a big fella but a terrific player.*

*'I've fond memories of all the players, such as Jimmy Fiddler and Jackie Austin, and Derek Parker from Bramley. Not stars or world beaters but they could play, and they'd give you everything.'*

# Chris Caisley

'We were bottom of Division One, shortly before the Super League era in 1991–92, and we went to Hull KR in the last game of the season. We had to win but even then the question was whether Featherstone would prevail at Wakefield. If they did, we were relegated whatever we did at Hull KR.

'I seem to recall we'd won something like 11 games either on the bounce or 11 out of 13 to even get into a position whereby at the last game of the season we still had to win and another team had to lose.

'It was quite remarkable really, there was a lot of pressure on that day and I remember a Hull player intercepting a pass near their line and going the full length of the field. I thought, "Oh, bloody hell, here we go" but Neil Summers scored a 60-metre effort in the corner and basically won the game for us. And Featherstone lost at Wakefield.

'If we hadn't achieved that, perhaps we wouldn't have even been in Super League. It's a fine dividing line between success and failure.'

I've nothing to look back on and say I've done Bradford a disservice. They've had great service from me and maybe I haven't been treated with the respect I deserved." So I walked away.'

A legacy of the Fox era, which helped propel Bradford to the forefront of Super League, was the major asset that was Paul Newlove.

The Great Britain and former Featherstone centre had become unsettled at Odsal and the deal surrounding his departure to St Helens helped the Bulls start life in the new era with a bang.

Caisley and his former prop Kelvin Skerrett, who had since moved to Wigan, were in full agreement on the deal that brought Bernard Dwyer, Paul Laughlin and Sonny Nickle – and £250,000 – to Odsal in exchange for the powerful centre.

Both reckoned it represented excellent business from Bradford's point of view and Caisley enthused: 'We are delighted – we have swapped one international for three high quality players and a sum of cash. Careful management by us of a very delicate situation over the past few months has ensured that we have obtained the deal that we have been working towards since it became obvious Paul Newlove did not want to play for the club.

'We have always insisted that Newlove would only leave Bradford in return for a deal that was too good for us to refuse and that any deal was wholly dependent upon quality players being part of the overall package.

'St Helens were made to realise that to get quality you have to trade quality. We definitely do not want has-beens. I feel like the man who broke the bank at Monte Carlo, this is a tremendous piece of business for our club and is another big step along the way to our objective to become a major Super League contender.'

Skerrett felt the same way and in his 'Super Kel' column in the *Rugby Leaguer* said: 'Bradford Bulls pulled off what must be the deal of the century when they acquired three international-class players, plus a king's ransom, for a flagship player who wasn't even turning out.

'Saints must either be desperate for a centre, or have forwards coming out of their ears. Or maybe it's been done to show the fans that

*Looking on the bright side. Second row Paul Medley and coach Peter Fox share a joke.*

*Second row Roy Powell, a tackler almost impossible to bypass, denies Castleford prop Lee Crooks.*

*Bradford Northern, leading by example as the British game embraced the razzmatazz of Super League, changed their name to Bradford Bulls.*

*The new name quickly caught the imagination of younger supporters but older fans found the loss of the suffix 'Northern' – which had meant so much to the pioneers who had stood by the rugby cause when Bradford (Park Avenue) and Manningham switched to soccer – harder to swallow.*

*Bradford South MP Gerry Sutcliffe tabled an early day motion in the House of Commons aimed at persuading the Bradford board to rethink.*

*Sutcliffe, who had the support of Terry Rooney (Bradford North), Ian McCartney (Makerfield) and All Party Parliamentary Rugby League Group Secretary David Hinchliffe, the MP for Wakefield, said: 'We want the chairman and directors to reconsider their decision. We believe the decision is out of step with the wishes of the supporters and the wider community, who have not been consulted.'*

*Bradford Chairman Chris Caisley hit back: 'Gerry Sutcliffe would be better off spending his time pushing through the Super Dome project and getting Bradford back on its feet rather than worrying himself over our name'. Marketing executive Peter Deakin, meanwhile, pointed out that the company name remained Bradford Northern (1964) Ltd.*

they are willing and able to compete with Wigan.

'Have they paid too high a price to fetch Paul Newlove to Knowsley Road? They may have got a highly-rated player in Newlove, but they have severely weakened other areas in dispensing with the services of Sonny Nickle, Bernard Dwyer and Paul Loughlin as part of the deal.

'If I were a Saints fan I would be upset to see three good players and a fortune leaving the club, with just one player coming in; it's not as if St Helens have turfed out rubbish as part of the deal.

'On the other hand Brian Smith now appears to have one of the best jobs in Rugby League. In fact it may be THE best as he can build at Bradford and any success will be down to him.

'To have a good Premier League side, plus three top players, plus £250,000 – all before the Murdoch money arrives – represents good business. As I see it, it will now be difficult for Brian Smith to fail at Odsal.'

Smith, meanwhile, was pulling off another masterstroke by appointing teenager Robbie Paul as captain. Paul reflects: 'When I first came here the club seemed to be stuck in a rut. I didn't know a lot of what was going on in the background but since then I've found out that the Chairman Chris Caisley was a very busy

*Welsh winger Gerald Cordle. A wholehearted player whose commitment to the Bradford cause made a big impression on Chairman Chris Caisley.*

## Brian Smith
### interview (by Phil Hodgson, Rugby Leaguer)

*It turns out that he is the son of a farmer and the thought seemed to suddenly strike him that the lessons learned on the farm as a child may have influenced his coaching philosophy. 'Maybe it's had a bearing on my coaching style,' he mused. 'I never wanted to be a farmer myself but I watched my dad working his socks off, cultivating the land, sowing the seeds, and not expecting those seeds to grow into crops overnight. That upbringing probably taught me a lot, I think it must have influenced my attitude to Rugby League coaching.'*

*Compared favourably to predecessor Peter Fox as another coach whose teams appeared to be better than the sum of their parts, Smith said: 'It's a fair assessment of what I have tried to achieve. On top of that, one of the real values of a coach to a club is to leave it in a better position than when he took over. That is what I have done everywhere I have been – I have left my clubs in a strong position.'*

*Bulls fans can rest assured that, like his father, Brian Smith is sowing the seeds from which, given normal conditions, a rich harvest will most certainly grow.*

man. He was putting a structure in place and luckily I've become a part of that.

'It was a bit of a strange time in 1995–96, quite tough really, because every week there was a different team. So many players were coming and going as Brian Smith put his Super League squad together that we were constantly on our toes.

'At one training session I was asked if I wanted to be captain. I said yes.

'I was 19. I was a bit naïve really, you think you can take on so much. But it was a case of leading by example rather than saying anything, because every player in the club was a senior player to me. There was really nothing I could tell them about Rugby League so it was a matter of just getting out there and doing it.

'It was also a good marketing ploy. We were targeting children at the time and in a lot of respects I was still a kid myself so I was definitely someone that the younger supporter base could relate to.

'He must have also seen leadership qualities in me, and it worked out in the end. I learned a lot from the senior players that I had around me at the time, players like Graeme Bradley, and previously from such as Deryck Fox, Roy Powell – an amazing man – Neil Holding and Gerald Cordle, who really took me under his wing. He

taught me a lot about the ins and outs of life in England, about the culture. He made me streetwise.'

*Bernard Dwyer joined Northern, with Sonny Nickle and Paul Loughlin, as part of the record deal in which Paul Newlove moved to St Helens. Bradford had great service from the trio, particularly tireless tackler Dwyer.*

# 10.
# Embracing Super League

The advent of Super League in 1996, and the switch from winter to summer, was tailor-made for Bradford.

Odsal, a setting of bleak windswept frozen wastes between the beginning of December and the end of March, was likely to be a totally different prospect for matches played in June and July.

The possibilities were not lost on the board which, led by Chairman Chris Caisley, immediately recognised that a wonderful opportunity was there to be grasped.

Caisley remembers: 'We needed to have a whole new concept. We imagined that Super League was going to be all-singing, all-dancing, and real razzmatazz. Rupert Murdoch was coming and he would insist upon certain criteria as a result of putting his money in. So we thought well, we have to do something; if we wait for somebody else to do it for us, it would never happen.

'What we wanted to do was create an atmosphere in which, even if we lost, people had had a good day out.

'We devised the name Bradford Bulls, although we kept the company "Bradford Northern 1964 Limited" to retain the "Northern" name as a link with the past. We got a restaurant facility in there so that we could at last entertain people, and we set about changing the whole place.

'I recruited Brian Smith in Sydney and he sent Matthew Elliott over beforehand on a bit of a scouting mission.

'Appointing Brian Smith, getting him out of Australia, was a bit of a coup, although he had a bit of a culture shock when he arrived! But I sold him the dream of the all-singing all-dancing club

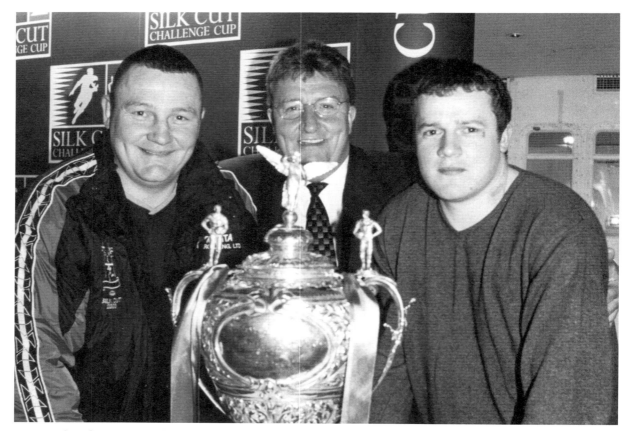

*Peter Deakin, the inspirational marketing guru behind the Bradford Bulls dream, pictured with family members Chris and Michael and the Challenge Cup.*

# A match to remember
## Challenge Cup Semi-Final

*Bradford Bulls 28 Leeds Rhinos 6*
*McAlpine Stadium, Huddersfield*
*23 March 1996*
*Bradford ended a 23-year Wembley absence with a thundering victory founded on a blistering opening in which three tries were scored in the first 12 minutes. To add extra lustre to the success, a couple of Headingley cast-offs had a central role in the assault, led by hat-trick winger Jonathan Scales.*
*Scales, extra to requirements at Leeds in the view of Rhinos coach Doug Laughton, crossed after second row Jeremy Donougher and scrum-half Robbie Paul had linked with hooker Jason Donohue and centre Paul Loughlin. Full-back Paul Cook (another discard) converted from the whitewash.*
*Paul and the incisive Loughlin set up Scales for his second score and the writing was on the wall for Leeds when centre Matt Calland, in his first outing after a three-month ban, raced over in the corner after supporting yet another Donougher break.*
*The Rhinos hit back with their only try, Francis*

*Cummins crossing off giant Kiwi Kevin Iro's pass, and added a Graham Holroyd penalty when Donohue was sin binned for holding down.*
*Paul had a 'try' ruled out for spilling the ball in a despairing tackle after having done all the hard work in a 50-metre attack, before Scales powered over for his third score, helped by Laughlin's astute pass.*
*A date with St Helens in north London was booked when Simon Knox popped up on the end of Calland's prompting ball, Cook wrapping an emphatic and historic win with his fourth goal of the afternoon.*

*Bradford: Cook; Christie, Calland, Loughlin, Scales; Bradley, Paul; McDermott, Donohue, Fairbank, Donougher, Nickle, Knox. Subs: Longo, Medley.*

*Leeds: A Gibbons; Fallon, Iro, Cummins, Hassan; Mann, Holroyd; Harman, Shaw, Howard, Morley, Field, Forshaw. Subs: Golden, Shultz.*

*Referee: Mr S Cummings (Widnes).*

that would put on entertainment. The motto that we had right the way through, which I insisted upon, was that anything we did had to be done properly, with style and to the best of our ability. Otherwise we wouldn't do it. The dance team, the pre-match entertainment, the food kiosks and everything else had to be good quality; sub-standard was not acceptable. I think that rubbed off on Brian who wouldn't accept anything less than he'd asked for; if that wasn't forthcoming, players wouldn't stay very long.

'We brought Peter Deakin in to sell the story for us. You can have the best plans in the world but if nobody knows about them you're wasting your time. We had to get the message across that the Bulls was the place to be when it came round to game day and Peter did that better than anybody else that I could ever imagine.

'That stemmed to a large degree from his

tremendous affection for the sport; and Peter would say that he'd learnt with us as well. The big thing about him was that he would talk to anybody and everybody and sell the story to them. The worst thing I used to hear about us before Super League was that we were unfashionable. Peter helped us to overcome that; we got rid of the negatives and became brand leaders on and off the field.

'We did pretty well in the sense that we got to the Challenge Cup final in 1996, the first year of Super League. That kick-started the process but the key was that we were good at getting the right people involved. In Peter Deakin, we got the right person. In Brian Smith, we got the right person. In Matthew Elliott, we got the right person.'

The Bulls also got the right people in Bernard Dwyer, Paul Loughlin and Sonny Nickle who,

*Second row Paul Medley on the rampage against Castleford.*

leading players all, were rather more than makeweights in the deal that sent Paul Newlove to St Helens. It was still a shock for the trio, however, as Dwyer revealed on the eve of the first Super League season. He lamented in the *Rugby Leaguer*: 'I went in to Saints on the Monday and signed for Bradford on the Tuesday. There was no warning at all.

'It wasn't a matter of wanting to go to Bradford. It was either "want" or that was it; we would have been playing A-team football at Saints.

> *Former Bradford prop Kelvin Skerrett, since transferred to Wigan, on the likely impact of summer rugby at Odsal: 'Bradford was the only team I ever felt happier playing away from home for.'*

'I only had a contract until June 1996; the other two had just signed new deals. I was told that if I didn't sign for Bradford I would not have a contract at Saints when it ran out.

'I'm St Helens born and bred, I thought I had been called in to sign a new contract, but it turned out to be something completely different. Saints had offered me a Super League contract the previous June and I'd turned that down because a lot of different things were happening at the time. I had a testimonial, and I

thought I could have got a better contract. As time passed the testimonial, which did very well for me, finished. I thought, "I don't want to leave Saints, I will sign the contract they offered me." When I went back they said it was no longer available. Little did I know, but all this had already been decided. The directors didn't even tell me then what was going to happen. It was a fortnight later that it all happened with Bradford.

'But you have to move forward. I am a Bradford player now and I'm going to give them 120 per cent and get on with the rest of my career. The way in which the move was done left a nasty taste in my mouth but I don't want to dwell on that side of things, at least I'm wanted somewhere.

'I don't think in the next 12 months we are going to be challenging for the Super League title. We will, though, make it very hard for teams to beat us.'

**Building**

The Bulls were spreading their casting net in all directions in the bid to build a side to challenge for the Championship, which was to be seen in the new era as the main prize, above the Challenge Cup. Classy loose forward Steve McNamara, signed from Hull, says: 'I was fortunate that I came to Odsal when I did, at the launch of Super League. It coincided with

*Former Odsal centre Paul Newlove, a huge signing from Bradford by St Helens, goes past the Bulls' Brian McDermott and Sonny Nickle (one of the three players who headed from Saints in part-exchange) in the 1996 Challenge Cup Final.*

# A legend remembers
## Robbie Paul

'Wembley in 1996 was my first appearance on a big stage and what a place for the experience. I've never seen any stadium like it; the only other ground with the same type of energy is the Millennium Stadium with the roof on. The way Wembley was created, so squat and flat, probably wouldn't be allowed these days. It just wouldn't pass safety rules.

'It was amazing when you walked out of the tunnel. The atmosphere physically touches you. I guess in my naivety it took me to another level. You have to have that type of belief in yourself because if you don't then you'll deliver well under par.

'I've always found that the greatest sportsmen in the world are the ones that have the most self-belief. You can go far outside your limitations if you ask your body; sometimes it's really happened for me and sometimes it hasn't.'

Northern changing to the Bulls and all the excitement surrounding that. Brian Smith, together with Peter Deakin, really changed a lot of things at the club.

'The overwhelming thing was the excitement from the fans and the way that the Odsal club was transformed from a "Northern flat cap" sort of thing to probably the most progressive club around. It was just fantastic; that groundswell of support dragged along the team. We put in some really good performances and started to win trophies.

'Brian Smith was really shrewd in his signings. We all had different strengths and weaknesses and we all complemented each other.

'I was brought in to help move the side around the park and be probably a little bit of a leader. It brought my strengths out and because of the fantastic athletes around me it made me look a better player; hopefully I helped make them look better players as well.'

Another key player was snapped up in the shape of hooker James Lowes from Leeds for an undisclosed fee. Phil Hodgson reported in the *Rugby Leaguer*: 'The former Hunslet star has joined the Bulls on a three-year contract, leaving the Rhinos stunned after having appeared to agree terms at Headingley only days earlier.

'The hard tackling Lowes has been the rock in

*Full back Nathan Graham was unfairly criticised after the Bulls' 1996 Challenge Cup Final defeat.*

what has sometimes been a weak Leeds defence in recent seasons and Smith is ecstatic at the acquisition of a man who can also call the shots in the middle of the park.

'Smith said: "Lowes caught my eye when I looked at videos of Bradford-Leeds games when I first came here, but I couldn't sign him. He nearly came to Odsal when we were working on Carl Hall's move to Leeds last year but Leeds weren't prepared to let him go. But then we found out that his contract was expiring at the end of January and we were delighted to do the business this time.

"'James is more than perhaps the best defender in the country. He has tremendous vision and, playing at hooker, he will handle the ball more than anyone else. I think he will improve everyone else's game at Odsal; in my opinion he is one of the most important ingredients we have added to the team. I have spoken to our current hookers, Bernard Dwyer and Jason Donohue, who would both prefer to play at hooker. I have told them that Lowes has

more ball talent around the ruck; but his ability to play in different positions is a big bonus."

'Leeds were taken by surprise. Football Manager Hugh McGahan said: "We are very disappointed. We thought we had sorted out a deal but if James wants to go to Bradford there is nothing we can do. We only want players who are committed to Leeds."

'Lowes, 26, revealed that a key factor in his decision was the chance to play at hooker on a permanent basis. He added: "I was very impressed by what Brian Smith had to say, and the contract's good!" He is, however, cup-tied and unable to take part in this season's Challenge Cup. "I had to think about that," he said. "But I wanted to get things done and I've sacrificed this season's Challenge Cup for the next."'

Paul Medley, meanwhile, jumped at the chance to go full time. 'When I first came to Bradford, coach Barry Seabourne said that he was going to play me in the centres. A week later, he packed in, so that threw things into a bit of turmoil. But I fitted in and when Super League took hold it became a 17-man game and that just suited me down to the ground really. The opportunity to go full time was fabulous. Somebody said that technically you had to take a pay cut to go full time but my reaction was, "where do I sign? You've saved me 40 hours a week working!"

'Later, coach Brian Smith called me in and said, "We're clearing the decks, getting rid of everybody that's been here before. Featherstone are in for you if you're interested in going." I said, "No, I want to stay here." He said, "I can't guarantee you a place," and I said, "I don't expect you to. I want to fight for my place." Smithy replied, "Good, that's what I wanted to hear, but you need to go full time. What are you earning at work, and what are you earning here?" I told him and he said, "Well, we can't afford to pay that. This is it, you're going to have to take a pay cut." I think it was about £8,000 but I just said, "Fine, where do I sign? I want to stay at this club." You could see things were

## Sonny Nickle

*interview (by Phil Hodgson, Rugby Leaguer,*
*1 April 1996)*

happening. It's not about money sometimes; it's about being a part of the place and a part of what's going on.

'The club had been good to me at the time when I needed them, in getting me away from Halifax. I felt I needed to repay a bit of that faith, accept the deal that they were giving me, and have a shot at this full time Rugby League thing.'

Northern legend Brian Noble was also brought on board. The former Great Britain hooker had earned plaudits for the quality of his captaincy on the 1984 tour to Australasia and he recalls how his return to Odsal owed something to the fluctuations of fate.

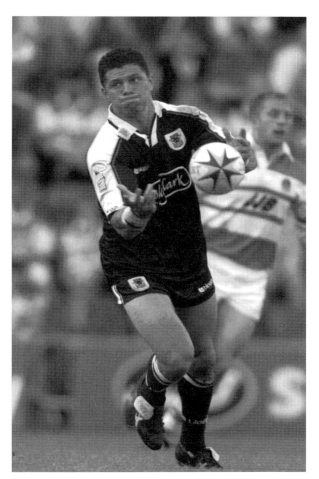

*New Zealand international Henry Paul, with brother Robbie, lit up the Odsal scene after his switch from Wigan. Paul, pictured in action against his former club, subsequently took the professional Rugby Union ticket.*

'Leafing through an old scrapbook the other day, some figures from the late Sixties stood out. On the same weekend, Bradford had played Featherstone, while Wigan had entertained Warrington. The crowd at Odsal in those heady Northern days was nearly 14,000; less than 7,000 turned up at Central Park. 'The feeling is that, with summer rugby upon us, a wind of change could be about to blow through the game. Odsal, dreadfully inhospitable in winter with the old stand gone, could become the place to be in the heat of June, July and August. And with Brian Smith's new side promising entertainment the equal of anywhere else, it's not too fanciful to imagine Bradford once again housing massive crowds, week-in, week-out.

'Sonny Nickle, first a Phoenix, then an Eagle, then a Saint, now a Bull, would enjoy that. And the fans, quickly taking him to their hearts, are certainly enjoying having the wholehearted grafter around in their rejuvenated side; a side which could be on the brink of great and sustained success.'

'My appointment as assistant coach under Brian Smith and Matthew Elliott came about through a chance meeting in the Odsal office. I'd agreed to join Steve Simms at Halifax and I came back to claim my boots. I bumped into Matthew Elliott who asked me what I was up to. I said I was going to Halifax as a part-time coach and he answered that if I was doing that, why not at Odsal? Matthew rang Brian Smith and said, "There's a bloke here, a policeman, who wants to be a part-time coach." Six months later I'd left the police with an injury and Bradford took me on full time – on a pittance I might add! But they still got me.

'It's a tough job, coaching. The first year I didn't know if I was punchdrunk or countersunk. I thought "I'll never get this" and I wondered if I'd made a huge mistake, but in the end it worked out for me. I kept working and I got better and better. Matthew, a lifelong friend, was very certain of it and he was very patient with me.

'Brian left earlier than we anticipated and Matty got the head coach's job and offered me the assistant's job. Four years after that Matty left, I put my hat into the frame, and the club thought I was ready.'

### 'Stats'

Bradford, meanwhile, were also ready to embrace new technology. Steve 'Stats' Fairhurst had already been centrally involved for a couple of years: 'John Simpson, who was coaching the Academy in 1994–95, let me do some statistics for him. We were entering the era in which statistical support was seen, more and more, as a valued coaching tool.

'I implemented video analysis, as well as statistical support, linked to individual performance tapes for players.

'Matthew Elliott gave me every support in the transitional 1995–96 season between winter and summer rugby. He was heavily involved in the build up to the first Super League season pending Brian Smith's arrival and he put in place a whole new approach to training and a whole new approach to technical support, involving technical advances in terms of the key skills and the core skills of the game. Matthew, obviously working to Brian Smith's template, was injecting that directly into the club.

'The players, including the senior lads, were very receptive. People like Jon Hamer got Indian summers and Karl Fairbank continued when he might not have done. Such as Simon

---

# A match to remember
## Challenge Cup Final

*Bradford Bulls 32 St Helens 40*
*Wembley Stadium*
*27 April 1996*
*The Bulls, back in the Challenge Cup Final for the first time since 1973, played a full part in a pulsating decider. Both the victors and the losers recorded the highest-ever points tally for a final, and the 13 tries scored in the soaring heat was also a new high.*
*Kiwi scrum-half Robbie Paul, at 20 years of age the youngest man to captain a Challenge Cup Final team, became the first player to score a hat-trick at Wembley. But it meant little as St Helens fought their way back from 26-12 down to lift the Cup with a superlative display of tactical kicking by Bobbie Goulding. The scrum-half peppered the Bradford defence with a series of telling bombs that helped garner five of the Saints' eight tries, including three in seven minutes early in the second half.*
*St Helens hooker Keiron Cunningham, Simon Booth and Ian Pickavance pounced for converted touchdowns which transformed the Bulls' 14-point lead into a four-point deficit.*
*St Helens added a try for winger Danny Arnold before Bradford clawed their way back into the frame with Paul's hat-trick score, a sensational 40-metre solo effort.*

*But the Saints sealed their win when Western Samoan prop Apollo Perelini crashed over six minutes from time. Paul's consolation was the Lance Todd Trophy, by 36 votes from 37, and a £10,000 cash prize for his hat-trick. But he admitted that he would have swapped the lot for a winner's medal.*
*Centre Paul Loughlin, a three-time Wembley loser with St Helens, was once again a forlorn figure while on the other side of the coin former Bradford centre Paul Newlove enjoyed his first experience of the winner's rostrum.*
*Bernard Dwyer and Jonathan Scales scored the Bulls' other tries, Paul Cook totalling six goals.*

*Bradford: Graham; Cook, Calland, Loughlin, Scales; Bradley, Paul; McDermott, Dwyer, Hamer, Donougher, Nickle, Knox. Subs: Medley, Fairbank, Hassan, Donohue.*

*St Helens: Prescott; Arnold, Gibbs, Newlove, Sullivan; Hammond, Goulding; Perelini, Cunningham, Leatham, Joynt, Booth, Northey. Subs: Martyn, Hunte, Matautia, Pickavance.*

*Referee: Mr S Cummings (Widnes).*

*Hooker James Lowes was a central figure in the Bulls' sustained successes in the first decade of Super League.*
*A passionate player signed from Leeds, he is pictured squaring up for the Headingley outfit against Bradford duo Karl*
*Fairbank and Paul Dixon.*

Knox and Jason Donohue and Tommy Hutchinson came in and were very coachable. So much so that perhaps we overachieved in that first year by reaching the Challenge Cup Final.

'A lot of our success stemmed from Brian Smith's and Matthew Elliott's attention to detail. They didn't leave any stone unturned. I hear stories now of people like Jose Mourinho setting new standards in analytical support for new players and I firmly believe they're no further on, other than in technology, than we were in '97–'98.'

That attention to detail came into play as the Challenge Cup Final against St Helens approached. Bradford's bid for a rule change floundered, however, when the Saints declined to play ball.

The Bulls campaigned to overturn the signings deadline, which excluded players registered after 2 January, with the aim of clearing scrum-half Glen Tomlinson and hooker James Lowes for Wembley.

Loose forward Steve McNamara, snapped up from Hull only a couple of weeks before the final, could also have come into contention.

St Helens would, by agreeing, have possibly opened the way for Aussie Derek McVey to feature but the prospect of Bradford benefiting by three players to one could have been a factor in their stance.

Saints Chief Executive David Howes said: 'Even if we had agreed it would have needed a council decision to change the byelaws'.

Bradford Chairman Chris Caisley said: 'McNamara was not part of the equation when the rule change was discussed. We were talking about us gaining two players and St Helens one. But I understand Saints' point of view and I don't have a problem with it. Our thinking was to put the best teams on the park for the benefit of spectators'.

**There but for the grace of God**

The Bulls slipped to defeat, largely through Saints scrum-half Bobbie Goulding's intelligent kicking game. Full-back Nathan Graham – unfairly criticised for his display – was interviewed three days later by Phil Hodgson for the *Rugby Leaguer*.

'If a prop forward spills a couple of passes; if a second row misses a tackle or two; or if a stand-off slices a kick to touch, the damage to that

135

player's side is not usually too serious.

'It's different for those on the edges, however. The winger who drops the ball with the line at his mercy can cost his side victory – and so can the full-back, cruelly exposed at the rear and subjected to criticism not only when things go wrong but also, sometimes, when they don't go quite as well as expected.

'Most people felt for Nathan Graham eight days ago. The Bradford No 1 was generally held to be at fault when the Bulls snatched defeat from the jaws of victory at Wembley and the former Dewsbury man cut a forlorn figure immediately after the final whistle.

'With hindsight each and every one of the 76,000 in the ground, not to mention the millions watching on TV, would have taken that first bomb on the full. In that first split-second, though, the ball looked as if it was going out, then it dipped alarmingly, then it took a cruel bounce; almost as if it had been sent down the wicket by the master leg-break bowler Shane Warne.

'Just as Mike Gatting was deceived by that famous, phenomenal delivery, so Nathan Graham was exposed by Goulding's rugby version of the googly. And anyone who has ever played at full-back, at any level, would have muttered to themselves "There but for the grace

of God go I".

'Many full-backs, aware as they might be of the golden rule – never allow the ball to bounce – will consider themselves fortunate that they weren't called upon to deal with that first Goulding bomb. And the feeling is growing that the two later tries could be pinned down as much to Graham's colleagues as to Graham himself.

'Speaking in the lull after the storm –

*Charismatic Australian winger Danny Peacock races over for a spectacular try in the 1997 Challenge Cup Final.*

interrupted in fact by the *Leaguer* while in the middle of a first viewing of the match video – Graham said: "I left that first bomb because I thought it was going out, either on the full or after a bounce. Unfortunately it didn't, and then it took a wicked bounce. And when I tried to jump for it, Keiron Cunningham had the momentum which helped him get there first."

'Saints were naturally going to kick again. Because they scored on each occasion Graham has carried the can for the next two tries, which might be a shade unfair. A number of defenders were under Goulding's second hoist and if Graham had been left to his own devices the chances are he would have taken it. And the third came down on a Bulls defence which seemed, at that stage, to be in a state of panic.

'Several judges have pinpointed the Bulls' tactic of harassing Goulding with three or four players as a factor which left Graham more exposed at the back. With a little more luck, however, it was a strategy that could have worked, as Graham himself insists: "One of Robbie Paul's tries, and Bernard Dwyer's score, came from us harassing Goulding. And Goulding's speciality is kicking to the corner, I didn't expect any pressure from him.

"'It was only the rugby papers, really, which read the game right. The rest tended to take the simplistic option of seeing three tries scored from kicks and blaming the full-back."

'If Graham could be blamed, nerves weren't a factor. He was the man who fielded each Saints kick off directly after each try, and he did it with aplomb. "I didn't feel nervous. I thought I would but when the match came around I reasoned that it was my big day and I should just enjoy it. And coach Brian Smith reckoned

that my first half display was one of the best offensive performances I've given him.'"

The Bulls, rated as fourth-favourites at 16-1 preseason by William Hill to secure the inaugural Super League title, fared rather better than that by finishing third and enjoyed a spell after the Challenge Cup Final defeat of 14 wins in 15 games.

Castleford, who won 26-23 at the Jungle, were the only side capable of halting the juggernaut before Halifax Blue Sox staged an upset with a 27-26 victory at Odsal. The sequence included a 50-22 demolition of St Helens, a 20-12 win over Wigan at Odsal before a mid-July 17,360 crowd and a 56-18 thrashing of Leeds at Headingley in which Robbie Paul (who topped the Bulls' try scoring list with 23 touchdowns from 28 appearances) scored a hat-trick and Paul Loughlin crossed twice.

**Reflections**
As the first Super League season of 1996 headed towards its close, marketing guru Peter Deakin reflected, in an interview with the *Rugby Leaguer* in late July 1996, on the first summer of Super League and the Bulls' success in embracing the concept.

That success was helped by a first appearance

| *1996: Stones European Super League Championship* | P | W | D | L | F | A | Pts |
|---|---|---|---|---|---|---|---|
| St Helens | 22 | 20 | 0 | 2 | 950 | 455 | 40 |
| Wigan | 22 | 19 | 1 | 2 | 902 | 326 | 39 |
| Bradford Bulls | 22 | 17 | 0 | 5 | 767 | 409 | 34 |
| London Broncos | 22 | 12 | 1 | 9 | 611 | 462 | 25 |
| Warrington | 22 | 12 | 0 | 10 | 569 | 565 | 24 |
| Halifax Blue Sox | 22 | 10 | 1 | 11 | 667 | 576 | 21 |
| Sheffield Eagles | 22 | 10 | 0 | 12 | 599 | 730 | 20 |
| Oldham Bears | 22 | 9 | 1 | 12 | 473 | 681 | 19 |
| Castleford Tigers | 22 | 9 | 0 | 13 | 548 | 599 | 18 |
| Leeds | 22 | 6 | 0 | 16 | 555 | 745 | 12 |
| Paris St Germain | 22 | 3 | 1 | 18 | 398 | 795 | 7 |
| Workington Town | 22 | 2 | 1 | 19 | 325 | 1021 | 5 |

*Matthew Elliott, a thoughtful coach who maintained the Super League progress instigated by his fellow Australian Brian Smith.*

*Brian Smith oversaw a nine-try, 50-22 win over St Helens – and then announced that he was leaving at the end of the season after agreeing a two-year contract with Parramatta.*

*Chairman Chris Caisley said: 'It's a very sad occasion for Bradford but we are positive at this club and I firmly believe our success will continue after Brian's departure.*

*'We will become the biggest name in this country and we will have a damned good try to be the best club in world rugby.*

*'It has been a very amicable parting of the ways. We understand Brian's position and he understands our position. Life goes on and it will be a good life at Odsal.'*

*Smith admitted: 'I am an Australian and that is where my heart is. I had no intention of anything like this happening, but it is an opportunity which I cannot turn down. The past 12 months have been the most exciting of my career and leaving a club with the potential of Bradford is disappointing. But I am excited by the prospect of being the head coach of a club with the potential of Parramatta. Money had nothing to do with this deal. It was an opportunity that might never come my way again.'*

in a Challenge Cup final for 23 years but Deakin insisted: 'What a lot of people forget, especially now we have won 11 of our last 12 games, is that apart from our semi-final win over Leeds we won just two of our previous eight matches up to the end of April.

'We went into Super League and beat Castleford and London but lost to Sheffield, St Helens and Wigan. So we came back to Odsal the week after Wembley on the back of four consecutive defeats; yet we had a 9,000 crowd for the visit of Warrington.

'You can't put everything down to Wembley. My analogy is with a racing car. The team is the engine, but it won't work without the other little parts; the marketing operation, the fans, and the vision of the club itself are all important.

'It helps to have Damon Hill behind the wheel and we have our Damon Hill here in Chris Caisley. But it's got to be a team effort if any success is to be achieved.

'We try to pack a whole host of events into the

*Matthew Elliott, 31, was appointed as head coach on a two-year contract to replace the departing Brian Smith.*

*Elliott stepped up from the role of Smith's assistant and Chairman Chris Caisley said: 'It would have been easy for us to bring in big names from overseas – a lot of people with outstanding CVs had approached us.*

*'But we had no doubt that Matthew was the man for us. We are in the early stages of creating a dynasty here at Bradford and we are keen to continue the forward momentum commenced by Brian Smith. His philosophy about playing the game had to be continued and the board felt that Matthew's appointment would continue that trend.'*

*The Bulls celebrated the appointment by winning 56-18 at Headingley; Leeds' biggest ever home defeat. Brian Smith lauded prop Brian McDermott and full-back Stuart Spruce and pushed their claims for Great Britain selection, enthusing: 'Brian's workload is tremendous and the quality of that work is outstanding. As for Spruce, if there's a better player in his position in the country then Phil Larder is looking for different things in a full-back than I am. He's not had a bad game since he joined us.'*

*Chief scout Eric Hawley, credited with enticing a host of talent to Odsal.*

game-day, with the match the highlight. While a winning team will always be significant, we are trying to achieve an overall philosophy at Odsal.

'Of course we want to win, but we want to do it in style. And if we happen to lose, we want to do that in style too.

'We are not overconfident. We know that at some time in the future – it may be in two months, in six months or in three years, but it will happen – we will hit a losing sequence. We want to make sure that everything here is so good, that everybody is having such a good time, that they will want to come anyway. That's the key.'

He added: 'Rather than sit back and almost apologise for playing on a summer Sunday, we said to our fans from the outset: "All games will kick off at 6pm. Make sure you plan around us. If you've got to go to the pub or do the garden or

visit your granny do it – but be sure you are at Odsal for 4pm.

'We now have a lot of people coming two hours before kick off. We have everything to entertain them, from crafts to jugglers to face painting. We have a resident DJ, quality cheerleaders, the lot.

'We believe you should do it properly or not at all. I have nothing but total excitement for the game and the whole thing can be encapsulated in a three-letter word: FUN.

'I had what almost amounted to hate mail after we'd introduced the changes, with some people saying they didn't need the music and the razzmatazz. To be fair, some have since put their hands up and said what a fabulous day out it is at Odsal now. Many blokes, instead of coming on their own or with their mates, are now fetching the wife and kids.'

Deakin was keen to deflect praise for the Bradford boom to what he fervently believed was its rightful place. He said: 'The strategist is Chris Caisley. My function is the marketing; I am the implementer.

'It's no good having good thinkers and people

# A match to remember
## Challenge Cup Final

*Bradford Northern 22 St Helens 32*
*Wembley*
*3 May 1997*
*Northern's immediate return to Wembley resulted in another defeat at the hands of the Saints who, on this occasion, fought back from 10-4 down midway through the first half to finish comfortable winners. Bradford had few problems in the early stages, thrilling their supporters in the capacity 78,022 crowd by responding to an early try by Lance Todd winner Tommy Martyn with a touchdown fit to grace any final. Loose forward Steve McNamara set the scene with a smart ball to second row Sonny Nickle who charged from half way to send centre Danny Peacock down the touchline and in at the corner.*
*That score was followed by an interception touchdown for centre Paul Loughlin, McNamara converting, but Bradford were on the back foot by the break, through tries for Saints' duo Martyn and Karle Hammond, who atoned for the pass that led to Loughlin's effort by crashing through a posse of defenders.*
*Bobbie Goulding added both goals, passing the '1,000 points in a career' mark in the process, and St Helens were in control when Martyn sent Chris Joynt over and then fired the kick for a controversial touchdown to winger Anthony Sullivan who was subsequently shown to have not grounded the ball properly.*
*Bradford hit back with a try for Glen Tomlinson, courtesy of James Lowes' precision kick, and a late try for Lowes himself who burrowed over to give McNamara the chance to kick his third goal. But the latter score came too late to affect the outcome, Goulding's five goals having put the Saints beyond reach.*

*Bradford: Spruce; Ekoku, Peacock, Loughlin, Cook; Bradley, Paul; McDermott, Lowes, Reihana, Nickle, Dwyer, McNamara. Subs: Medley, Calland, Tomlinson, Knox.*

*St Helens: Prescott; Arnold, Haigh, Newlove, Sullivan; Martyn, Goulding; Perelini, Cunningham, O'Neill, Joynt, McVey, Hammond. Subs: Pickavance, Matautia, Northey, Morley.*

*Referee: Mr S Cummings (Widnes).*

with vision unless you've got it at senior management level – that's crucial. We have done a lot of work, and Odsal lends itself perfectly to summer rugby and the Super League. To use Maurice Lindsay's quote: you ain't seen nothing yet!'

**In League with the Union**
Robbie Paul, voted the 1996 Super League Player of the Season at 20 years of age, went into his winter loan spell with the Harlequins Rugby Union team aiming to improve his game.

The Kiwi half-back, who had agreed a £250,000 deal which would keep him at Odsal until the year 2000, planned to focus on his kicking and said: 'I don't want to leave Harlequins in January the same player I joined them. I want to return to Odsal a better player.

'I will be able to learn from them. The kicking game in Union is so strong. It might not be so attractive for the fans but I'd like to polish up on that aspect of my play. I'm sure I can pick up a few tips from the Harlequins players.'

The agreement between the Bulls and the London-based Union club which allowed Paul to head south also offered Bradford first option for the 1997 season on any possible converts to Rugby League. Said Paul: 'I could emerge as Bradford's biggest scout. I will take a good look at the players and if any want to play League I'll tell them about it. But that's not the reason I'm joining Harlequins.'

Said Chris Caisley: 'Robbie Paul will show the Rugby Union world how to play rugby and will help to raise the profile of the Bradford Bulls wherever he plays.'

Less than a month later, Caisley was reacting angrily to a bid by Harlequins to sign Paul on a permanent basis after the expiry of his loan period. He insisted: 'Even if they bid £2 million, we would turn it down. Robbie is not for sale.'

Caisley also had harsh words for Harlequins director of football, Dick Best. He said: 'We allowed Robbie to play Union on a short-term basis as a favour and it ill befits someone in

*Graeme Bradley, an abrasive captain whose commitment to the cause was beyond question. The Aussie's forthright comments regularly got him into trouble with the authorities.*

# Phil Hodgson
### *Rugby Leaguer 12 May 1997*

'Robbie Paul had been in great pain when I glimpsed him, alone and forlorn, clutching a stanchion for support in the Wembley tunnel.

'That pain had not eased minutes later, when he had been helped into the Wembley press conference by Peter Deakin and Matthew Elliott. "It's the foot, the whole foot and nothing but the foot," he told the assembled hacks. "We do a lot of strange little things to our bodies. We've got to take the knocks and the bumps, and a lot of the time it's a mental thing. You can push through the pain barrier. When you pick the ball up you get a shot of adrenaline and you can't feel any pain at all. If someone's running at you, you get another shot of adrenaline. It's just those moments in between when you feel the pain."

'Which was hurting most: the foot or the defeat?

"They are different types of pain. The foot is a physical pain, the defeat is an emotional pain. It's hard to say which is the greater, but I would say the emotional.

"I'm hungrier than ever, now, after two defeats at Wembley. I want to come back and put it right, but that's for next year."'

Best's position to mouth off to the press about the permanent capture of the best player in Rugby League.

'If Best put all his energy into decent coaching and bringing through some of his own players, they might not have to pay exorbitant sums for Rugby League stars.'

Best said of Paul: 'He is fantastic. He gets right up into the tacklers' faces and then waltzes away. He ran rings around the Swansea centres in the Anglo-Welsh Cup match – and he was not playing against monkeys.'

Paul, meanwhile, categorically denied telling the *Mail on Sunday* that Rugby Union was a better game than Rugby League.

Insisting that he had been 'quoted out of context' Paul, who confirmed that he would be returning to Odsal when his winter contract with

# A legend remembers
## Steve McNamara

*'Wembley 1997 has to be the highlight of my playing career. We got beat but I think it's everybody's boyhood dream to play in the Challenge Cup final. We'd been there the year before but Glen Tomlinson, James Lowes and I were cup-tied so we missed out on that great occasion.*

*'Although the result and our performance was disappointing, getting the chance to be there with a wonderful club like Bradford was fantastic. Obviously we won the championship that year as well, I think we went 20-odd games unbeaten at the start before missing out in the last two matches, and that was up there along with the Challenge Cup.*

Harlequins expired, said: 'I am a Rugby League player. I have always been a Rugby League player and I would never say anything against a game which has made me what I am today.

'The *Mail* reporter wanted to know how I was going on in Union and I told him. He took from the interview what he wanted. The question of which was the better code was never put to me.

'I can't say which is the better game because I have not been playing Union long enough to compare them in this way. I am not going to say a bad word about either sport. In League, you get the ball more and my only problems in Union have been technical; four months is not long enough to learn about the game.'

Paul admitted to having said that League is defence-orientated in comparison to Union and added: 'I did not say that is a bad thing. League is physically harder but that is not a problem either.'

Back in Rugby League after his sabbatical in the 15-a-side code, the Kiwi played his part as the Bulls eased through the early rounds of the Challenge Cup to book a semi-final tie with Leeds to confirm that Bradford would remain a force under new coach Matthew Elliott.

Elliott, in preparing for the 1997 season, had said: 'People say I'm on a hiding to nothing and that it could be the house that Brian built which Matthew knocked down, but that doesn't worry me.

'I've been wanting to coach a top team for a long time. I'm 31, my playing career was cut short by injury but with a little good management and some luck I now find myself in the hot seat at Bradford. I'm sure I've made the right decision and I'm confident in my own ability.'

Repeating the previous year's third-place finish was not going to be good enough for the new boss who added: 'It was a fantastic achievement when you consider where we came from but my chairman and my players are not content. I arrived at Odsal on July 13 1995 and if you look at our style of play then, you will see it has developed. That won't change much but the philosophy will. I'm different to Brian Smith, whose background and experiences are different from mine. There will be some change, we need to tweak a few aspects.'

Tweak them they did, as Bradford secured the championship for the first time since 1980–81.

**Ban**

The Bulls beat Leeds Rhinos 24-10 in a physical Challenge Cup semi-final. Director of referees Greg McCallum said he was concerned over three incidents and would be studying the match video. Bradford prop Brian McDermott single-handedly floored three players – Terry Newton, Damian Gibson and Martin Masella – in a rousing cameo five minutes from the end which earned him a four-match suspension by the RFL.

Chris Caisley had strong words when the Disciplinary Committee refused to reduce the ban, sidelining the prop until the Challenge Cup Final.

St Helens had already called for a soccer-style points system aimed at introducing consistency to sanctions and Caisley said: 'We support them.

I can't see any argument against a reduction in Brian McDermott's ban. There should be no discretion in the imposition of a sentence.

'The Disciplinary Committee's discretion is far too wide ranging. They treat punching with greater severity than a high tackle which, along with the use of the elbow, is the most serious offence a player can commit.'

He added: 'Leeds' Barrie McDermott received three matches for a high tackle – with a previous five match ban behind him – while our Brian McDermott is handed a four-match ban when all he has behind him is a one-match suspension for an offence while playing for the Alliance side.

'The committee says he wasn't provoked in his attack. Surely everyone can see the incident which provoked him if they look at the TV replay? He let his temper get the better of him and there is no excuse for his behaviour. But there appears to be little fairness in the matter.'

McDermott had served his sentence by the time the final came around but his return couldn't lift the side beyond a 32-22 defeat. A little-known factor helped scuttle the Bulls' hopes that day, as Paul Medley relates. The packman, who had won the Man of the Match award in the semi-final, was looking forward to the greatest day of his career. It turned out to be the worst.

'We'd all been measured up for our playing kit, which we wore tight-fitting to make it harder for opponents to tackle us. When it came through the shirts were too tight, so the club got onto the suppliers and it went back; fair enough.

'Our opponents, St Helens, won the right for choice of colour and they wouldn't budge, which again was fair enough.

'That meant we had to order predominantly amber shirts from the original manufacturer. No problem; there was plenty of time.

'When I was getting stripped at Wembley, ready for the biggest occasion of my career, I got a real shock. I couldn't get my shirt on properly. And neither could most of the other players,

## A match to remember
### Super League

*Sheffield Eagles 12 Bradford Bulls 32*
*Don Valley Stadium, Sheffield*
*17 August 1997*
*Bradford won the championship for the first time since 1981, and became the first Yorkshire side to finish top of the table for 11 years, after battling back from a six-point deficit at half time to win 32-12 at Sheffield Eagles.*
*A 10,500 crowd, a record at Sheffield, witnessed the Bulls batter the Eagles into submission in the second period with tries by Bernard Dwyer, Mike Forshaw, James Lowes and Jeff Wittenberg, with Steve McNamara adding six goals.*
*It had all been so very different in the first 40 minutes when Bradford had been limited to a try for Danny Peacock. Coach Matthew Elliott said: 'My mind had turned to jelly! The scoreline really did flatter us but I will take the victory. I am very humbled when I think about how much work has gone into this.'*
*James Lowes said: 'The Eagles made it very difficult for us and we had to be at our best, which is just how it should be when a trophy is at stake.*
*'Sheffield owed it to the rest of the league to give it their best shot and nobody can accuse them of not doing just that.*
*'At 10-4 up they looked in a strong position but we were never over-worried. We have a tendency to finish strongly and that's how it proved on this occasion.'*

*Sheffield: Sovatabua; Pinkney, Morganson, Taewa, Crowther; Mycoe, Aston; Broadbent, Vassilakopoulos, Thompson, Senior, McAllister, Doyle. Subs: Gacia, Laughton, Wright, Erba.*

*Bradford: Spruce; Ekoku, Loughlin, D Peacock, Scales; Bradley, R Paul; Wittenberg, Lowes, McDermott, Donougher, Nickle, McNamara. Subs: Tomlinson, Forshaw, Dwyer, Reihana.*

*Referee: Mr S Ganson (St Helens).*

including Glen Tomlinson. The suppliers had worked to their original – wrong – measurements.

'My shirt was so small I was unable to wear my shoulder pads and I had to cut away some of the fabric under the armpits.

'Even that didn't get rid of the problem. The shirt was so tight across my chest that I couldn't breath, it was terrible. Our coach Matthew Elliott asked me what was wrong but I just couldn't cope, I was all over the place.

'I had to come off. It was dreadful, the biggest day of my career had been turned into the worst. I was so devastated I couldn't go to the post-match party that night. I just went up to my hotel room at 8 o'clock that night with my kids. In fact I retired as a player there and then. But I was picked for the A team – ironically at St Helens – the following Thursday. I agreed to play and although – maybe because – there were a few boos and jeers I got my appetite back and kept on going. But Wembley, instead of being the dream come true I'd hoped for, was a nightmare.'

The Bulls, in 1996, ended Wigan's 12-year reign as the best-supported side in the game with an average attendance of 10,346, ahead of the Central Park club's 10,152. Bradford eased further in front in 1997, a massive 46 per cent increase – following a 12.5 per cent hoist the previous year – resulting in a total of 166,793 easing through the Odsal turnstiles to produce an average home crowd of 15,163. Wigan's average had dipped over four years from 14,561.

Bradford Marketing Executive Peter Deakin had said in 1996: 'At the beginning of the year our aim was to hit 8,000 so we are delighted to have ended with what was going to be our second year target.' And Chairman Chris Caisley had added: 'I think it's not unreasonable to expect over 10,000 for every game soon, and our long term aim is to average over 15,000.'

There were no excuses, as far as James Lowes was concerned, when the Bulls lost 30-10 at home to Cronulla in the 1997 World Club Championship, visiting winger Mat Rogers

*Darrall Shelford, a motivated second row forward who joined the Bulls' development team.*

scoring a hat-trick. He said: 'Cronulla are a very good team. They were well-drilled, and they got what they deserved. Unfortunately, so did we.

'It's now back to the welcome distraction of the Super League programme. There's no doubt that the plate's piled high to the point of everybody being outfaced. The Bulls for example face four games in 10 days before we travel Down Under for the second leg of the World competition.

'No doubt our Australian opponents will have played only two matches in the same spell; and we'll be nice and fresh as well, I don't think.

'It's crazy, to say the least. Our domestic fixture programme needs sorting out.'

Lowes was, however, delighted if not surprised to discover that British fans are far more vocal than their counterparts Down Under. While with the Bulls for the return trip for the World Club Championship, he took in an

'There has been some comment about my reaction after coming off against London Broncos.
'I have to admit it – sometimes my mouth does a bit of wandering. It's not something I'm happy about, in fact it's something I'm actively trying to control. But it seems to happen in the heat of the moment. On reflection it seems to be my way of letting off steam, and maybe it comes out of frustration as much as anything else.
'At the end of the day, people can read more into these incidents than is perhaps needed. Certainly, as far as I'm concerned, everything is forgotten after the game, at least by me.
'It just seems to be part of my make up. As I say, I'm trying to control it. But the last thing I want is for anybody to take personal offence.'
*James Lowes in his Rugby Leaguer column 'Lowe Down' (September 1997).*

*Lowes was sent off for foul and abusive comments to referee Stuart Cummings in the home defeat by Wigan in June 1998. The hooker lost his composure when Denis Betts was allowed to tackle him despite not standing square at a play-the-ball. Coach Matthew Elliott said: 'James shouldn't have called the referee but I don't think he deserved to be sent off.'*

*No-nonsense prop Brian McDermott relished the task of making the hard yards. There's no way through this time against Warrington, as Mike Forshaw looks on.*

# A legend remembers
## Paul Medley

*'To win the title in 1997 was the pinnacle of my career. I'd been in a lot of finals and lost, but to actually win a championship was a great thing.*
*'We came back here to Odsal to play Paris and paraded the trophy round the field. The atmosphere was unbelievable. I've played in front of big crowds, but there's just this friendly community spirit and atmosphere round here. That's why the timing was special for me, because the supporters were not so fickle, they were genuine supporters and they just loved the place.'*
*The Bulls had been crowned Super League champions in front of an ecstatic 17,128 crowd after routing Paris St Germain 68-0. The 14-try thrashing kept unbeaten Bradford on course for an unprecedented clean sweep which was thwarted by defeats in the last two games, at home to Wigan and at London Broncos.*

Aussie game or two and revealed in his column in the *Rugby Leaguer*: 'I went to watch Manly play Parramatta, when there were 22,000 fans packed into a smallish stadium. If I'd closed my eyes I could have imagined I'd been on my own, it was that quiet.

'The hundreds of Bradford fans who made the trip made us all aware of their presence – they were the only ones singing. They deserve a big rap from everyone at Odsal.'

## Championship

The hooker was able to write, after Bradford had clinched the Super League title: 'The people I feel happiest for are the fans. They've been tremendous all season and they were just the same at Don Valley. Eight thousand made the trip down from Bradford and they were unbelievable, it was just like being at home.

'The championship is just as much for them as for the players. It's a big boost for the fans and for the city. I suspect, though, that the hard work

is about to begin. People will be trying to knock us off our pedestal but everyone at Odsal is relishing the challenge.'

That included Bernard Dwyer, Sonny Nickle and Paul Loughlin who, 21 months after having switched from Knowsley Road to Odsal, were delighted to be interviewed on their title win.

The *Rugby Leaguer's* Phil Hodgson wrote: 'When the record-breaking transfer of Paul Newlove from Bradford to St Helens was completed, the 'makeweights' in the deal did not seem to be particularly happy chappies.

'What a difference 21 months has made for Bernard Dwyer, Sonny Nickle and Paul Loughlin.

'The Bulls might not have gone through the season unbeaten, as hoped, but the Championship is safely on the Odsal sideboard, the St Helens-based trio are on top of the Rugby League tree, and all in the bullring is lovely.

'Asked how they had felt when being told they were going to Bradford, Dwyer admitted to having been "gutted" while Loughlin looked away soulfully and made no reply. Nickle said: "I

# Chris Caisley

*'Bernard Dwyer was brilliant. One of the final games, if not the very last, he played for us was away at Hull. He'd had a bicep injury, a significant tear, and he'd come back from that in that match. He then did his other one and there he was, at the Boulevard, unable to raise his arms. But he stayed on the pitch – he just wouldn't come off. What a fantastic player, unbelievable.*
*'Dwyer and Paul Loughlin were great for us. Sonny Nickle, who was the one Brian Smith really wanted out of the deal, was maybe a bit of a disappointment, I think he would agree that he didn't play his best rugby at Bradford. But the other lads, plus the money that we got from St Helens, enabled us to recruit a squad for Super League. We recruited something like 23 players in the close season and we got rid of probably as many. It was that big a transformation.'*

was a bit surprised but I took the view that I was doing the same job in a different coloured shirt."

'And on their feelings now, Dwyer said: "It's worked out, I've never been happier in my life." Nickle reflected: "The move turned out to be the right one," and Loughlin said: "Winning the championship is probably the proudest moment, bar none, of my career."

'Nickle first began to realise that the move may not have been such a bad one after all when the Bulls set about signing a few other players. "I could see that the squad was being strengthened and team spirit started to become really good. All the preparation was right and I started to believe that something big was going to happen."

'Dwyer said: "Things started to come together at the beginning of the first Super League season. It was clear that everything was falling into place, and that's when it began to dawn that coming here could become a really positive step."

'Loughlin reflected: "When the milk started to go chocolatey."'

Things didn't go quite as chocolatey for Great Britain half back Shaun Edwards who left the Bulls in June 1998, only eight months after moving to Odsal from London Broncos. The background to the 31-year-old's departure remained shrouded in mystery, although the former Great Britain captain was described as a 'bad apple' by Bulls skipper Graeme Bradley. Edwards, who returned to London, was a central figure as the Broncos beat Bradford 22-8 at Heart of Midlothian's Tynecastle ground three weeks later in a Super League 'on the road' clash. Chris Caisley had said, the previous October: 'We want to be the number one club in World rugby and the signing of Shaun Edwards, the best half-back in the British game, will help us do just that'.

Bradford, however, were continuing to attract quality. Balmain centre Michael Withers was the hero as his side held Brisbane Broncos to a 10-10 draw and then the villain as he revealed he had agreed a two-year deal with Bradford Bulls

*Former Bradford and Great Britain second row Roy Powell collapsed and died at training with Rochdale Hornets.*
*Powell, who was walking towards the session with old friend and Hornets coach Deryck Fox, was singing 'I Feel Good' when the incident happened.*
*Said Chairman Ray Taylor: 'He suddenly collapsed onto his knees, with Deryck saying, "I know you have a bad back, Roy, but come on," and after he had struggled to his feet he just keeled over on his face.*
*'Mick Coult, our close season signing from Hunslet who is a fireman, gave him mouth to mouth and heart resuscitation but he was dead on arrival at Rochdale Hospital.'*

from 1999. 'It appeals to me as the chance to travel and should be a great experience,' he said.

Elliott, meanwhile, added centre Nathan McAvoy and prop Neil Harmon to his squad and vowed: 'If Nathan doesn't end up being the best centre in this country then it won't be my fault. I would never have paid the money for him if I didn't believe what he could achieve for Bradford. He is a young and exciting player with the potential to be a great player.'

McAvoy, 21, had joined the Bulls from Salford for a reported £140,000 in a three-year deal. Harmon, 28, had switched from Huddersfield Giants on a 30-month contract.

Added Elliott: 'They are two deliberate recruits. I have been working on both signings for the past two months and their arrival is not just a knee jerk reaction to events of the past few weeks.

'The recruitment is the start of our enhancement of the squad and, over the next few months, there will be other players to join them'.

# 11.
# On Centre Stage

After a relative lull in 1998, Bradford entered a period of heady success from 1999 to 2001.

The Bulls, under coach Matthew Elliott and then Brian Noble, embarked on a new era with a style of enterprising play founded on the impact of a heavyweight pack. Established with Leeds, St Helens and Wigan as one of the 'big four', Bradford were cemented as a firm favourite for major honours. The success, moreover, was earned through a strong team spirit which permeated the entire club – as Stuart Duffy, Media Manager from 1998, relates.

*The Bradford Bulls logo, launched in 1996, encapsulated the new era of Super League. The change of name from 'Northern' met with initial resistance; by 1999, all but the diehards had succumbed.*

'It was a tough decision to come to Bradford. I'd been a Leeds fan all my life and it was a dream come true when I got the job at Headingley.

'Things, however, weren't working out particularly well at Leeds and I got the call from Gary Tasker asking if I'd like to work for Bradford Bulls. Peter Deakin had been gone for about a year and I think the club felt that they weren't getting the exposure in the media that they deserved.

'Within five minutes of the interview I knew that if they offered me the job I'd take it. It was the best thing I ever did. Every player that's played at Bradford Bulls will tell you this is the best club they've been at because of the way that they're treated by the Board, by the coaching staff and by the other staff.

'The way that this club was run in the early days of Super League set the standard for every other club, with a very supportive chairman, great coaching staff, and players who are all aware of their responsibilities to the media and to the game. That makes the media manager's role very easy.'

Bradford Bulls were also underpinned by the results of an early and pro-active decision to link the euphoria over Super League to a strong development drive.

Steve Fairhurst, a volunteer schools Rugby League worker in the city, was one of the enthusiasts who joined a Bulls outfit who fully appreciated the value and importance of supporting the grass roots and the community.

Fairhurst, with Andy Harland, was involved with Bradford Schools Under-11s' appearance in the curtain-raiser to the 1995 Challenge Cup final at Wembley. And training sessions before the event with Northern stars such as Roy Powell, Neil Summers and Jon Hamer led to many of those youngsters remaining in the sport into adulthood.

The Bulls were, and remain, focussed on the wider development of children and a development team was formed which visited

*The Bullettes, Bradford's cheerleaders. The advent of Super League brought a touch of glamour to Rugby League. The wheel had, however, come full circle at Odsal where the concept had been introduced to the sport four decades earlier.*

schools in the area, working alongside teachers to help improve standards of literacy and numeracy through the National Curriculum.

A booklet – *Bullman and the Mystery of the Missing Boot* – was a huge success during the Bradford Year of Literacy in 1997–1998 when reading standards among children throughout the city improved significantly.

Bradford Bulls, with a policy of offering match-day packages through schools, also helped regenerate youth interest in the game, from both playing and spectating perspectives.

Says Fairhurst: 'Although Bradford is traditionally a strong Rugby League city it wasn't at that time a place that you could say was steeped in development tradition. There weren't a lot of Bradford players around, especially at Under-11s and Under-12s. Ten years later, after nearly a decade of in-your-face Super League development, there's a total contrast.'

Brian Noble, too, appreciates the value of proactive development. The man who guided Bradford to four trophies in 2003–04 says: 'Some principles of rugby don't change and I've always managed to pick something off everybody I've played under or with; I've an element of all of them in me. Barry Seabourne taught me a lot, and Peter Fox certainly did. My first two Colts coaches, Garth Budge and Mick McGowan, were brilliant. Mick McGowan sorted my life out really because I was bit of a firebrand. He made us play in every position; sometimes he'd stick me at full-back, say, and I'd think "What am I doing here?" but you do get an appreciation of what everybody else has to do.

'Mick was the forerunner of modern-day coaches, his depth and understanding of the game was terrific. He changed my life in rugby terms, he made me realise that there's a lot more to the game than just turning up and firing yourself out of a gun. Rugby League is a very technical game and I certainly started picking things up then. I didn't know it at the time, but people make impressions on you – and Mick made a massive one on me.'

*Mr and Mrs Walter Paul, parents of Henry and Robbie, were delighted by the news early in 1999 that Henry had joined his brother at Odsal.*
*Robbie confided: 'Mum has never liked the idea of us playing against each other, and dad's pleased because he only has to watch one match now instead of two. Rugby League is a business for us, however, and Henry came to the Bulls because it was a good career move for him.*
*'At the end of our contracts we would still go separate ways if that was in the best interests of our families.'*

Hooker James Lowes also made an impression and was at his inspirational best as the Bulls carved out a 22-14 victory at a cold and wet Warrington in April 1999.

The hooker created two of Bradford's four tries and his running and creativity from dummy half posed persistent problems for the Wolves.

Noble enthused: 'When Lowes is in this form he is up there with the best players in the world. He led from the front and made the right decisions at the right times'.

### Fish and chips?
As did Trevor Foster who, 61 years after having left south Wales for Odsal, was honoured by his adopted city. Foster, who had been expecting a family fish and chip supper at Harry Ramsden's, was instead presented with a Lifetime Achievement Award by the Lord Mayor,

*New skipper Robbie Paul promised 'peace and goodwill' in 1999 to all referees.*
*Paul had taken over from Australian Graeme Bradley, who had had a stormy relationship with match officials culminating in his controversial dismissal by Stuart Cummings in the last match of his career. Said Robbie Paul: 'I hope to be on good terms with referees and give them a better time than perhaps they have had in the past. I've never seen a referee change his decision for a player. I can't see the point in arguing with them.'*

# Phil Hodgson

*interview (Rugby Leaguer 5 July 1999)*

'As a veteran of an era of constant change, James Lowes is well placed to provide an insight into why so many matches in Super League between top sides made up of full time professionals become one-sided affairs. He pinpoints the advent of summer rugby, and midweek matches, as the cause. 'The game is also faster,' he says, 'although I don't think it's any more physical than when I first played. I think the warmer weather and the firmer grounds help teams get on top more, and I believe that tackling techniques have improved with full-time professionalism. In some ways it's hard to put your finger on why we get these big scorelines, for example St Helens and Leeds flogged us but we then beat Saints easily. But midweek games definitely take their toll now. A side which hasn't had a midweek game and is a bit fresher has the chance to turn over the opposition and usually takes it. You can't play three games in a week any more, the body just can't take it in summer and with the pace of the current game.'

Councillor Tony Miller. The first person to be so recognised, Foster was given his award at a surprise presentation at the Bradford City Banqueting Hall in April 1999.

The former second-row forward would have been delighted by the emergence at Odsal of youngster Stuart Fielden. Bradford, despite lacking the Paul brothers, who were representing New Zealand in the Anzac Test against Australia, denied Halifax a hat-trick of victories with a 20-2 win at Odsal highlighted by a 48-metre solo try by the 19-year-old prop.

Fielden continued his rich vein of form the following month, starring in the Bulls' 22-12 win at Gateshead which ended the Thunder's run of home victories. Coach Matthew Elliott said: 'If you have seen a better front row performance than Stuart Fielden's, please give me the video.'

Less than two months later Elliott was calling for protection from high tackles for his protégé after an illegal challenge by St Helens' Vila Matautia, who was suspended for two games.

Fielden, out with concussion and a shoulder injury, was sidelined for three weeks. Elliott said: 'I'm concerned about the number of head shots he is receiving.

'We are working on his running technique, but a smack to the head is a smack to the head. And we are wary of changing his running style bearing in mind we had a player sent off for using a high forearm earlier in the season.

'My concern comes from the fact that I have

*The Community Development team that helped galvanise support for the Bulls.*

*Stuart Fielden, a young forward who made an instant impact.*

Lowes was the catalyst behind much of the Bulls' best work and in Phil Hodgson's *Rugby Leaguer* interview with the hooker in July 1999 he enthused: 'Any lingering doubts that James Lowes is back at the top of his form were surely dispelled by his superb performance in last week's hammering of St Helens.

'The Bradford packman, under some pressure last season from critics who pinpointed an alleged lack of self-discipline as a perceived weakness, and dropped from the Great Britain squad, has been back at his best this time. And he confirmed with his outstanding display against Saints that he ranks alongside any hooker in the world.

'A keen tactical awareness – vital in the hooker's pivotal role – allied to an alertness in attack honed in his days as a scrum-half or stand off with Hunslet make him a handful for any defence. And his own resilient, uncompromising tackling style lifts him onto a plane to which most other number nines can only aspire.

'Lowes could so easily have had a hat-trick against Saints. Two early disallowed efforts failed to faze the Ireland international, however, and a couple of touchdowns in the second period

an association with Adam Ritson, a similar type of player to Fielden. Ritson was a tough and uncompromising forward who played within the rules but who had to retire because of a head injury.'

Bradford lashed London 47-12 and opposing coach Dan Stains, who was to part company with the Broncos two days later, lamented: 'The Bulls were far too good for us. They weren't red hot, they were white hot.'

Matthew Elliott's charges followed up the rout with a 42-14 victory over Hull Sharks, again at Odsal, in which 22-year-old centre Nathan McAvoy helped himself to four tries. The win, secured without regulars Paul Anderson, Mike Forshaw, Henry Paul and Stuart Spruce, took Bradford's try tally to 29 in three games.

# A match to remember
## Super League
## Grand Final Play-offs

*Bradford Bulls 40 St Helens 4*
*Odsal Stadium, Bradford*
*26 September 1999*
*The Bulls crushed the Saints – who had been rated as favourites beforehand because of their impressive success over Leeds Rhinos – with a stunning performance founded on a blistering first half.*
*St Helens, inept by comparison, struggled from the outset and were under pressure in the first few minutes when winger Chris Smith made a hash of a couple of kicks to gift Bradford possession.*
*Prop Stuart Fielden and centre Scott Naylor took the opportunity to register the Bulls' opening tries, loose forward Steve McNamara converting each score. Bradford, switching their focus to St Helens' left wing, continued their assault when Henry Paul raced over after Tevita Vaikona had palmed a kick back for Naylor to hack on, and Paul added another touchdown before former Northern centre Paul Newlove crossed for the visitors.*
*Centre Michael Withers beat Smith to a McNamara bomb to cross early in the second half and Vaikona raced over from 70 metres, courtesy of a Paul Deacon pass, after St Helens' Anthony Sullivan had knocked on. McNamara, in superb kicking form, landed his eighth goal from as many attempts to confirm to any doubters Bradford's rating as the best side in the British game.*

*Bradford: Spruce; Vaikona, Naylor, Withers, Pryce; H Paul, R Paul; Fielden, Lowes, Anderson, Boyle, Dwyer, McNamara. Subs: Deacon, McAvoy, Peacock, McDermott.*

*St Helens: Atcheson; Smith, Iro, Newlove, Sullivan; Sculthorpe, Martyn; Perelini, Cunningham, O'Neill, Clark, Nickle, Joynt. Subs: Tuilagi, Hoppe, Matautia, Wellens.*

*Referee: Mr S Presley (Castleford)*

*Chris Caisley, a steady and clear-thinking chairman whose single-minded resolve underpinned the Bradford Bulls success story. Caisley stepped down after the 2006 Carnegie World Club Challenge victory over Wests Tigers.*

added weight to his claims for a place in the Great Britain squad.

'One, in particular, epitomised his strength, his vision and his sheer will.

'Most acting half-backs would have settled for moving the ball wide when a Bulls move was halted on the visiting line. Lowes, however, stood well back from the action, darted forward to collect as the ball left the heel, and burrowed over in unstoppable fashion for a try which looked simple enough but which in reality could have been scored by few players.

'And Lowes created a fine score, redolent of his early Hunslet days, when he collected his own astute kick before feeding Henry Paul who sent Leon Pryce over for his second touchdown.

'Lowes said: "It's good to be back to something like my old form. Last year I felt I had a decent season but it did seem as if people were at me all the time. I just needed to regain my consistency and hopefully I've done that."

# A match to remember
## Super League Grand Final

*Bradford Bulls 6 St Helens 8*
*Old Trafford, Manchester*
*9 October 1999*
*The Bulls, who had finished five points clear at the head of the Super League table, were denied the title that the majority of supporters – including many from outside Bradford – believed was rightfully theirs as St Helens ground out a notable win.*
*Former Bradford stand-off Ellery Hanley, now coach of the Saints, guided his side to a hard-fought verdict which, in the wet conditions, owed more to sheer resilience than quality or enterprise.*
*St Helens, beaten 40-4 by the Bulls in the play-offs only two weeks earlier, turned the tables with a result that left many questioning the wisdom of the play-off system as a means of settling the championship.*
*Superb performances by Henry Paul – the Harry Sunderland Trophy winner as Man of the Match – and his brother Robbie weren't enough to deny Saints.*
*Henry Paul grabbed the contest's first score after winger Tevita Vaikona had been halted by Saints full-back Paul Atcheson and St Helens half back Tommy Martyn had been wide with a drop goal attempt.*

*Paul's touchdown, a 60-metre solo effort, was almost thwarted by former Bradford second row Sonny Nickle, the Kiwi sliding over the tryline despite Nickle's tackle. But his conversion proved to be the Bull's last score as St Helens took control following the introduction in the 25th minute of scrum-half Sean Long, who quickly landed a penalty and went on to convert, crucially, Kevin Iro's second half touchdown.*
*Iro had a later 'try' ruled out for a knock on while Bradford's Leon Pryce also had a score vetoed, Michael Withers being judged to have knocked on in the build-up.*

*Bradford: Spruce; Vaikona, Naylor, Withers, Pryce; Henry Paul, Robbie Paul; Anderson, Lowes, Fielden, Boyle, Dwyer, McNamara. Subs: Deacon, McAvoy, Forshaw, McDermott.*

*St Helens: Atcheson; Smith, Iro, Newlove, Sullivan; Sculthorpe, Martyn; Perelini, Cunningham, O'Neill, Tuilagi, Nickle, Joynt. Subs: Long, Wellens, Hoppe, Matautia.*

*Referee: Mr S Cummings (Widnes)*

---

'Lowes feels consistency should also be rewarded at team level and that the side finishing top of the table should be awarded the championship. He said: "I'm all for the game going forward and I'm no traditionalist. I'm not against the top five play-off, but I believe it should have replaced the Premiership. The current system is not, in my view, the best way."'

Many outsiders, meanwhile, clearly saw little amiss with the sport as exemplified by Leicester Rugby Union Chairman Peter Tom, who called for his club to stage a game in the 2000 World Cup.

Tom fired out the message following the success of London Broncos' 'home' Super League clash with Bradford, which attracted 8,233 to Welford Road.

Said Tom: 'It was wonderful to see so many here, including many Leicester supporters who were watching League live for the first time. It was a fantastic occasion for both codes.

'We were a little apprehensive beforehand as we were not too sure how many people would turn up. In hindsight we should have opened up more turnstiles and we apologise to those fans who had to join long queues for tickets.'

**Removal van**
Wigan Warriors appeared to have failed in their bid to persuade Bradford to sell Henry Paul back, and an approach for the Bulls' 20-year-old forward Stuart Fielden had also been thwarted.

Bradford, meanwhile, denied rumours that Wigan and Great Britain skipper Andy Farrell was set to move to Odsal.

Rumours were rife that Farrell had even booked a removal van to move house to the Bradford area but the speculation was laughed off by Chairman Chris Caisley.

Bradford, though, were unable to laugh off either the 1999 Grand Final defeat or the aftermath.

James Lowes and Brian McDermott were on the carpet with Super League chiefs for failing to collect their runners-up medals after the Bulls went down 8-6 to St Helens in the Old Trafford

# Awards

*In a flurry of off-field activity in early 2000 Bradford Bulls:*

- *became the first professional sports club to receive a 'Mentor Award' aimed at helping individuals through mentoring in line with the government's education plans*

- *were honoured by the Encyclopaedia Britannica which named the Bulls' website as 'the best in Rugby League'*

- *secured the first European Regional Development Fund grant.*

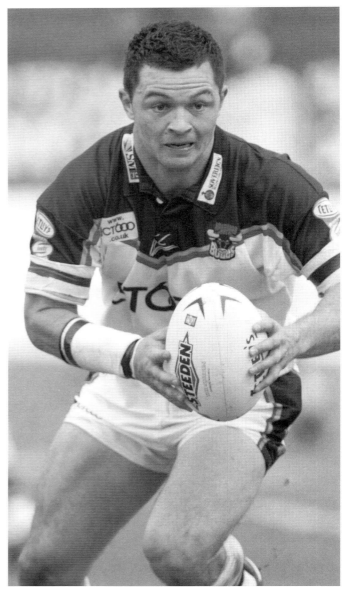

*Robbie Paul in action. The charismatic Kiwi, appointed captain at the age of only 19, was a wonderful ambassador for the club throughout a decade of service.*

decider. McDermott walked straight past sponsor Dave Whelan of JJB, who was handing out the medals, without shaking hands, simply grabbing his momento from a box in front of Super League boss Maurice Lindsay before striding away. Lowes, although on the pitch, took no part in the presentation at all and was given his medal later.

Stuart Duffy attributed the lapses to 'sheer disappointment'.

The Rugby Football Union was also throwing cash at Rugby League, albeit for different reasons. England RU coach Clive Woodward was allocated £2 million in his bid to entice League stars to switch codes but Bradford and Super League (Europe) Chairman Chris Caisley said: 'We are talking about no more than two or three players and I'm sure our game has enough money to keep them with our clubs.

'We have taken players from Union and made them into better players, the Union code has taken some of our best players and sent them back to us as worse players. We have had to do a lot of work on them to restore them to their previous ability.

'I'm not so sure that players will want to play Union when they have enjoyed the free-running in our game. I recently attended the Rugby Union's World Cup Final in Cardiff and was completely bored out of my mind.'

The Rugby Football League, meanwhile, took no action after Bulls coach Matthew Elliott apologised for a 'clerical error' which left him limited to only five substitutions instead of the

*The 2000 Challenge Cup Final, played at Murrayfield because of Wembley's redevelopment, came close to being the first in Rugby League history to being postponed.*
*Heavy rain in Edinburgh on the Thursday led to flooding in the Scottish capital and left the famous pitch under three feet of water.*
*With the dressing rooms awash and the power down, there was a real possibility that Bradford and Leeds would have to wait.*
*But a massive effort by stadium and RFL staff, backed by the Emergency Services and members of the Royal Navy Rugby League team, ensured that the match could go ahead as scheduled.*

regulation six in the 32-4 2000 Challenge Cup victory over Huddersfield-Sheffield Giants.

Elliott had included Paul Anderson in his starting line-up after having named him as a substitute. Anderson came up with a powerhouse performance before being replaced by Stuart Fielden – the man scheduled on the official team sheet to be in action from the start.

The RFL's Director of Referees, Greg McCallum, liased with other officials at the interval before explaining the situation to Elliott, who limited his subsequent substitutions to stay within the rules.

Elliott said: 'It was entirely my error and I apologise to the officials and to the BBC. It was not tactical – it was down to me not checking the team sheet.'

## Style and substance
The Paul brothers excelled as the Bulls won 39-10 at Castleford in July 2000. Phil Hodgson's report for the *Rugby Leaguer* ventured: 'Style over substance is what the game is now about. Rugby League, at Super League level, brings to mind the style of Sevens play adopted so successfully by Salford 30 years ago with the ball kept moving until a gap appears then – bang!

'The meat and two veg of scrums, battles of attrition between scrum-halves and referees – not to mention the darker side of the game – is now largely absent and we are left with little but the sweet course.

'It has to be said, though, that it's a hell of a sweet course when the Paul brothers are present. Henry and Robbie represent style in the best possible way, built on the substance of raw talent, intelligence, courage and awesome athletic ability.

'The pair were the key to Bradford's overwhelming victory, with Henry to the fore. The elder Paul has retained his habit of catching the ball one handed (the first time I saw him, playing for Wakefield against Wigan in a mudbound Christmas fixture, he coolly collected a huge bomb in the palm of his hand) and those

# A match to remember
## Challenge Cup Final

*Challenge Cup Final*
*Bradford Bulls 24 Leeds Rhinos 18*
*Murrayfield, Edinburgh*
*29 April 2000*
*The Challenge Cup returned to Odsal after a gap of 51 years as stand off Henry Paul turned the Murrayfield dream for Leeds winger Leroy Rivett – the Lance Todd Trophy winner with four tries against London 12 months earlier – into a nightmare.*
*Paul, who succeeded Rivett in the roll of honour as the Challenge Cup Final's Man of the Match, kicked the Rhinos' ambitions away with a series of punishing bombs that the winger, with little support, was unable to defuse.*
*Bulls centre Michael Withers benefited with two opportunist tries while substitute packman Stuart Fielden also touched down when Leeds full-back Iestyn Harris failed to smother yet another testing kick.*
*Bradford, with prop Brian McDermott running Paul very close for the Lance Todd Trophy with a barnstorming performance in attack and defence, led 14-2 at half time with the help of a Nathan McAvoy try but were rocking when Leeds hit back with touchdowns for loose forward Andy Hay and substitute Marcus St Hilaire, Harris adding five goals.*
*But the Bulls, for whom Paul kicked four goals, withstood the rally and were grateful when hooker James Lowes pouched a late Harris bomb to finally end Leeds' hopes of retaining the Challenge Cup.*

*Bradford: Spruce; McAvoy, Naylor, Withers, Vaikona; H Paul, R Paul; McDermott, Lowes, Anderson, Peacock, Forshaw, Mackay. Subs: Pryce, Fielden, Dwyer, Boyle.*

*Leeds: Harris; Rivett, Blackmore, Senior, Cummins; Powell, Sheridan; Fleary, Lawford, McDermott, Morley, Farrell, Hay. Subs: St Hilaire, Mathiou, Jackson, Barnhill.*

*Referee: Mr S Presley (Castleford)*

*Former Bulls favourite Paul Loughlin was an inspiration behind Bernard Dwyer's first Challenge Cup winner's medal.*
*Loughlin held the unenviable record of having lost in five finals, including two with Bradford in 1996 and 1997, and Dwyer revealed: 'Paul rang me during the week and told me to make sure I got a winner's medal at Murrayfield.*
*'I had four loser's medals before Saturday and he told me to win so that he could stay in the record books!'*

exquisite handling skills, which must give coach Matthew Elliott's heart the occasional flutter, were again on full display.

'There was one occasion when, under pressure from Castleford tacklers, he calmly collected the bouncing ball in his left hand from behind his own line and battered his way across the whitewash in a combination of class and sheer grit.'

Henry Paul continued his fine form the following week as Bradford rewrote the record books with a 96-16 victory over Salford City Reds.

The scoreline eclipsed the 92-0 win against Workington the previous year in the Challenge Cup, while full-back Henry Paul kicked 14 goals to match the total set by fellow Kiwi Joe Phillips in 1952.

The Bulls also equalled the best winning margin in Super League, set 12 months before by Leeds with an 86-6 hammering of Huddersfield. The success followed earlier victories in the 2000 campaign over Warrington (58-4) and Halifax (62-2), both at Odsal, and by 60-2 against Huddersfield at the McAlpine Stadium.

It was no surprise, given his rampant form, when Henry Paul broke the Super League record for goals in a season in the 52-20 victory against Huddersfield–Sheffield Giants in August. Paul, needing five at the start of the game to match Iestyn Harris' total of 129, slammed over eight goals to establish a new high of 132. But the Bulls came crashing back to earth at the end of August. Coach Matthew Elliott was left fuming as his side, with Scott Naylor and Stuart Spruce both in the sin bin, lost 20-19 at Wigan with the last kick of the match.

Warriors loose forward Andy Farrell landed the crucial score, a conversion from in front of

the posts of a Kris Radlinski try to complete an amazing fightback from 19-2 down before a record crowd at the JJB Stadium of 17,737.

Elliott, set to return home to Australia at the end of the year, was denied the 'double' when Bradford, despite a promising opening in which their big pack gave their Wigan counterparts a 'torrid time,' went down 40-12 in the 2000 Final Eliminator. Bradford had announced, earlier in the week, that long-serving Brian Noble would step up from his role as Assistant Coach to replace Elliott. Noble had signed a two-year contract, ending speculation that former Newcastle Knights boss David Waite, who had recently embarked on a three-month appointment with the RFL as an international coaching co-ordinator, would be handed the reins. His appointment reflected the stated aim by the board for continuity at Bradford epitomised by none more than Trevor Foster who, in the same month, was made an MBE in the Queen's New Year's Honours List in

*Media and General Manager Stuart Duffy, a key capture from Leeds. Duffy, who left home at the age of 15 to join the circus, slotted in smoothly to the carnival atmosphere at Odsal. The Manager of Yorkshire in 2004, he is pictured (right) leading the side out against Lancashire at Odsal.*

# A match to remember
## Challenge Cup Final

Bradford Bulls 6 St Helens 13
Twickenham
28 April 2001
Perhaps fittingly, every point scored in the first Rugby League game to be played at RFU headquarters came directly or indirectly from the boot.

The only two tries of the match, for St Helens stand off Tommy Martyn and hooker Keiron Cunningham, followed astute kicks by scrum-half Sean Long, the Lance Todd Trophy winner, as the Lancastrians added the Challenge Cup to the Super League title and the World Club Championship.

St Helens also had three 'tries' disallowed, each from a kick, in emulating the Wembley victories over the Bulls of 1996 and 1997.

Bradford's defeat stemmed from an unusually under-par performance by their much vaunted pack as few players, loose forward Mike Forshaw excepted, hit anything like form.

Kiwi duo Robbie and Henry Paul were unable to prosper on mere scraps as the Bulls regularly frittered away possession in promising positions.

St Helens took the lead when Bradford were down to 12 men, centre Shane Rigon having been sin binned for obstructing Martyn as the half back pursued a Long kick to the line.

Saints' opening try went to Martyn who, unfettered, beat the Bradford defence and the dead ball line for a well-worked score.

Cunningham grabbed the next touchdown, after the ball had bounced off Robbie Paul, Long adding his second conversion.

Martyn landed a drop goal but Henry Paul raised Bradford's hopes as half time approached with his second penalty.

The Bulls, though, were limited to Paul's third goal in a closely-fought second half, St Helens deservedly prevailing with arguably as fine an exhibition of close-to-the-ground kicking as Twickenham has seen.

Bradford: Withers; Vaikona, Naylor, Rigon, Pryce; H Paul, R Paul; Vagana, Lowes, McDermott, Peacock, Gartner, Forshaw. Subs: Deacon, Fielden, Gilmour, Anderson.

St Helens: Wellens; Hoppe, Iro, Newlove; Sullivan; Martyn, Long; Fairleigh, Cunningham, Nickle, Joynt, Shiels, Sculthorpe. Subs: Hall, Matautia, Stewart, Jonkers.

Referee: Mr R Smith (Castleford)

*All-action Leon Pryce, authoritative in any outside back position.*

recognition of his services to the community in Bradford.

Foster said: 'From the moment I arrived in 1938 and went into digs in Toller Lane the people of Bradford have been fabulous to me.

'I am a proud Welshman and I know the news will bring a lot of happiness in the Valleys today, but when my rugby days were over with Bradford Northern I stayed here because the city means so much to me. Life is all about people and I don't think they come any better than here in Bradford.'

An education welfare officer with Bradford Council throughout his working life, Trevor Foster's charitable works included voluntary endeavours for the Catholic Housing Society, Bradford Police Young People's Club, the Friends of Bradford Royal Infirmary and the Millennium Scanner Appeal. A year before his honour, he had donated £600 in prize money to

An anonymous Bradford fan, after the 2001
Challenge Cup Final defeat at Twickenham. 'I've had
enough. I'm wet through, Bradford didn't play and
I've dropped my programme in a puddle. On top of
that the wife told me not to come so I'll be in trouble
when I get home. I'm off to Soho to get drunk.'

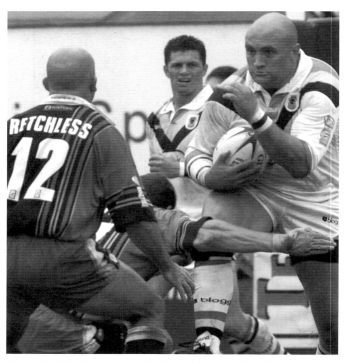

*Henry Paul looks on in awed admiration at Paul Anderson in
action. The heavyweight prop, at his best, was almost unstoppable
– certainly by a single man. London Broncos' second row Steel
Retchless, one of the best defenders in the business, was once
credited with 55 tackles in a game and braces himself for
Anderson's arrival*

Aussie full-back Michael Withers, who had played for
Ireland in the 2000 World Cup through grand-
parentage, ruled himself out of selection for Great
Britain.
He said: 'I would love to play Test football but it just
wouldn't be right. I did think about it but I know I
would have copped too much stick.'
Withers was subsequently called up by Great Britain
coach David Waite, another Australian. The duo's
involvement attracted the ire of all-time great Alex
Murphy who blasted: 'Withers has done exceptionally
well for Bradford but I always thought that if you are
born an Aussie you are an Aussie. You should be 100
per cent Australian or 100 per cent Great Britain and
not come in the back door with your granddad, your
grandma or your Uncle Ted.'

the Temple Bank School for the Partially
Sighted.

**Valley Parade**

'I'm not lonely,' said Brian Noble, who was the
only non-Antipodean British coach in Super
League as the 2001 season approached.

The new Bradford boss said: 'I'm trying not to
focus on being the only British coach in Super
League. The team is far more important as a
body than any individual, whether he be a Kiwi
or a True Brit.

'Sometimes I do think of the responsibility but
it's hard enough getting the team to play how you
want it to play. My focus is on the team and the
players first.'

Noble also had to contend with a switch of
venue for home games. As multi-million pound
plans for the redevelopment of Odsal Stadium
for the start of the 2002 Super League season
appeared to have become a reality, the Bulls
moved into their temporary new home at Valley
Parade. Bradford launched their tenancy with a
54-10 demolition of Widnes Vikings in their first
match in defence of the 2001 Challenge Cup,
Aussie centre Michael Withers leading the way
with a hat-trick in the 10-try romp.

The Bulls, with substitute prop Paul Anderson
in rampaging form, steamrollered Warrington with
a 39-22 victory in the semi-final at the McAlpine
Stadium, Huddersfield. Wolves stand off Lee
Briers, who scored a hat-trick, said: 'We gave our all
but Bradford are class, they are a big side. '

The Bulls, though, slipped to defeat at the
hands of St Helens as Twickenham hosted a
Rugby League game for the first time. A crowd
of just 9,663 – Bradford's lowest for two years –
turned up for the home game four days later
against Warrington and Chairman Chris Caisley,
revealing that an average gate of 15,000 was
needed to enable the Bulls to hold onto their
strong squad, attacked the stay-aways.

Bradford's chairman also criticised supporters
who left Twickenham before his players had
been presented with their medals.

He said: 'Had we been parading the Cup, I

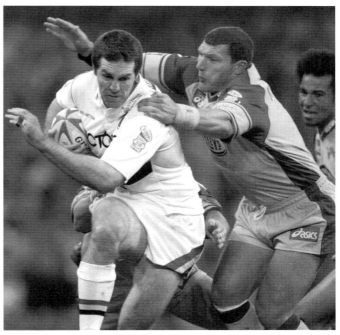

*Workaholic second row Daniel Gartner forged an effective partnership with the young Jamie Peacock. The Australian attempts to escape the clutches of Leeds prop Barrie McDermott.*

# A match to remember
## Super League Grand Final

*Bradford Bulls 37 Wigan Warriors 6*
*Old Trafford, Manchester*
*13 October 2001*

*The Bulls ripped Wigan apart before a record Super League crowd of 60,124 to confound concerns that a season's fine work could come to nothing.*

*Bradford rocketed to an unassailable 26-point interval lead which owed much to a hat-trick by full-back Michael Withers that, allied to his rock solid defence, secured him the Harry Sunderland Trophy. Robbie Paul and Henry Paul, together with such as try-scoring hooker James Lowes and centre Scott Naylor, were other serious contenders for the accolade while Brian Noble, in his first full season in charge, fully vindicated the Bulls board's decision to buck the Super League trend by offering the coaching role to an Englishman.*

*Wigan, limited to a Terry Newton try and David Furner goal, suffered their biggest-ever final defeat. Half backs Matthew Johns and Adrian Lam were left floundering and loose forward Andy Farrell withdrew in the second half with a dead leg – ending his hopes of scoring in a 49th consecutive match – as the Bulls dominated in terms of both power and panache. Henry Paul kicked five goals and a drop goal in his final game before switching to Gloucester Rugby Union while Stuart Fielden and Graham Mackay scored late tries, Mackay adding a conversion.*

*Bradford: Withers; Vaikona, Naylor, Mackay, Pryce; H Paul, R Paul; Vagana, Lowes, McDermott, Gartner, Peacock, Forshaw. Subs: Deacon, Anderson, Rigon, Fielden.*

*Wigan: Radlinski; Dallas, Renouf, Connolly, Carney; Johns, Lam; O'Connor, Newton, Howard, Cassidy, Furner, Farrell. Subs: Cowie, Betts, Johnson, Chester.*

*Referee: Mr S Cummings (Widnes)*

feel sure we would have been pushing the 20,000 mark, although we have to accept that fans were faced with the cost factor after having forked out for Twickenham.'

Those supporters who continued to support the Bulls had plenty about which to enthuse. Leon Pryce, 19, raced over for a hat-trick as the side went back on top of Super League with a 64-12 stroll against Halifax Blue Sox at Valley Parade. Seven days later centre Lee Gilmour produced his best performance since his winter move from Wigan, scoring a hat-trick and creating two others in Bradford's 42-10 win over Salford.

Meanwhile, Henry Paul agreed a four-year contract, reported to be worth £1.2 million and part-funded by the Rugby Football Union, with Gloucester. The New Zealand half-back, eligible for England through an English grandfather, was to switch codes at the end of the Super League season.

Early press speculation offered Leon Pryce as

*Kiwi stand-off Henry Paul on his immediate reaction to Bradford's 2001 Grand Final win over Wigan.*
*'At the final whistle I was nearly going to cry. We get a fine if we cry but I was pretty emotional.'*

## 'Words fail me'

*Coach Brian Noble, before giving the Rugby Leaguer nine paragraphs of quotes, after the 2001 Grand Final success.*
*'I spoke to Michael Withers in the week and he told me he'd had a dream about scoring a hat-trick in the final. I told him I'd had the same dream, too. That's what you do, visualise things like that, and it came true.'*

*Unadulterated joy for Scott Naylor and congratulations from full back Stuart Spruce after the threequarter's late touchdown ended Warrington's hopes in the 2001 Challenge Cup semi-final at Huddersfield.*

his likely replacement, while there were broader concerns over the future of Rugby League itself amid reports that some League clubs could consider switching to Rugby Union in the future.

Brian Noble, though, gave the idea short shrift, saying after his side's 44-22 win over Leeds before a 15,000 crowd: 'The obituary column was a bit premature in my opinion. I'm sick and tired of hearing about Rugby Union. We've seen a magnificent spectacle which shows we've got the product and we've got the people who watch the product.'

Nevertheless, crowds dipped by an average of over 2,000 following the move to Valley Parade. Some fans pinpointed higher admission prices as the cause of lower attendances. Others felt that supporters living on the south side of the city were loath to travel across Bradford for games, while a third group blamed the Bulls' disappointing defeat against St Helens in the Challenge Cup Final as a factor.

Hull coach Shaun McRae, meanwhile, hit out at the pitch, claiming that its narrow confines gave Bradford a massive advantage. Insisting that the distance from the half way line to the try line was only 42 metres McRae said: 'How many

*Harry Sunderland Trophy winner Michael Withers after the 2001 Grand Final.*
*'I nearly went back home this year but a few things persuaded me to stay. I've signed a new two-year deal and I'm pretty happy where I am.*
*'I knew where my dad was sitting and when I looked up at him I was nearly in tears. I'm very proud of my family and to have them here is very special. Dad's got the Cup and he's had a few beers out of it.'*

goals would Henry Paul have kicked (or even attempted) if he had been playing on a regular-sized ground? The result of last week's game against St Helens could have been completely different without some of Henry Paul's goals or Paul Deacon's drop goals.'

Absolving Bradford themselves from criticism McRae, writing in the *Hull Daily Mail*, added: 'It's not the Bulls' fault that they have to play temporarily at Valley Parade. But the Rugby Football League should have looked at the ground and realised how small it is.

'We should have standard fields of the same width, length and in-goal areas. When you are used to playing on that size pitch it is a big advantage; even more so when you are up against a side used to playing on a full-sized pitch.

'The markings put you off. Kicking is an obvious problem because you tend to kick the ball dead.'

Markings and other technical issues meant little as the Bulls demolished Warrington 84-12

*New Zealand prop Joe Vagana, a dynamic power up front for the Bulls.*

*Lee Gilmour, a gifted second row forward or centre.*

at Wilderspool to continue their push for top spot – only five weeks after having been beaten 18-14 on the same ground.

It was the home side's biggest-ever defeat; before a crowd of 8,393, their best of the season.

Wolves stars Tawera Nikau and Danny Nutley were making their last appearances at the famous ground and there were allegations in the following days that the Warrington squad was in no shape to face the Bulls after a leaving party the night before.

Henry Paul scored a try and 10 goals to set a new club record for the season of 457 points. Michael Withers and Graham Mackay both had hat-tricks, Leon Pryce and Scott Naylor bagged two tries apiece, and the rout was completed with tries for Robbie Paul, Jamie Peacock and Shane Rigon.

Brian Noble called for the Minor Premiers to be rewarded with silverware after the Bulls clinched top spot in Super League – the Minor Premiership – with a stunning 62-18 win over Leeds the following week.

It was the sixth occasion on which the Bulls had topped the half-century during the season, and the side had totalled 25 tries in two games.

The win assured Bradford of home advantage in the qualifying semi-final and Noble said: 'There should be some recognition, a championship medal or trophy, for whoever finishes top.'

The Bulls, 38-8 ahead at half time, had totalled 11 tries with Henry Paul setting a new Super League record of goals in a season of 168 with nine successes.

Naylor, Paul and Withers scored two tries each, with loose forward Mike Forshaw, second row Daniel Gartner, winger Tevita Vaikona and substitute Paul Deacon also crossing. Leeds had been limited to a first half try for Marcus St Hilaire and second half touchdowns by Danny Ward and Chev Walker, with Rob Burrow adding goals.

*Successful goalkickers need to be cool and unflappable. Scrum half Paul Deacon epitomises the breed.*

Chairman Chris Caisley, reflecting on the highlight of his term of office after announcing his forthcoming resignation in December 2005.
'My best memory is of the night we had a world record Super League crowd for the visit of Leeds in September 1999. There were over 24,000 supporters at Odsal, and we won the game in a sensational manner with a late drop goal by Michael Withers. The fact it was against Leeds made it all the sweeter. It was a super night which encapsulated what our dream, when we had focussed on the launch of Super League in 1996, had been about. We'd set about increasing crowds, creating a superb match-day atmosphere, and creating a good team. I looked around the ground that night and I felt fantastic. We'd beaten the Rhinos in a great game, there were women and children really enjoying the occasion, both the match and the razzmatazz, and I thought: "This is what we've been working towards." It was terrific.

# 12.
# A Noble Cause

Bradford, settled under coach Brian Noble, embarked on a period of unprecedented success as the side reached new heights.

With players such as Robbie Paul, Michael Withers, Lesley Vainikolo, James Lowes, Jamie Peacock, Paul Deacon, Leon Pryce, Stuart Fielden and Lee Radford around, the Bulls were packed with power, pace and panache. And the trophies continued to pile up as a result.

Fittingly, given Noble's strong local roots as a Manningham lad, the team matched the deeds of the fine Bradford and Manningham outfits of the Rugby Union and Northern Union era. And the achievements of the redoubtable Northern sides of the 1940s and late 1970s were also emulated in style.

The records, indeed, suggest that rugby in the city has never enjoyed a finer period than the Noble epoch with all four major available trophies nestling in the Odsal boardroom in 2004 after the Bulls had pulled off a clean sweep of the Challenge Cup, Championship and Minor

*Threequarter Jamie Langley, a 'protégé come good' at Odsal, displays his attacking skills with prop Joe Vagana in support.*

Premiership in 2003, followed by the World Club Championship the following February.

That accomplishment, it could be argued, elevated Bradford Bulls to the plane occupied by All Four Cups sides Hunslet (1907–08), Huddersfield (1914–15) and Swinton (1927–28), while Wigan picked up every available trophy in 1993–94.

It was a triumphant trilogy, capped by the victory over Penrith, of epic proportions and former Bull Henry Paul, who missed out on being part of that glory after his switch to Rugby Union, seemed to have early doubts as to the wisdom of his decision.

Finding himself dropped by Gloucester Rugby Union during a difficult transitional period he lamented: 'Moving here from Bradford feels like I have taken a step down.

'I don't think the coaching at Gloucester is good enough. There needs to be more technical work. It is holding me back and the side in general.'

Bulls Chairman Chris Caisley said: 'We would be very interested in taking Henry back, if we could extricate him from his contract. We didn't want to lose him in the first place and money didn't come into it, he was simply looking for a new challenge after having won so much with Wigan and Bradford.

'I have seen him playing a few games in the centre at Rugby Union were he did not get the service he needs. He is a stand off and that is where they should play him all the time. Give him the ball in his hands and he is a mercurial player, but he isn't seeing enough of it. That is the big advantage that Rugby League has over Rugby Union for a player of his abilities. League encourages players to play with the ball.'

Wigan, hungry for early revenge after the previous year's 2001 Grand Final mauling, were denied in a notable 18-4 Super League success at the JJB Stadium.

James Lowes masterminded the victory, supported by his powerful pack, as the Bulls bounced back from a disappointing Challenge

*Paul Johnson. Capable of playing in the second row or in the threequarters, a key cog in the Odsal machine.*

# A match to remember
## World Club Championship Final

*Bradford Bulls 41 Newcastle Knights 26
McAlpine Stadium, Huddersfield
1 February 2002
The Bulls, adapting far better to the monsoon-like conditions at Huddersfield, eased past the Knights with an awesome display in which Leon Pryce, introduced at stand off following the departure of Robbie Paul with a neck injury, excelled.
Hooker James Lowes collected the Man of the Match award for his telling contribution at dummy half, while loose forward Mike Forshaw was another thorn in the Knights' side.
The Bulls took control when it mattered, when the sides were locked at 14-14 late in the first half.
Paul sent Michael Withers over and the full-back returned the favour shortly before the break, scrum-half Paul Deacon's two conversions helping establish a 26-14 interval lead.
Bradford were in control within minutes of the restart, Deacon adding a penalty and Lowes sending winger Lesley Vainikolo through.
That score was followed by a sensational try for Withers, who was first to centre Lee Gilmour's clever kick. And a drop goal and a penalty by Deacon were enough to thwart a Newcastle rally involving two tries and three goals by the mercurial Andrew Johns and a touchdown for hooker Danny Buderas.
Paul – off a Deacon kick – and Daniel Gartner, from Paul's inside pass, scored the Bulls' opening tries, Deacon landing three goals, while the Knights responded with touchdowns for Josh Smith, Matt Gidley and Johns, who added a goal. Paul, whose injury turned out to be a trapped nerve in his neck, said: 'I expected to win by 20 points and we only won by 15. I might be just greedy though'.*

*Bradford: Withers; Vaikona, Naylor, Gilmour, Vainikolo; Paul, Deacon; Vagana, Lowes, McDermott, Gartner, Peacock, Forshaw. Subs: Anderson, Pryce, Fielden, Costin.*

*Newcastle: O'Davis; Smith, M Gidley, Hughes, K Gidley; Rudder, Johns; Parsons, Buderas, Perry, Abraham, Simpson, Peden. Subs: O'Brien, Newton, Morris, Jobson.*

*Referee: Mr S Cummings (Widnes).*

Cup defeat at the hands of Leeds.

Bradford scored three tries to Wigan's one and also had touchdowns for Daniel Gartner and Robbie Paul ruled out for forward passes. Two of the Bulls' scores went to Warriors' discards in centre Lee Gilmour and loose forward Mike Forshaw with Wigan-born Paul Deacon kicking three goals, while powerful winger Tevita Vaikona scored the other off a smart Deacon pass.

Gilmour and full-back Michael Withers sustained hamstring and groin injuries respectively and coach Brian Noble said: 'It's like a MASH unit in the dressing room.

'But anyone who thinks we are just a bish and bash team should take a look at the video of this game. We played some fantastic rugby.'

The Bulls repeated the medicine in the return at Valley Parade, when scrum-half Paul Deacon landed one of the most impressive goals in history to help the Bulls to a 28-26 success.

The sides were level when Bradford were awarded a penalty just inside the visitors' half and only 15 metres away from the touchline. Deacon, ignoring coach Brian Noble's exhortations to kick for touch and then seek a

# A match to remember

## Super League Grand Final

*Bradford Bulls 18 St Helens 19*
*Old Trafford, Manchester*
*19 October 2002*

*A final overladen with controversy closed with the most contentious incident of many as St Helens back row man Chris Joynt, aware that the seconds were ticking away and with his side hanging onto a one-point lead, went to ground prior to Paul Deacon's challenge without a hand being laid on him. Bradford players pleaded a voluntary tackle but Russell Smith declined to award a penalty that would have been within the range of hotshot Deacon.*

*The Bulls, who had fallen behind with 51 seconds remaining on the clock when St Helens scrum-half Sean Long landed a drop goal, also had cause to regret a penalty awarded against Stuart Fielden for what they insisted was accidental offside. And Deacon, who had crossed in the first half, had had his 'try' ruled out for a Jamie Peacock knock on in the build up – the resultant scrum feed going to St Helens despite what had appeared to be a previous 'spill' by the Saints' Paul Newlove.*

*Deacon, who had stretched Bradford's lead after having converted Scott Naylor's opening try, added a penalty before St Helens bounced back with a try and two goals by Long and a Mike Bennett touchdown for a 12-8 interval advantage.*

*The Bulls, though, restored their lead in the second period with tries for Robbie Paul and Michael Withers, Deacon kicking a conversion. But Bradford were to be thwarted as Saints paved the way for a sensational finish with a Martin Gleeson try.*

*Bradford: Withers; Vaikona, Naylor, Costin, Vainikolo; R Paul, Deacon; Vagana, Lowes, Fielden, Gartner, Peacock, Forshaw. Subs: Gilmour, Anderson, McDermott, Pryce.*

*St Helens: Wellens; Albert, Gleeson, Newlove, Stewart; Sculthorpe, Long; Britt, Cunningham, Ward, Bennett, Jonkers, Joynt. Subs: Hoppe, Shiels, Stankevitch, Higham.*

*Referee: Mr R Smith (Castleford).*

**In the Land of my Fathers. Sixty-five years after heading north from Newport, Trevor Foster prepares to lead the Bradford team out at the 2003 Challenge Cup Final at Cardiff.**

drop goal, elected to finish the opposition off in one fell swoop. And, with typically cool aplomb, the Wigan product scuttled his hometown club with a massive goal measured at 43 metres.

The scrum-half, who had previously landed a touchline conversion and fired a 40–20 kick that led to a try, said: 'I looked at the clock when we got the penalty and I knew I was going to go for it. It was a bit nerve racking, but that's what I'm paid to do, kick goals. Luckily it went over.'

### Absent friends?

St Helens and the Bulls engaged in a war of words over whether Bradford fans had 'gone over' in any numbers to the Friday evening Super League clash at Knowsley Road later that summer. Bradford sold only 800 tickets of the 12,297 gate and Saints coach Ian Millward blasted the 'stay aways', alleging that Bulls supporters had acted in retaliation to Saints having fielded a weakened side for the April clash at Odsal; a game that had taken place only days before St Helens faced Wigan in the Challenge Cup Final.

Millward said: 'It was unsportsmanlike. Now we will put the next game against Bradford on in our bar for our supporters to watch, and not go to Bradford.'

Bulls Media Manager Stuart Duffy retorted: 'Millward is talking absolute nonsense. We returned so many tickets because St Helens suddenly decided on Wednesday that the match would not be all-ticket.

'The Bradford end of the ground was packed and we must have had twice as many fans there as tickets sold.

'There must have been at least 2,000 Bulls fans at Knowsley Road and I would like to bet that they will not get a better away attendance this season.'

Chris Caisley, meanwhile, continued to be concerned by lower home crowds following his club's temporary switch to Valley Parade and pinpointed the regular presence of SkyTV cameras as the prime factor, suggesting that coverage of home games be 'blacked out' in the city. His analysis, however, was given short shrift by the fans and Sam Grundy of the Bradford Independent Supporters' Association (BISA) said: 'The main factor behind the fall in attendances has been the move to Valley Parade. Many fans just don't like the place and coercing supporters to go to games by withdrawing TV coverage will only antagonise them further.'

Bradford fans subsequently called for a return to Odsal. A

## A legend remembers
### Paul Deacon

*One penalty that ace kicker Paul Deacon didn't get the chance to take was in the 2002 Super League Grand Final. He was, though, more involved than most in the incident when the Saints' Chris Joynt was tackled – or not, according to perspective – in the closing seconds.*

*The Harry Sunderland Trophy winner admits, nearly three years after the incident: 'That would have been a pressure kick. I was going to tackle Chris Joynt and he sort of fell on the floor and I thought, and I still think to this day, it was a voluntary tackle. I would have loved the opportunity to have a go at it but it just never happened unfortunately.'*

survey conducted by BISA during the second half of the 2002 season revealed that 93.6 per cent of supporters craved a return to the club's home of nearly 70 years, with fewer than 5 per cent preferring to stay at Valley Parade.

Crowds over the first 13 weeks of the season had dropped by 14.9 per cent although some

*The dangerous Australian full back Michael Withers, with Lesley Vainikolo in support, breaks a tackle.*

165

*Parramatta coach Brian Smith dedicated his side's victory in the World Sevens to his old Odsal colleague Peter Deakin, who passed away on 1 February 2003 at the age of 49 after a long battle with cancer.*
*The former Bradford boss said: 'The World Sevens epitomised everything about Rugby League that Peter liked. He would have enjoyed being here.'*
*Smith learned of Peter Deakin's death on the way to the ground when his brother Tony, the Huddersfield coach, phoned with the news. 'I had to pull over to the side of the road. I burst into tears. I was shattered. We all knew of his illness, but thought he was improving. We had no idea he was so bad.'*

fans indicated that they appreciated the roof, view, bars, toilets and seating facilities at Bradford City's ground; 28 per cent of the respondents cited relative lack of protection from the elements as Odsal's worse feature.

Hooker James Lowes welcomed the eventual return, saying in September 2002: 'It's a real boost for everyone. It means everything to the fans and it means a lot to the players as well. When I played for Leeds, we feared the place. As Bradford players, we enjoy the intimidation factor. It is the natural and spiritual home of the club and we are looking forward to playing there next season.

'We train at Odsal and we only go to Valley Parade to play games. It's Bradford City's home and like an away game for us.'

**Taking Twickenham**
The Bulls emulated Wigan's feat of six years earlier by easing past all opposition to win Rugby Union's 2002 Middlesex Sevens at Twickenham – despite having played St Helens the previous night and only arriving in London at 4.30am.

Bradford beat Leeds Tykes, Gloucester and the British Army on the way to the Final in which London Wasps were brushed aside 42-14, to take the £50,000 prize and the Russell Cargill Memorial Trophy.

Captain Robbie Paul said: 'It wasn't as hard as we thought it would be because the opposition played patterns similar to Rugby League. We frustrated teams with our defence and capitalised when they panicked and made mistakes.

'We were tired in the opening rounds but once we sensed we could win the tournament everybody was on a high and nobody wanted to be substituted.'

The Bulls squad was: Robbie Paul, Tevita Vaikona, Leon Pryce, Mark Sowerby, Lesley Vainikolo, Michael Withers, John Feeley, Nathan McAvoy, John Skurr, Brandon Costin, Lee Gilmour, Rob Parker.

The defeated Wasps captain, gracious in defeat, said: 'They are all very clever players and when they got the ball in open play they are simply fantastic.

*Goalkicking scrum half Paul Deacon, the undemonstrative orchestrator at the rear of the pack, sets up an attack.*

# A match to remember
## Challenge Cup Final

*Bradford Bulls 22 Leeds Rhinos 20*
*Millennium Stadium, Cardiff*
*24 April 2003*

*Leeds skipper Kevin Sinfield's decision to tap a penalty rather than attempt the goal that could have secured a draw was one of many talking points in a controversial final played, for the first time, under cover.*

*Sinfield was pilloried for his decision and so was referee Russell Smith as Leeds took issue with several rulings. Many neutrals in the 71,212 crowd, however, believed that Bradford were worthy winners for a performance founded on grit, power and skill.*

*No one illustrated those qualities more than second row Jamie Peacock who was a colossus in defence, scored a try through sheer willpower and popped up several times to nullify Leeds kicks.*

*Peacock's try, recorded despite the attentions of several Rhinos, helped the Bulls – with Paul Deacon's touchline conversion – to a 20-14 lead.*

*Bradford escaped conceding a penalty try when Lesley Vainikolo was deemed not to have impeded Mark Calderwood in a chase for the ball, and the Bulls were back in the ascendancy when Deacon landed a penalty. Leeds, though, hit back when David Furner crashed over, Sinfield tagging on the goal to reduce the score to 22-20 and pave the way for his subsequent misery.*

*There had, however, been drama in the previous 80 minutes to match the late pathos, never more so than when Vainikolo sent Robbie Paul through for a first half try with what looked like a forward pass.*

*Bradford, though, could point to doubts over Gary Connolly's touchdown, which could have been ruled out for double movement, and a try by Chris McKenna when Shontayne Hape had got his arm under the ball. There was nothing better in the game – other than the sight of Welshman Trevor Foster leading Bradford out – than Vainikolo's touchdown, scored from a precision kick by Deacon who had executed a telling run-round with Hape, the scrum-half adding a towering conversion.*

*Bradford: Paul; Vainikolo, Hape, Naylor, Vaikona; Pryce, Deacon; Vagana, Lowes, Gartner, Radford, Peacock, Forshaw. Subs: Pratt, Gilmour, Parker, Anderson.*

*Leeds: Connolly; Cummins, Senior, McKenna, Calderwood; Sinfield, Dunemann; McDermott, Diskin, Bailey, Adamson, Walker, Furner. Subs: Burrow, McDonald, Ward, Poching.*

*Referee: Mr R Smith (Castleford).*

'Their defence was awesome and though we had the ball for long stretches of time we couldn't break them down.

'The Sevens game really does suit Rugby League sides. They were easily the best team in the tournament.'

### Differing views

Back home, over 13,000 fans balloted by text message for the Bradford Bulls 2002 Player of the Year.

Prop Stuart Fielden topped the poll and collected his award before 2,000 supporters on the evening of the Bulls' 28-26 Qualifying Semi-final win over St Helens at Knowsley Road in 2002.

The victory had been a tactical masterstroke for Brian Noble who had declined to introduce substitutes Leon Pryce and Lee Gilmour. Noble claimed afterwards to have deliberately kept them in reserve in case the game had gone to extra time.

The Bulls boss had bravely maintained his coaching composure despite a strong Saints rally from 24-4 down at half time.

Bradford went on to lose the Grand Final in the most controversial of circumstances. Opinions were polarised on whether St Helens second row Chris Joynt should have been penalised for a voluntary tackle in the closing seconds but RFL Technical Executive Stuart Cummings, the Referees Supremo, backed Smith and said: 'The definition of a voluntary tackle is: "A player in possession shall not deliberately and unnecessarily allow himself to be tackled by voluntarily falling on the ground when not held by an opponent."

'Chris Joynt was quite clearly trying to make sure that St Helens retained possession with only 10 seconds to go.

'He had one arm wrapped securely around the ball and ran towards Paul Deacon. He was using his other arm to fend off the tackle. He is seen to lean forward and protect the ball from any impact as he leans forward into the tackle.

'Paul Deacon is directly in front and, as Joynt leans into the expected tackle, Paul Deacon deliberately moves out of the way, causing Joynt to fall to the ground.

'As soon as he realises that he has not been tackled, Joynt gets up and attempts to make further progress. Therefore, it can be seen that Joynt did not deliberately fall to the ground but he ended up on the ground as a result of the Bradford player moving out of the way.

'In my opinion the decision by Russell Smith to allow play to proceed was the correct one.'

Bulls coach Brian Noble, after being told in the post-match press conference that Bradford scrum-half Paul Deacon had caused Joynt to fall by moving out of the way, blasted: 'Have a look at the tape, it's there for all to see. I've tried my best not to focus on that but it's real hard to stomach this one. I thought we'd done enough, played the football and scored the tries, and had the Man of the Match performance.

'It was a gutless performance from the official in the last eight minutes. It was great play by

---

# A match to remember
## Super League

*Bradford Bulls 22 Leeds Rhinos 21*
*Odsal*
*7 September 2003*
*Scrum-half Paul Deacon was the match winner with a 30-metre drop goal two minutes from time as the Bulls sealed the Minor Premiership before a 21,102 Odsal crowd.*

*Deacon, who had landed a previous one-pointer, also scored a try and four goals for a 14-point haul.*

*Leeds had looked like snatching a draw with a late try and goal before Deacon's intervention. Deacon had opened Bradford's account with a 20-metre solo try and added the extras off an upright after video referee Ian Ollerton, who had reviewed two incidents in the opening 12 minutes, ratified the score to leave Rhinos fans fuming.*

*Leeds had been granted a penalty rather than the penalty try they would have preferred when Francis Cummins was obstructed by Tevita Vaikona, and the Rhinos were denied shortly afterwards when Keith Senior pounced, Ollerton ruling that Cummins had taken Vaikona out in the build-up.*

*The Rhinos levelled when Matt Adamson powered over, Kevin Sinfield goaling, but the Bulls looked in control after Deacon kicked a penalty and Leeds' Willie Poching had a 'try' ruled out.*

*Full-back Stuart Reardon crossed four minutes into the second half, Deacon again improving but Leeds – after having a Cummins effort vetoed – were level when Poching raced over, Sinfield added the conversion and a subsequent penalty awarded against Joe Vagana for ball stealing.*

*James Lowes, sin binned for disputing the decision, had to watch from the sidelines as Sinfield put the Rhinos ahead with a drop goal.*

*But the hooker, back in the fray, fired the kick that gave Lesley Vainikolo the chance to score, Deacon improving after another video referral. And Sinfield's try and touchline conversion meant little in the light of Deacon's late clincher.*

*Bradford: Reardon; Vaikona, Naylor, Hape, Vainikolo; Pratt, Deacon; Vagana, Lowes, Anderson, Gartner, Peacock, Forshaw. Subs: Gilmour, Langley, Radford, Parker.*

*Leeds: Connolly; Calderwood, McKenna, Senior, Cummins; McGuire, Dunemann; Adamson, Diskin, McDermott, Furner, Poching, Sinfield. Subs: Jones-Buchanan, Burrow, Ward, McDonald.*

*Referee: Mr S Ganson (St Helens).*

them for the drop goal, but the reality is that we were the better team on the night.'

Paul Deacon, the Harry Sunderland Trophy Man of the Match, lamented: 'It doesn't mean anything if you don't win the gold ring. I know I will look back on it and feel honoured but at this moment I'm so gutted that we didn't win that I can't think of anything else. I really thought the best team lost.'

St Helens' Aussie prop Darren Britt admitted: 'We were never in it. We've pulled off a Houdini trick, really.'

Bradford full-back Michael Withers said: 'If it had been Bill Harrigan, he'd have done it. The

| 2003: Tetley's Super League (leading seven) | | | | | | | |
|---|---|---|---|---|---|---|---|
| | P | W | D | L | F | A | Pts |
| Bradford Bulls | 28 | 22 | 0 | 6 | 878 | 529 | 44 |
| Leeds Rhinos | 28 | 19 | 3 | 6 | 751 | 555 | 41 |
| Wigan Warriors | 28 | 19 | 2 | 7 | 776 | 512 | 40 |
| St Helens | 28 | 16 | 1 | 11 | 845 | 535 | 31 |
| London Broncos | 28 | 14 | 2 | 12 | 643 | 696 | 30 |
| Warrington Wolves | 28 | 14 | 1 | 13 | 748 | 619 | 29 |
| Hull FC | 28 | 13 | 3 | 12 | 701 | 577 | 27 |

coach and the club can't say anything because they get fined but when you play for 80 minutes and you get let down like that by someone who hadn't got the bottle to make a decision it's hard.'

Withers also contested the penalty awarded 15 minutes from time which enabled Long to land the equalising goal. 'It was accidental offside and should have been a scrum,' he said. 'They were gifted two points. And the disallowed try of Paul Deacon's should have been given; the referee went back two plays and you can only go back one.'

James Lowes, in his column in the *Spenborough Guardian*, explained why he had to be restrained by Withers from making contact with referee Russell Smith. He said: 'I think there were some vital decisions made incorrectly, both by Russell Smith and by the video referee, and they affected both sides.

'What Smith did was to look away and not give the penalty for the voluntary tackle in the last few seconds.

'My reaction at the end was borne out of frustration and disappointment. Perhaps it was a little bit of an over-reaction, but that's the way I am. I call a spade a spade and if, looking back at it now, it seems like over-reaction, it didn't feel like that at the time.'

Karl Pratt's career, meanwhile, was on an upwards curve following his switch from Leeds, where he had been deemed surplus to requirements. He said: 'Everyone reckons that when you're at a club like Leeds there is only one place to go, and that's down. But I feel as though I've gone up a gear, and I do feel as if I'm at a bigger and more professional club than

*Model Nell McAndrew, a welcome guest of the Bulls, adorned the team shirt with perhaps more style than one or two of the players!*

# A match to remember
## Super League Grand Final

*Bradford Bulls 25 Wigan Warriors 12*
*Old Trafford, Manchester*
*18 October 2003*
*The Bulls became the first team in the Super League era to record the Cup and League 'double' with a masterly display.*
*Full-back Stuart Reardon collected the Harry Sunderland Trophy for a near-faultless performance in attack and defence and hooker James Lowes scored his 99th try for the club in the last game of his career.*
*Bradford opened, in the words of coach Brian Noble, like 'rabbits caught in headlights' but finished well on top to end Wigan's 12-match unbeaten run under new coach Mike Gregory and leave Warriors hooker Terry Newton in floods of tears.*
*It was all smiles, though, for Newton's opposite number Lowes who brought the curtain down on a memorable career with a superlative performance.*
*Bradford, 6-4 down at half time after responding to a Danny Tickle try and Andy Farrell conversion with two Paul Deacon penalties, responded magnificently to Noble's half time promptings for a massive effort.*
*Wigan winger Brian Carney departed the scene shortly after the restart, sustaining concussion under Leon Pryce's heavy challenge, and the Bulls added to another Deacon penalty when Reardon raced over after a raid involving Daniel Gartner, Shontayne Hape and Joe Vagana.*
*Hape was next to cross, off a telling Deacon ball, and Deacon's conversion gave Bradford a 12-point cushion with a quarter of the game remaining. That was extended when the scrum-half landed a drop goal in the 70th minute but Wigan showed they weren't finished with a touchdown by Kris Radlinski, who popped up on Martin Aspinwall's shoulder when the centre was hauled down by Reardon after a 70-metre chase.*
*Farrell's conversion, though, was Wigan's last fling and Lowes sealed the Bulls' win with a trademark try on the last tackle, which the unflappable Deacon improved.*

*Bradford: Reardon; Vaikona, Withers, Hape, Vainikolo; Pratt, Deacon; Vagana, Lowes, Fielden, Peacock, Gartner, Forshaw. Subs: Pryce, Paul, Anderson, Radford.*

*Wigan: Radlinski; Dallas, Aspinwall, Hodgson, Carney; O'Loughlin, Robinson; Pongia, Newton, Craig Smith, Cassidy, Tickle, Farrell. Subs: Johnson, Hock, Mark Smith, O'Connor.*

*Referee: Mr K Kirkpatrick (Warrington).*

Leeds where we always promised to win trophies, and had the squad to do it, but for some reason never did.'

He added: 'One of the reasons I came to Bradford was because you are going to win stuff. I want to be part of a winning team and a winning club.'

**A welcome home**

The chances of that being the case increased significantly when the Bulls returned to Odsal on 9 March 2003 with a 22-10 victory over Wakefield before a 20,283 crowd – a record gate for the opening day of a Super League season – which included Pop Idol runner up Gareth Gates, the club's special guest for the afternoon.

A two-year exile at Valley Parade was ended in carnival style but Trinity almost played the role of party poopers, easing to a 10-point lead early in the second half with tries for Adrian Vowles and Gareth Ellis, Ben Jeffries adding a goal.

Bradford, though, made certain of their celebrations when Leon Pryce, Lee Gilmour and Shontayne Hape crossed, Lee Radford adding three goals. Karl Pratt had nipped over in the first half.

Chairman Chris Caisley, boosted by the homecoming and very much 'hands-on' following the departure of Chief Executive Abi Ekoku, said that he wanted Bradford to be 'like the Australian cricket team'.

He insisted: 'People say that success comes in cycles. I don't want that to happen here. I want continued success, as enjoyed by the Australian cricket side.

'I don't want this to be the beginning or the middle or the end of a golden era for the Bulls. I want this to be continued success that we build on consistently.'

Second row Jamie Peacock also appreciated the importance of steady progress and said, during his final season at Odsal in 2005: 'I think if I'd been at any other club I might have struggled to get where I am now. But the coaching set-up at Bradford is geared to

*Lee Radford, a hard working and alert back row forward and an integral factor in the Bulls' accumulation of silver, attempts under the watchful gaze of hooker James Lowes to escape the grasp of Wakefield Trinity Wildcats full back Martyn Holland.*

# A match to remember
## World Club Challenge

*Bradford Bulls 22 Penrith Panthers 4*
*McAlpine Stadium, Huddersfield*
*12 February 2004*
The Bulls, in winning their fourth trophy in 12 months, ensured that all the available silverware was resting on the Odsal sideboard; despite being without regular half-back pair Robbie Paul and Paul Deacon.

Worries that the Bulls would struggle in their absence proved ill-founded as stand in duo Karl Pratt and Leon Pryce tormented Penrith with astute kicking games which allowed the powerful Bradford pack to dominate. Full-back Michael Withers, in perhaps his finest game for Bradford, prospered against his former junior club. Withers, constantly overlooked at Penrith, had felt it necessary to move to Balmain to kick start his career, subsequently switching to Odsal, and the Panthers were made to lament their error in front of nearly 19,000 fans and millions of TV viewers.

The full-back also repaid the faith shown in him by coach Brian Noble, who far from showing him the door during an injury-troubled 2003 had handed him a three-year contract.

Withers almost sent Lesley Vainikolo over in the early stages, his pass eluding the winger, before Penrith had a Paul Whatuira try disallowed. Vainikolo made up for the earlier lapse by putting Bradford ahead, leaping above Rhys Wesser, and Pryce extended the lead with an audacious solo try. Withers added a penalty and a conversion after he had sent loose forward Logan Swann over, and landed another goal before half time when Luke Swain was penalised for a high tackle on Vainikolo.

Penrith hit back early in the second half with a Luke Priddis touchdown but the Bulls, despite having a Stuart Fielden try ruled out, were not to be denied and sealed their win with another Withers goal and a late Rob Parker try after a Pratt break.

*Bradford: Withers; Vaikona, Johnson, Hape, Vainikolo; Pryce, Pratt; Anderson, Smith, Fielden, Radford, Peacock, Swann. Subs: Vagana, Parker, Langley, Reardon.*

*Penrith: Wesser; Howland, Lewis, Whatuira, Rooney; Campbell, Gower; Clinton, Priddis; Lang, Guluvao, Puletua, Waterhouse. Subs: Ross, Rodney, Ward, Swain.*

*Referee: Mr S Ganson (St Helens).*

*Prop Rob Parker, a valuable member of Bradford's squad.*

'It was a pleasure to be playing in that match. I thought I played well and to just hold on and win in that way was a really, really good feeling – the best feeling I've had winning any game.

'I managed to get back when they kicked it for Calderwood. I don't know whether my legs took Calders out but I managed to get back on the ball. We did everything possible to win that game, there was a lot of heart and spirit, it was particularly special.'

Oddly, however, Bradford took some time to settle after returning to Odsal and coach Brian Noble lamented the 'fickle' fans who booed his side off at half time in the 35-0 home defeat by St Helens at the end of June 2003.

The reverse was the third on the trot at Odsal and followed a narrow win at Warrington after which Noble had asked supporters to get behind his side.

Noble said: 'The players and I share the fans' disappointment. I want them to know we are doing everything we can to fix the problem. It is disappointing to lose but we are working hard to put things right.

'I'd like to think they are booing the performance and not the players. I can appreciate they are used to success here but I

rewarding hard work and that's shown with me, the way I've come through. If you're prepared to listen you can go as far as you want.

'Everything I've learned at Odsal has helped make me a better player. At other clubs I might not have been coached so well, or have been able to learn so much from other players. Maybe I wouldn't have got to the kind of level I've reached. It's not just about the coaches. One of the things that was good about the 2003 season was that we had people like Danny Gartner, Mick Forshaw, Jimmy Lowes and Scott Naylor around. Before, there were such as Brian McDermott and Bernard Dwyer. They were all players you could learn a hell of a lot from. Hopefully I'm now passing that on myself; there seems to be an everlasting cycle of good players coming through at Bradford.

'The 2003 side was a great side. We built towards it for three or four years and the team then won everything.

'I'd come back early from a broken hand for that season's Challenge Cup final and I was playing against my hometown club, Leeds, who I had supported as a kid.

## A legend remembers

*'If you can't join 'em, beat 'em!' It's very sweet, in fact it's a beautiful feeling – Michael Withers on the 2004 World Club Challenge win*

*'I have been itching to get back and this is the ideal start for me. The high balls kicked up in the opening minutes were tricky as these new balls move about in the air. But I caught the first one and I was set for the game.*

*'I've put a nightmare year behind me and now I can look forward to the rest of the year. It was a great team display from one to 17 and even the boys that have left the club – this was down to them putting it in all last season. We weren't given a chance but we came through.'*

don't think it's helping the situation. I feel sorry for our spectators if they are that fickle'.

Chris Caisley added: 'The funny thing about British sport is that people's expectations actually become higher the more success you have. It becomes more difficult to please people than it does if you've had no success or if you've had limited success. So as we've gone through the

*Iestyn Harris controversially opted to join Bradford instead of Leeds – who argued that they had first claim on his services – when he returned to Rugby League from Welsh Rugby Union in 2004. Harris was appointed Bulls captain in 2006, lifting the World Club Challenge Cup in his first game at the helm.*

---

## A legend remembers
### Stuart Fielden

'I cherish the memory of our victory over Penrith in the World Club Challenge in 2004. Robbie Paul and Paul Deacon were out, and we had Leon Pryce and Karl Pratt at half back. We were completely written off, but we absolutely dominated a team seen as best in the world.

'The forwards were given a great platform by a superb kicking game by Leon and Karl. It's kind of chicken-and-egg. Which comes first – the platform set by the forwards for the backs or the platform provided by the backs for the pack? On that day we had both. I think that was one of the most complete performances with which I've been involved at Bradford.'

---

period people have become more choosy, more picky about what they actually want to see. It certainly becomes more difficult every year instead of becoming easier, it's bizarre really.'

Robbie Paul broke his arm in the defeat – an injury that threatened his bid to feature in the play-offs. And there was bad news for the fresh-faced Paul Deacon when the Bulls got back into gear the following month with a 60-12 win at Halifax. The squad celebrated with a trip to Blackpool but Deacon had to have an early night when the bouncers at a night club refused to believe he was over 18.

A month later, a restless evening battling with sickness didn't dent the impact of Lesley Vainikolo in the Super League clash with Hull FC. The awesomely powerful winger defied his condition to race over for a hat-trick, including two second half tries, in the 36-22 victory.

Vainikolo also helped set up two tries for Lee Gilmour but coach Brian Noble revealed afterwards that the 'Volcano' almost didn't appear. 'Lesley phoned me last night and this morning and he didn't think he should play,' said Noble, 'but we got him in early at 3.30pm to see the doctor and it was a case of we didn't have anybody else. He was initially going to play for just 30 minutes.'

The delight of Bradford's fans at the return to top form was increased when Iestyn Harris was tipped to move back from Rugby Union – but to Bradford, not Leeds.

*Powerful winger Lesley Vainikolo dives over for a typical try.*

The Welsh Rugby Union, struggling to meet Harris' six-figure contract, was set to release the former Warrington and Leeds star after the 2003 Rugby Union World Cup; and the Rhinos had expected him to return to Headingley under the terms of the deal in which he originally departed to the Principality.

Harris, though, was about to join a side on top of the world, with the Challenge Cup and the Minor Premiership on board and sitting astride Super League as comfortable 2003 Grand Final winners. And the Bulls would be recognised as the best club side in the world with the victory over Penrith the following January.

A relatively unsung hero, youngster Stuart Reardon, was selected by Noble at full-back in place of the injured Michael Withers for the

# A match to remember
## Super League Grand Final

*Bradford Bulls 8 Leeds Rhinos 16*
*Old Trafford, Manchester*
*16 October 2004*
*An impressive surge towards the end of a season dominated by the Rhinos ended in disappointment as Leeds lifted the championship for the first time since 1972. The Rhinos benefited from a tactical masterstroke by coach Tony Smith who, far from seeking to avoid the threat of Super League's top try-scorer Lesley Vainikolo, sapped his energies with a series of telling kicks.*
*The strategy worked and it was the Rhinos' supposed weak link Mark Calderwood who, in direct opposition to Vainikolo, was a key figure.*
*So was hooker Matt Diskin who collected the Harry Sunderland Trophy for a dominant display.*
*It says much, however, for Bradford's abilities that, despite their problems, they could have won a purist's match before a 65,537 crowd.*
*The issue was in the balance until five minutes from time when an error by Robbie Paul – the kind only a player of true quality can make – helped seal Leeds' win. The hooker, seeking to prise open the Rhinos' defence in his own half, got caught in two minds and*

*allowed the ball to slip from his grasp. Leeds won the scrum and Danny McGuire, previously under wraps, finally found space to send Keith Senior over, Kevin Sinfield converting.*
*Bradford had opened with a try for Vainikolo, who finished off a run-round involving Paul and Lee Radford, and their only score of the second period went to Shontayne Hape – who had had a previous try vetoed – who crossed after good work by Paul, Iestyn Harris, Paul Deacon and Logan Swann.*
*The Rhinos' other try went to Diskin while Sinfield kicked four goals from as many attempts.*

*Bradford: Withers; Reardon, Johnson, Hape, Vainikolo; Harris, Deacon; Vagana, Paul, Fielden, Peacock, Swann, Radford. Subs: Anderson, Pratt, Langley, Parker.*

*Leeds: Mathers; Calderwood, Walker, Senior, Bai; Sinfield, McGuire; Bailey, Diskin, Ward, McKenna, Lauititi, Furner. Subs: Burrow, McDermott, Poching, Jones-Buchanan.*

*Referee: Mr S Ganson (St Helens).*

Stuart Fielden on the 2004 Grand Final defeat

'They kicked us to death. They turned us around to our 20-metre area and that's what winning Rugby League is all about. You need to keep your opponents from your try line and dominate them; we just didn't do that.

'The last 10 minutes of the match was a battle and that was epitomised when Paul Deacon broke through a gap and no one other than Rob Parker was able to get with him. If someone quick had managed to get alongside him, we might have scored. But that just shows how everyone was tired. We were forced to have four drop-outs in the second half while they had none. It takes it out of you.'

Grand Final and did his coach proud, collecting the Man of the Match award in the process.

He said: 'To win the Harry Sunderland Trophy in my first year is a dream come true. Brian has always shown his faith in me and I just hope I have repaid him for that.

'I am always nervous before a game and tonight was no exception. But when I got the ball near the try line I just wanted to go for the line and score. Luckily, I did'.

Noble added: 'To win all three trophies really takes some doing. I'm fully in favour of a League Leaders' trophy as recognition of what a team goes through in a season to finish top of the pile. A treble is history, especially a first one.

'Three weeks ago people were telling me that I should leave Stuart Reardon out of the team. But Stuart showed that he is an outstanding full-back and I had every confidence in him. He works hard and he does the extra work in training.'

## Chris Caisley

'You're either for the cause, as Gerald Cordle once said, or you're against it. It's something that's always stuck in my mind as a great slogan, what a tremendous thing to say. He was 110% Bradford Northern was Gerald. He came from the Valleys and I think he lied about his age when we signed him but what a great person. He was dead right and that's an ethos that we've taken right the way through the organisation from way back in 1989.'

*Second row Jamie Peacock, captain on the night, delights in hoisting the 2004 World Club Challenge Cup.*

Skipper Robbie Paul, another key figure after returning from injury, assessed: 'The key to the game came in the second half was when James Lowes came back onto the pitch. His short passing around the ruck area enabled our big forwards to move the Wigan team back towards their own try line.

'The doctor ruled me out for the rest of the season when I broke my arm. But I told Brian I wouldn't be giving up on this game and that I would do everything in my power to take part in it.

'It meant spending a month in a steel case, in a hyperbaric chamber, but it was all worth it.'

**Towards greatness**

The 2004 Super League campaign opened with an awesome personal performance by giant winger Lesley Vainikolo, who crashed over for five tries at a freezing Odsal to single-handedly beat Wigan 34-6 in the first game of the season.

The Volcano warmed up the 17,267 crowd and supermodel Nell McAndrew with a scintillating power-packed display.

Wigan, who had perceived Vainikolo as a weak link, had adopted a tactic of kicking to him but

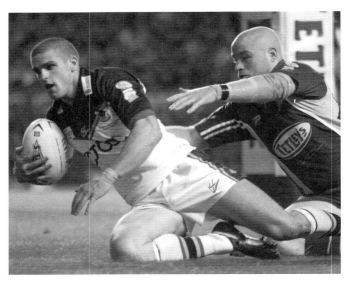

*Utility man Stuart Reardon scores against Leeds in June 2004. Equally effective on the wing or at full back, Reardon also impressed for Great Britain against Australia.*

## A legend remembers
### Brian Noble

'The 2004 season was one of adversity but I think I improved more as a coach in that year than I did in the previous three.

'We still got to the Grand Final, we finished second in the league but we were still disappointed; that's how high our expectations are at Bradford, because in reality it was a really successful year.

'In my first year, 2001, I was confident we were going to beat St Helens in the Challenge Cup final at Twickenham but we lost. We thought we'd prepared well, but we were so tense. I learnt from that that you've got to have an element of relaxation about a Final team, you can be too focused.

'The occasion will look after that; you have to suck the crowd in, enjoy them, otherwise it becomes too much for you. Just 15 minutes before the kick-off before the 2003 Grand Final we were playing cards on the stage that they'd put up. They had to kick us off. The players were a lot more relaxed and went out and blew a team away. They were ready for that – you could sniff it in them.

'The 2004 Grand Final defeat was tough because we'd turned the corner as a team. We'd got ourselves back into a bit of form and we'd beaten them at Headingley. Maybe over-confidence played a part but for some reason we got very stifled and tense again. And Leeds kept kicking us into a corner so it was very difficult for us to get to the parts of the field where we wanted to be.'

coach Mike Gregory admitted: 'He showed pace and he showed strength. Part of our job was to show that we could control him and we came up short there'.

Noble glowed: 'On his day he's the best winger in the world and that's not an understatement. The guy is a handful, he enjoys himself, he's a character and he brings colour and excitement to the game. Rugby League is lucky to have him'.

Rugby League was also lucky to have Trevor Foster who, in May 2004, was inducted into the Welsh Sports Hall of Fame Roll of Honour.

Fellow Welsh great Billy Boston was also at Cardiff's City Hall to witness Foster receiving the accolade from Wales Rugby League manager Mike Nicholas.

Meanwhile talented youngster Chris Bridge came off the bench to steer Bradford to victory at Salford after the home side had led 16-10 at half time. Bridge scored a try, sent Lesley Vainikolo over, and kicked four goals in the mid-June 35-28 win. Barnsley referee Ronnie Laughton came under fire from both camps and Salford boss Karl Harrison, formerly Brian Noble's assistant at Odsal, was angry that a try had been ruled out for an incorrect play-the-ball, claiming that similar offences had been overlooked throughout the game. Noble said: 'If Karl gets hauled over the coals by the RFL I will go with him. I don't think refereeing standards have improved this season.

'There were some big individual performances today but I cannot praise Chris Bridge enough. Teams that come to Salford need to understand that they are in for a fight and we knew that.'

It was just as tough in the September clash at Warrington as the Bulls, out of contention for the Minor Premiership in a season dominated by Leeds Rhinos, set their sights on the runners-up spot. Deacon, with two late drop goals including one effort with the very last kick of the game after Lee Briers had equalised for the Wolves, helped Bradford record a 28-27 win. The Bulls,

*New Zealand centre Shontayne Hape formed a highly effective partnership with left-winger Lesley Vainikolo. Hape's injury in the 2004 Tri-Nations Series seriously hindered the Bulls' bid for the Super League title in 2005.*

# A legend remembers
## Paul Deacon

*'There can be just as much pressure kicking for your Under-13s team as in a Super League or Challenge Cup game. When you're 12 you don't want to let your team mates down; when you become professional and you've got the same kick to win a game it's no different, you still don't want to let the fans and the other players down.*

*'Most pressure kicks are the ones that are 10 metres in from touch or in that area, that everyone expects you to get every time. If you kick the ball straight it will go over, it's just a goal kick and you've got to look at it that way. They can go over, they should go over, but sometimes they miss. Luckily most of mine have gone over.'*

ahead 22-6 at half time, had almost thrown the match away and Noble said: 'It must have been a fantastic spectacle. We put a lot of ball down in the second half and that was the difference. But we knew from the final kick off that there was about 45 seconds left and it sounds strange but when we got the ball back I was pretty confident we would get there or thereabouts.'

Vainikolo, meanwhile, had been a huge success throughout the season and shattered the Super League try-scoring record with 37 touchdowns in league games, edging Leeds stand off Danny McGuire, to finish top of the listings.

The giant winger passed the previous best in the 64-24 win over St Helens in September, scoring a hat-trick including one try presented by centre Shontayne Hape who fed his winger after having crossed the Saints' line in an illustration of the strong team spirit at Odsal.

That spirit was founded on the philosophy of the club's Chairman. Chris Caisley said: 'The view I've always taken is that loyalty is a tremendous thing and whether or not you're the best, if you've got that loyalty and that togetherness and feeling for the job you want to do then it makes up for any deficiencies you may have.

'Neither Matthew Elliott nor Brian Noble were the finished article when they started their jobs with us, that's for sure, and they would accept that. But I think that they both had committed backing from the board, and I think they've more than repaid that with the work they've put in. Both worked tremendously hard. I think Matthew was tremendous, to the point where he probably worried a bit too much about the job. He thought about it nearly every hour of the day that he was awake. Brian is very much of the same mould.'

With that strong work ethic underpinning the undoubted talent that abounds at Odsal it's highly likely that Chris Caisley's dream of sustained success will be realised. Robbie Paul, in his last season at the club in 2005, said: 'Everything snowballed from 1996 and 1997. With the success came money and with that money we were able to buy a world-class team. We've had a world-class side for a long time and the interesting thing, I think, is that we're nearing the end of this era. What's the next dimension, which is the next direction for the Bulls, for the club and the company?

'That's the thing that's going to be most entertaining over the next few years.'

# 13.
# Magicians

The 2005 Engage Super League season encapsulated, in nine short months, the wild fluctuations in fortunes that have typified rugby in Bradford since the pioneering days of 1863.

Perhaps drawing on the folk memories passed down by their illustrious predecessors, the class of 2005 pulled off one of the most amazing feats in the sport's history to win the championship in exhilarating fashion.

A visit to Old Trafford in mid-October seemed to be way off the agenda in any capacity other than as hapless spectators when the Bulls, already in a dismal spell which belied the form that took them to a Grand Final appearance the previous season, slumped to a crushing home defeat at the hands of St Helens in early June.

SkyTV viewers, and Bradford fans in the 15,260 crowd, could only watch in stunned bemusement as the Bulls conceded 12 tries in a 66-4 hammering.

The possibility of relegation, albeit remote given Leigh's struggles from the start, nevertheless appeared to be a far more likely option than any kind of serious assault on the play-offs and coach Brian Noble was under no illusions in the immediate aftermath.

Even allowing for the dismissal in the 29th minute of centre Leon Pryce for a high tackle on his opposite number, Saints' imposing Australian Jamie Lyon, the Bulls were abject. St Helens had already mounted a 12-4 lead by the time of Pryce's departure and it was one-way traffic

---

## A match to remember
### Engage Super League
### Qualifying semi-final

*St Helens 18 Bradford Bulls 23*
*Knowsley Road*
*7 October 2005*
*The Bulls mounted the final hurdle of the Minor Premiers in a rousing clash in which the Saints' performance belied the absence through injury of such as loose forward Paul Sculthorpe, scrum-half Sean Long and stand off Jason Hooper.*
*St Helens' commitment was vividly illustrated by an awesome start in which Bradford prop Stuart Fielden, harried at the kick off by four tacklers, was forced to offload to Shontayne Hape who was bundled into touch by Mike Bennett, Keiron Cunningham and Jamie Lyon. That approach was again in evidence when the home side bounced back from 12 points down, after Bradford had notched converted tries for Hape and second row Paul Johnson, to lead 14-12 at half time with two touchdowns for stand-in half-back Jon Wilkin and three goals for outstanding Australian centre Jamie Lyon. Centre Jamie Langley put the Bulls back in front with a craftsman's try, Paul Deacon ensuring Bradford were on level terms with his third goal after Wilkin had grabbed*

*his hat-trick score. With nerves beginning to fray, Deacon edged his side ahead with a drop goal after St Helens had gifted possession in attempting to force a pass. And victory was sealed when Hape crossed the whitewash three minutes from time.*
*St Helens were left in a state of despondency after becoming the first team in the Super League era to top the table yet fail to reach the Grand Final. Bradford, by contrast, were on their way to their fifth successive Old Trafford decider.*

*St Helens: Wellens; Hardman, Lyon, Talau, Gardner; Wilkin, Moore; Fozzard, Cunningham, P Anderson, Gilmour, Bennett, V Anderson. Subs: Higham, Roby, Fa'asavalu, Graham.*

*Bradford: Withers; L Pryce, B Harris, Hape, Vainikolo; I Harris, Deacon; Peacock, Henderson, Fielden, Johnson, Meyers, Radford. Subs: Paul, Langley, Morley, Vagana.*

*Referee: Mr K Kirkpatrick (Warrington).*

*Two members of the Bulls' accomplished coaching team in the early part of the 21st century pictured in their playing days. Steve McNamara, then with Hull, tackles Brian Noble.*

thereafter as depleted Bradford showed little stomach for the fight.

The absence of such as winger Lesley Vainikolo, centre Shontayne Hape and full-back Michael Withers cut little ice with frustrated boss Brian Noble who lamented: 'I didn't think the Pryce incident was quite as bad as some people made out and it certainly didn't help us

*Jamie Peacock, perpetual motion in the second row in attack or defence, with Karl Pratt in support.*

# A match to remember
## engage Super League
## Grand Final

*Bradford Bulls 15 Leeds Rhinos 6*
*Old Trafford, Manchester*
*15 October 2005*
*Bradford, who had been in 11th position in the table after having lost their first two games of the season and for much of the campaign appeared to be in grave danger of missing out on the play-offs, completed the fairy-tale recovery with a richly deserved victory over the side that had beaten them in the previous season's Grand Final.*
*The Bulls secured their third Super League title in five years for a dominant display before a 65,537 crowd against a Rhinos outfit that had taken the lead in the opening quarter when stand off Danny McGuire was first to an Andrew Dunemann kick. Leeds were, however, limited to a Kevin Sinfield penalty thereafter as Bradford's defence, with prop Adrian Morley outstanding, held firm.*
*Scrum-half Paul Deacon, who replied with a couple of early penalties, helped the Bulls to an 8-6 interval by firing the long pass that sent over winger Leon Pryce – the Harry Sunderland Award winner as Man of the Match.*
*Bradford extended their lead when, after Shontayne Hape and Leeds' Chev Walker had had tries ruled out, winger Lesley Vainikolo went in from dummy half in the 53rd minute after Jamie Langley had gone close. Deacon added the extras to extend the Bulls' lead to eight points and, after the scrum-half was wide with a subsequent penalty, stand off Iestyn Harris sealed the issue with a drop goal five minutes from time to ensure that skipper Jamie Peacock, who was to join Leeds the following season, collected the urn at his future employers' expense.*

*Bradford: Withers; L Pryce, B Harris, Hape, Vainikolo; I Harris, Deacon; Fielden, Henderson, Peacock, Johnson, Meyers, Radford. Subs: Paul, Morley, Vagana, Langley.*

*Leeds: Mathers; Calderwood, Walker, McKenna, Bai; McGuire, Burrow; Bailey, Dunemann, Ward, Ellis, Poching, Sinfield. Subs: Diskin, Lauititi, Jones-Buchanan, McDermott.*

*Referee: Mr A Klein (London).*

*Young ball handling forward Andy Lynch, a capture from relegated Castleford prior to the 2005 season, escapes the attentions of Wigan's Lee Hansen.*

throughout the game, but I'm not using that as an excuse. They were far better than us.

'We've six days to turn this around for the game against Huddersfield. It's a big test of our character now but I'm pretty confident in that respect. Some things out there from some of the players were simply unacceptable and we, as coaches, have got to decide what action to take.

'At the start of the game we just couldn't find our last play and this has been an issue for us before; when we do address it we are a totally different team. But some of the players have got this "score-a-try-every-set" mentality and you can't have that. The guys in the dressing room are pretty subdued.'

Noble's assessment of the strength of character within his squad proved to be justified. The quality of the players within the side, too, was never seriously in doubt and the manner in which the Bulls battled back from that humiliating nadir confirmed his own abilities as a coach. His own future was also under speculation in an era in which any coach, regardless of his previous achievements, is only three successive defeats away from media debate over whether he should be sacked.

Matters, however, hardly improved in the next month. There was, admittedly, an improved performance the following week with a 38-20 victory at Huddersfield but that success was followed by a 25-25 home draw with Widnes, who withstood a late Bulls rally to share the spoils, and defeats at Leeds (albeit by a more acceptable margin, in a 36-26 thriller) and at Wakefield.

The reverse at Belle Vue, by 44-34, was Trinity's second win of the campaign over Bradford and set the scene for the Wildcat's rise

*Second row Brad Meyers excelled in his first season at Odsal in 2005. Noted for his defence, the Aussie creates an opening from which half back Paul Deacon hopes to prosper.*

from the relegation zone.

It also proved to be the Bulls' last acquaintance with defeat in 2005.

Significantly New Zealand centre Shontayne Hape, who had been injured in the previous autumn's Gillette Tri-Nations Series, returned to action the following week for the visit of basement outfit Leigh Centurions when supporters confirmed their commitment to the club with a 10,294 gate despite the disappointments of the previous month.

His winger Lesley Vainikolo, who had been out of action since the game at Hull in late May, returned to action a fortnight later, and the duo were central to Bradford's astonishing transformation from title write-offs into eventual champions.

Hape, who admitted after the 58-12 win over Leigh, 'It has been a long eight months since the Tri-Nations. I'm glad to have got the game under my belt,' was an absentee from the hard-earned 24-18 win at Salford the following weekend, but he was back in

*Australian Ian Henderson solved a problem with his arrival at Bradford, filling a void that until then had not been adequately dealt with following the retirement of James Lowes.*

Bradford Bulls, the sport of Rugby League and the wider community in Bradford lost a man of the highest standing when Trevor Foster passed away on 2 April 2005.

The Welshman, who died on the same day as Pope Paul II, had joined Bradford Northern from Newport in 1938 and had remained in, and enriched, his adopted city for the rest of his life.

Rarely, if ever, can a capture from Rugby Union have ploughed so much back into the League code and it was fitting that the funeral service at St Cuthbert's Church, Heaton, for Foster, who was awarded the MBE in 2001, was packed with people from all sections of the various communities to which he had given so much.

Trevor Foster played for Bradford Northern from 1938 to 1955, making 462 appearances and scoring 140 tries, including a record six for a forward against Wakefield Trinity in 1948, and one goal. His career was interrupted by the war but following the cessation of hostilities he earned three caps with Great Britain and played for Wales on 16 occasions.

Those bare statistics, however, pay scant justice to a player whose sportsmanlike qualities were of the highest order, in one of the most uncompromising of sports, with not a single suspension in his 17 years as a professional.

He was also a great man to have around, one of unimpeachable character, an attribute that was vividly illustrated on Great Britain's famous Indomitable tour to Australia in 1946 when his positive approach amid the deprivations of the immediate post-war period helped keep the tour intact.

Trevor Foster went on to serve Bradford Northern and the Bulls in many capacities. His finest hour was arguably in 1964 when, with New Zealander Joe Phillips, he was a guiding light in reforming the club after the collapse of the previous regime in 1963.

For that, alone, his name will forever be indelibly linked with Bradford and his commitment to the cause remained strong until the very end, in a host of capacities including that of timekeeper.

Sport, however, can be considered a mere frippery in the greater scheme of things. Trevor Foster, when in his nineties, would spend most Saturday afternoons standing outside his local supermarket on behalf of various charities, not returning home until his collection tin was full.

It was for such selfless work, added to his input with the Police Boys Club in Manningham and within the church, which helped persuade the Vatican to award Foster a Papal medal in 2001.

# A legend remembers
## Bulls coach Brian Noble

*'It's an amazing achievement, unprecedented in the modern era, to play in five consecutive Grand Finals and it was an unbelievable achievement to reach the last of those from fourth position. That kind of consistency reflects the very hard work ethic that permeates all sections of the club and what makes it more gratifying is that we've done it without a millionaire backer.*

*'We're a very stable organisation, and we try to look after everybody. The players, in turn, react to that and when the chips are down they come up with the goods.*

*'An interesting psychological study could be made of the Bradford Bulls, and of the strong characters within the club that have helped us achieve our success.'*

harness with Vainikolo in the next round and the pair duly took the remainder of the campaign by storm.

Vainikolo swiftly regained the form that had made him Super League's top try-scorer the previous season and, with Hape, grabbed two tries in the 74-24 slugging of a Widnes outfit that before kick-off had been regarded as something of a bogey side.

Skipper and second row Jamie Peacock, who had been strongly linked with Leeds throughout the summer and who would confirm his decision to switch before the close of the campaign, was also back to something approaching his best and full-back Withers emulated his colleagues with a top-notch performance.

The scintillating display heralded a remarkable transformation as Bradford Bulls battered away all opposition in the closing two

*The biggest date in the modern-day Rugby League calendar. Bradford Bulls and Leeds Rhinos wait to enter the Old Trafford arena for the 2005 engage Super League Grand Final.*

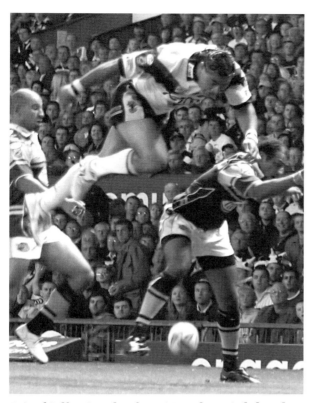

*Is it a bird? Is it a plane? No, it's Lesley Vainikolo – the nearest thing to Superman outside a comic strip – in 2005 Grand Final action*

months of the season with an unanswerable blend of power, pace, poise, precision and panache, mixed with the pragmatism necessary for all serious championship aspirants.

Salford, coached by former Odsal favourites Karl Harrison and James Lowes, were back at Bradford only three weeks after having tested the Bulls at the Willows but the match, this time, barely resembled a serious contest.

Bradford, who had occupied fifth spot in the table since slipping to fourth with that heavy defeat by St Helens, made almost as light of the Reds as they had Widnes, cruising to a 58-16 verdict.

Iestyn Harris, showing the talent that had persuaded the Bulls to secure his services ahead of Leeds – who had insisted that the half back was contractually obliged to return to Headingley after the end of his flirtation with Welsh Rugby Union – netted two tries in addition to orchestrating the side to fine effect.

High scoring wins against sides in the lower reaches naturally pleased the fans but there was sheer joy as superb victories were recorded in the next two games against opponents who each had major trophies on their respective

sideboards.

Leeds were given their comeuppance for the Grand Final defeat at Old Trafford 10 months before with a 42-10 result at Headingley that represented the Rhinos' heaviest reverse of the season.

The reigning Super League champions, it could be argued, may have been distracted by the following week's Powergen Challenge Cup Final against Hull but the fact remained that their players were playing for their places in Cardiff.

The astonishing scoreline, coupled with St Helens' 50-4 stroll over London, toppled Leeds off the top of the table and with hindsight the match could be seen, at the end of the season, as one that set the benchmark for the 2005 championship.

Hape continued his rehabilitation with a

# A legend remembers
## Bulls coach Brian Noble

*'A lot has been made of the contribution made by the men who were leaving and I wouldn't quibble with that. But there was also huge input from the players who were remaining at Odsal and their massive efforts shouldn't be overlooked.'*

# Chairman Chris Caisley

*'There was never any question of us not standing by our coaches. Brian Noble had won everything two years earlier and had already proved himself. Our problems were caused by a lengthy injury list that left us without Shontayne Hape, Lesley Vainikolo, Robbie Paul and Paul Johnson for much of the season. In addition, we hadn't replaced Jimmy Lowes, and there were issues involving the futures of several players, whereby we couldn't offer them terms at Odsal because of salary cap restrictions, which were out of our control. Other players were leaving anyway although it was very difficult, with such as Rob Parker and Lee Radford, to have to let them go.*

*'So there was some uncertainty in the camp but as soon as we got Ian Henderson in, and Vainikolo and Hape came back, we were a totally different team and we always knew that was going to be the case.*

*'It disappointed me to receive emails insisting that I should sack the coach. I'm one of the world's worst losers but if the game has taught me anything since I became Chairman in 1989 it's that you have to learn from defeat and turn the experience into a positive one. It's important, in that situation, to stand by your managers as best you can – it's only when you reach a situation in which he can no longer carry the dressing room that you should really look at it. The reality is that there are no guarantees that anyone else will do any better, and replacing Brian Noble was never remotely on the horizon. In fact, while people were advising me to sack the coach, I was offering him a two-year contract.'*

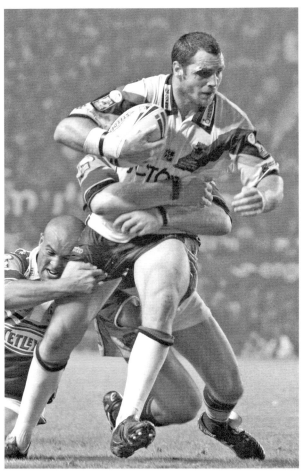

*Bradford snapped up Great Britain prop Adrian Morley on a temporary deal from Sydney Roosters in the middle of 2005. The signing was inspired. Morley is pictured in typically explosive action in the 2005 Grand Final victory over his old club Leeds.*

sparkling hat-trick, Vainikolo touched down and Harris ignored a hostile reception by sections of the home crowd to once again have a major impact.

There was a huge moment, too, when prop Joe Vagana bottled up Keith Senior in an awesomely robust tackle which led to the Great Britain centre being stretchered off with an ankle injury.

Noble, clearly sensing that something special could be on the agenda, was now focussing on securing a home tie in the forthcoming play-offs and working from that platform. He enthused: 'We've been building steadily and getting the troops back on board. Once they were all back on deck I knew they would be a force.

'We played well and it was good for our confidence but we'll keep a lid on it. Five other teams will be involved in the shake-up. We need to know we are playing the best we can but it is

# Chairman Chris Caisley

*'Our players and coaching staff deserve huge credit for our success in winning the 2005 engage Super League title. To achieve that, we had to win our last 11 games to get to the Grand Final. Defeat in any of those matches could have arguably left us in a position in which we would not have finished as champions. Our progress during that time illustrated the inner determination that permeates Bradford Bulls not to accept defeat.*

*'If something needs doing it's never a matter of saying "it can't be done," it's about finding a way of achieving our aim. In life, it can be too easy to do nothing. But our players and coaches did their bit and achieved what many outsiders, who were talking about us getting relegated, would have thought was impossible.'*

in our own hands.'

Two weeks later Bradford entertained Hull, who had beaten Leeds in a nail-biter in Cardiff to win the Challenge Cup for the first time in 23 years.

The Airlie Birds' party spirit was pooped by one man above all. Vainikolo powered over after only 30 seconds and raced over in the final minute in the 49-6 flagellation.

Fortunately for Hull, the giant winger was unable to maintain a rate of two tries every minute but the Volcano still managed a wonderful six touchdowns to break the previous

*The end of a difficult 2005 season and the Bulls celebrate in fine style, winning the engage Super League Grand Final.*

*Chairman Chris Caisley considers his term of office shortly after announcing his resignation*
*'Without a shadow of a doubt the 16 years since 1989 have been the most successful in the club's history. We've appeared in 18 finals, including such as the Yorkshire Cup, Regal Trophy and Premiership Finals in addition to Grand Finals and the Challenge Cup, and although I'd have liked to have been in more, it's a tremendous achievement. We've won our fair share of trophies and we've done it in style, going right back to the beginning of Super League when we lost in the classic 1996 Challenge Cup Final. I don't like looking back but I can do so with some satisfaction.'*

*Chairman Chris Caisley after confirming his decision to step down from the board following the 2006 World Club Challenge fixture with Wests Tigers*
*'It's the right time for me and for the club. It's been an enjoyable journey, but with what is going on at the Odsal Sporting Village, it's an opportunity for someone with a bit of cash to become involved in an organisation that can be successful and capable of diversifying.*
*'I will continue to support the club but it would be wrong to remain centrally involved and that's why I've stepped down from the board. I could only be an impediment to the new incumbent who will, naturally, wish to work in their own way.'*

# A match to remember
## Carnegie World Club Challenge

*Bradford Bulls 30, Wests Tigers 10*
*Galpharm Stadium, Huddersfield*
*3 February 2006*
*It was fitting that it fell to Ellery Hanley to present Stuart Fielden with the man-of-the-match award after the Bulls had brushed aside the challenge of the NRL Champions in a one-sided contest.*

*The Bradford prop had dominated the game in a manner rarely seen since Hanley had blasted onto the scene with Northern two decades earlier.*

*Hanley, for a heady period in the mid-1980s, had been close to unstoppable, certainly by a single defender. And Fielden's awesome performance against the best of Australia, crowned by two fine tries, was a wonderful echo of that era. The newly installed club captain simply tore stunned Wests apart in a devastating display founded on courage, commitment, power, experience and no little skill. Not to mention sheer stamina, coach Brian Noble opting to keep him on the field for the full 80 minutes.*

*Man of the match awards are invariably open to debate but on this occasion there could be only one selection, although several other Bulls stars made major contributions before the 19,207 crowd.*

*Scrum half Iestyn Harris, celebrating his appointment as team captain and switched from stand off because Paul Deacon was struggling with a hamstring injury, was a key figure and had a hand in both of debut winger Marcus Bai's two tries, full back Michael Withers supplying the final pass for the first.*

*Wests replied to Bai's opener with a touchdown by stand off Daniel Fitzhenry, but Bradford were in control by the break – despite the disappointment of having a 'try' for second row Brad Meyers disallowed.*

*That was thanks to Fielden, who powered and sidestepped through three tackles for his first try, Harris improving and adding a subsequent penalty for a high tackle by full back Brett Hodgson to set up a 12-4 interval lead.*

*Fielden crashed over within 12 minutes of the restart off hooker Ian Henderson's well-timed pass, and was only denied a hat trick when Hodgson somehow got underneath him shortly afterwards in a brave one-on-one tackle.*

*Bradford, though, sealed their win when Bai's fellow Papua New Guinean Stanley Gene, also on debut, bustled over from dummy half.*

*Bai, courtesy of a smart Harris pass, squeezed in at the corner for the Bulls' closing score, Harris landing the conversion from the touchline for a three-goal haul, one difficult attempt having bounced out off an upright. Wests had the last word with a late, and well deserved, try and goal by the irrepressible Hodgson. But the title of the best club side in the world deservedly went to Bradford Bulls. And the status of the best player in the world rested, albeit unofficially, with Stuart Fielden.*

*Bradford: Withers; Bai, B Harris, Hape, Vainikolo; K Pryce, I Harris; Fielden, Henderson, Lynch, Johnson, Meyers, Langley. Subs: Vagana, Cook, Gene, Ferres.*

*Wests: Hodgson; McDonnell, Collis, Whatuira, Lolesi; Fitzhenry, Prince; O'Hara, Farah, Skandalis, Laffranchi, Heighington, Galea. Subs: Fulton, Harrison, S Harris, Gibbs.*

*Referee: Mr S Ganson (St Helens).*

record, which he had set in 2004 against Wigan, of five tries.

Hape, prop Stuart Fielden, Vagana and Peacock also charged over in the 10-try romp, with half-back Paul Deacon adding four goals and, seconds before the interval, a drop goal that helped establish a 17-6 half-time lead after an opening period that had been closely fought after Vainikolo's early blast.

Continuing their role as killjoys, Bradford ended Huddersfield's bid for a top-six spot with a 52-34 result in which half-back Robbie Paul, in his last league game at Odsal, turned on a super

show after coming on as a substitute against the club he would join at the end of the season.

The Bulls duly closed the campaign in third spot with a 32-18 win at Minor Premiers St Helens, earned with a blistering spell of three tries in seven minutes which turned around a 10-point deficit as the match went into the closing quarter. Two of those touchdowns went to winger Paul Johnson while Vainikolo, who also registered a brace, notched the other try in the rousing rally. Pryce and Ben Harris also crossed for Bradford, Deacon adding four goals, in a display that would have been almost

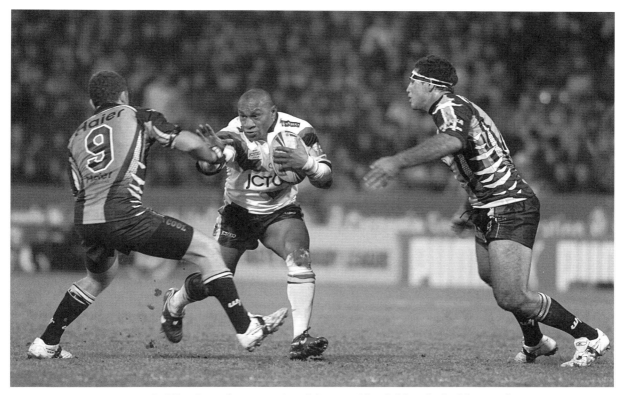

*Veteran Papua New Guinea half back Stanley Gene, signed from Huddersfield in the build-up to the 2006 campaign, was a revelation on his debut in the Carnegie World Club Challenge win over Wests Tigers. Gene, who continually tested the Tigers after coming off the bench into the hooking role, capped a fine performance with a try.*

unimaginable earlier in the season.

There had been precious little to celebrate in the first half of a campaign which had opened with disappointing defeats at home to Wakefield, who ground out a 28-16 result, and at Widnes where the Vikings won 31-22.

The third game of the season, at Wigan, appeared to be heading the same way when the Warriors established a 21-6 lead in the 54th minute. But the strength of character which would underpin the Bulls throughout 2005 was firmly in evidence in a pulsating finish, spearheaded by Peacock, which ensured that

## A legend remembers

*'We dominated them. Defensively, we were 100 per cent. We handled all their plays around the ruck, and their plays on the fringes. And we weren't slouches with the ball either.*

*'We showed enough to suggest we can be a little bit better and we have some players to come in, so we're highly delighted.'*

*Bulls coach Brian Noble after the 2006 World Club Challenge victory*

Bradford would not occupy bottom spot in the table.

Iestyn Harris netted the first try in the fightback after a wondrous one-handed back pass by Pryce and although Kevin Brown replied for Wigan to help put the home side 15 points ahead, the rest of the contest was to belong to Noble's men.

Robbie Paul, coming off the bench, marshalled Bradford's continuing revival. Fielden, with a powerhouse charge, set up the position from which Paul was able to send Peacock over with an exquisitely timed pass. The next score, with six minutes remaining, went to winger Stuart Reardon who squeezed in at the corner after Peacock, Paul (twice) and Johnson had combined. Deacon, who had converted Peacock's touchdown, couldn't add the conversion but the Wigan product was soon to be hailed as the match-winner, goaling full-back Michael Withers' 78th minute try for a dramatic 28-27 win after Iestyn Harris had tempted Wigan centre David Vaealiki out of the line.

That success, however, and the subsequent victories over London, Leigh and Hull, was undermined by a sequence of three league

*Full back Michael Withers adds to the pressure on West Tigers' defence in the 2006 Carnegie World Club Challenge.*

defeats on the trot, alleviated by an 80-14 stroll over Featherstone Rovers in the Challenge Cup at Post Office Road.

Leeds recorded a seventh win in as many outings in the 42-12 result at Odsal, St Helens edged a 34-27 clash at Knowsley Road, and it was a similar story in the 35-32 setback at Warrington in a period in which the club and the wider community, both in Rugby League and in the city of Bradford, was in mourning for Trevor Foster, who had given so much since coming north from his native Wales in 1938.

The home game with Huddersfield on Sunday 17 April 2005 was played in tribute to Foster and the Bulls reacted accordingly with a 54-10 victory in which Vainikolo scored a hat-trick.

Five days later, Wigan were turned over 40-8 at Odsal, and Bradford's season seemed to be back in gear with a remarkable victory at London in which the Bulls, 18-0 down at half time, hit back with 37 points in a blistering 24-minute spell to post a 41-26 win.

Bradford gave themselves another mountain to climb in the Challenge Cup at Hull but, on this occasion, time ran out in a valiant fightback from 20-0 down, the final hooter sounding with the Bulls deep in home territory but 26-24 adrift.

That setback could, in hindsight, have paved the way for the eventual title success as Noble

and his charges were able to focus totally on league football.

It certainly seemed that way as Salford were brushed aside 58-0 at the Willows, Deacon totalling 26 points with three tries and seven goals and young centre Karl Pryce scoring his first hat-trick for the club.

But a worrying trend towards inconsistency resurfaced with the 44-22 home defeat by Warrington.

The loss was made all the more painful by a Man of the Match display by former Bull Chris Bridge, who totalled 24 points with two tries and eight goals to overshadow Aussie three-quarter Ben Harris' debut for Bradford and raise questions as to why he had been allowed to leave Odsal.

Bradford were back in form six days later with a 42-24 revenge success at Hull, achieved despite Vainikolo being sidelined.

The unavailability of the giant winger for the next seven games would, with Hape's absence, be key factors in a dismal spell highlighted by the home hammering by the Saints. But the pair's return, together with that of second row Paul Johnson and the loan signing from Sydney Roosters of Great Britain prop Adrian Morley, would herald an achievement unprecedented in Super League. The title was won from third position after a season that would have been beyond imagining for most clubs but which, for Bradford, was perhaps simply par for the course.

*Iestyn Harris lifts the Carnegie World Club Challenge trophy as the Bulls continue their trophy haul into the 2006 season.*

# Index of Names in the Main Text